Guide to
Florida Historical
Walking Tours

Roberta Sandler

PINEAPPLE PRESS, INC.
Sarasota, Florida

To Marty

Always, All Ways

And to my "girls":

Jodi, Lori, Amy, Alyssa

Inquiries should be addressed to:
Pineapple Press, Inc.
P.O. Box 3899
Sarasota, Florida 34230

Library of Congress Cataloging in Publication Data

Sandler, Roberta, 1943–
     Guide to Florida historical walking tours / by Roberta Sandler. — 1st ed.
        P. Cm.
     ISBN 1-56164-105-7 (pbk. : alk. Paper)
       1. Florida—Tours. 2. Florida—History, Local—Guidebooks. 3. Walking—Florida—Guidebooks. I. Title.
F309.3.S254 1996
917.5904'63—dc20   96-28003
                                       CIP

First Edition
10 9 8 7 6 5 4 3 2 1

Design by Carol Tornatore

All photos not otherwise credited are by Roberta or Martin Sandler.

Printed and bound by Edwards Brothers, Ann Arbor, Michigan

NORTHWEST

NORTHEAST

CENTRAL EAST

CENTRAL WEST CENTRAL

SOUTH

CONTENTS

CENTRAL WEST

SOUTH

ACKNOWLEDGMENTS

Without the generous help of many people, I could not have written this book. My gratitude to Dr. Paul George for inviting me on his entertaining historic walking tours of Hollywood and the art deco district of Miami Beach. My thanks to Whit Rylee of Mango Tours, who escorted me through the Laurel Park district of Sarasota.

Thanks to Weona Cleveland for her delightful walking tour of Eau Gallie. I am indebted to Diane Pickett of Pickett's People Parade for her fascinating, anecdote-filled tour of DeFuniak Springs. She obviously loves her city.

My special thanks to Sandy Craig of Tour St. Augustine, whose guided walking tour was vivid with intriguing anecdotes about the pioneers of St. Augustine as well as the history of the city. My thanks also go to Cathy Slusser, Supervisor of Historical Records at Manatee County Courthouse, for patiently guiding me on four walking tours.

My deep appreciation goes to Dr. Wayne Wood for providing me with invaluable information, including that which appears in his books, "Jacksonville's Architectural Heritage," and "The Living Heritage of Riverside and Avondale." My thanks to Jean Orteaga of Cocoa, Bob Fisk of St. Cloud, Bob Hudson of the Historical Society of North Brevard, Beryl Willmot of Historic Ocala Preservation Society, and Carolyn D. Torrey of Fort King Realty in Ocala.

Also, thanks to Tom Muir of the Historic Pensacola Preservation Board, Pete and Mary Brandenberg of the El Cid Historic Neighborhood Association in West Palm Beach, Dr. Vin Fisher of Daytona Beach, and Dennison Tempel, curator of the Donkey Milk House in Key West, for their guided tours.

My thanks also to Alicia Clarke, curator of the Sanford Museum; Millie Bunnell of Vero Heritage, Inc.; Bill Morris, who guided me around Ybor City; Patricia Cayce, Historic Preservation Planner for the City of Delray Beach; Margie Ferrer, downtown coordinator for the Delray Beach Chamber of Commerce; and John and Fred Bistline, who have a lifelong knowledge of Longwood.

A nod of appreciation to Ed Shupe and historian Murray Laurie for guiding me around High Springs, and again to Murray Laurie for introducing me to the Northeast Historic District of Gainesville. Thanks also to Kathleen Martin for giving me a tour of Seaside.

I am grateful for the assistance of Shari, Jennifer, Traci, et al. at Geiger & Associates in Tallahassee, and for the help from Zimmerman Agency in Tallahassee and Kevin Hayworth at Moore Consulting Group in Tallahassee.

My thanks to Ellen Uguccione for introducing me to historic Coral Gables, to Stephanie Hofmeister for enlightening me about the Biltmore Hotel in Coral Gables, and to Anne Ford at the Downtown Redevelopment Agency for inviting me on the celebratory tour of Boynton Beach. Cookie Ellis at the Ybor City Chamber of Commerce provided me with great assistance and valuable information, as did Lori Burns, tourism administrator at the Vero Beach-Indian River County Chamber of Commerce.

I am most appreciative of the assistance of Alexandra Owen at the Bradenton Area Convention & Visitors Bureau and Mary Louise English and Jeanne Sullivan at the Greater Miami Convention & Visitors Bureau. Thanks to Jacqueline Whitmore and Dale Carlson at The Breakers in Palm Beach.

Thanks also to Kevin Russell at Sarasota Convention & Visitors Bureau, Stacie Faulds at Greater Fort Lauderdale Convention & Visitors Bureau, Colleen David and Candi Antonetti at the Tallahassee Area Convention and Visitors Bureau, and to Stewart Newman Associates for helping me to research Key West.

Thanks to Laura Hilderbrand at the Lee County Visitor and Convention Bureau, and to her assistant Delores Pomarico. Thanks also to Michele Albion, curator of the Edison and Ford Winter Estates, and to Cheri O'Mailia.

A note of appreciation to Beth Dabrowski, Helen Durian, Virginia Farace, Debbie Joyner, Jeff LaHurd, Wright Langley, Don Lanham, Kathleen Prewitt, Ruth Stanbridge, and Geri Zambri.

Thanks to Ron Haase for sharing his knowledge of historic architectural styles.

Thanks also to the Walton County Chamber of Commerce, the Pensacola Convention & Visitors Bureau, the Kissimmee/St. Cloud Convention and Visitors Bureau, the Daytona Beach Area Convention & Visitors Bureau, and the Palm Beach County Convention & Visitors Bureau. A special thanks to Michelle Brent and Mary Lou Janson at the Tampa/Hillsborough Convention & Visitors Association and to Mary Green-Hollas at Chernoff/Silver and Associates.

My love and thanks to my husband Marty, for his amazing and surprising patience. I am grateful to Pineapple Press for believing in my project. Thanks to all others who helped me during the research and writing of this book.

INTRODUCTION

The colorful threads of history, architecture, and culture are interwoven into the tapestry of Florida's sixty-seven counties. Walking through Florida's many historic districts provides a healthful, entertaining, enlightening way to explore the state's past and to glimpse the manner in which its people lived.

Local chambers of commerce, historical societies, preservation societies, convention and visitors bureaus, and tourist development councils throughout Florida will invite you to take walking tours of their historic neighborhoods.

Some walking tours are conducted by proud residents who have familiarized themselves with the birth and development of their city. For example, Sandy Craig, whose ancestors arrived in St. Augustine in the 1600s, leads guided tours of America's oldest city. Diane Pickett gives guided walking tours past the stately Victorian mansions in her town of DeFuniak Springs. Dr. Paul George, a Miami-Dade Community College associate professor of history, conducts guided walking tours of historic sections of Dade and Broward Counties. Weona Cleveland guides visitors past the old New England-like homes of Eau Gallie and Melbourne. Cathy Slusser leads guided tours through several areas of Manatee County. Whit Riley conducts similar walking tours in Sarasota.

Some tours are self-guided ventures in which associations provide a brochure or an area map that gives information about the points of interest in their historic districts and gives directions on how to find those points. For example, this is true of the Riverside and Avondale Preservation Society in Jacksonville, the Historic Ocala Preservation Society, and the St. Cloud Chamber of Commerce.

Some of the walking tours in this book, such as in Eau Gallie, Gainesville, West Palm Beach, and Coral Gables, focus on residential neighborhoods. Others spotlight historic commercial districts such as Sanford, Bradenton, Cocoa Village, Miami Beach, Ybor City, and Vero Beach. Still others, such as tours of Boynton Beach, Delray Beach, Quincy, High Springs, and Daytona Beach, combine the two.

The purpose of this book is to make it easier for you to locate such tours, or to experience them through your own self-guided exploration. As you will see, Florida is more than sunshine, beaches, palm trees, and theme parks. When you experience the walking tours described in this book, you will discover how much more substance there is to Florida, how rich and diverse is its past, and how beautiful is its landscape.

Although a city may have more than one historic neighborhood to visit, such as the downtown and the residential sections of Tallahassee, Gainesville, and Sarasota, I have described here specific guided and self-guided walking tours that I took at the suggestion of chambers of commerce or historical societies.

Explore the restored Pensacola Village; Key West's tin-roofed houses; Seaside's pastel, picket-fenced cottages; the grand 1920s Mediterranean revival homes of West Palm Beach; the kinetic Miami Beach art deco hotel district; and the tranquil neighborhoods of Hollywood, Gainesville, and Sarasota.

Learn about the pioneers of Bradenton, the wild beginnings of High Springs, the colonial settlement of St. Augustine, the charming antiques district of St. Cloud, and Tampa's lively and legendary Ybor City.

From one end of the state to the other, this book describes many of the walking tours that will help you to feel the pulse of Florida's history, its people, and its architecture, which are all intertwined. Each chapter lists the buildings you'll see on these guided or self-guided walking tours and, where available, a brief description.

The book also offers a bit of history about each area, and it suggests any nearby historic dining and lodging accommodations. You'll also find information about some additional historic attractions in these areas. Bear in mind that, in some cases, buildings that are part of a walking tour do get torn down, relocated, or altered in appearance. The structures listed here are described as accurately as possible, as of the writing of this book.

In many cases, people who conduct guided walking tours will offer an expanded, more detailed tour than what I have described in these chapters. It is highly recommended that you take their tours or at least contact them for directions and information.

Unless the homes on the walking tours have been converted into museums or advertise that they are open to the public, they are private residences, and must be viewed only from the exterior. Please do not ring doorbells and ask if you can see the inside of the house.

However, many of the commercial and residential buildings described in these walking tours have become museums that are open to the public. You can heighten your walking tour experience by taking time to visit these museums. Of course, doing so will lengthen the time it takes to complete a walking tour. The length depends also on how slow or fast you walk.

Ponce de Leon, Zachary Taylor, Andrew Jackson, Addison Mizner, Henry Flagler, Henry Plant, Osceola, the Chautauqua Society, Henry Sanford, George Merrick, Teddy Roosevelt — these names are carved into Florida's architecture and history. Pioneers cut a swath through palmetto scrub and swampland to give their names to towns such as Daytona, Ybor City, Boynton Beach, Titusville, and Gainesville as they bravely forged new settlements. They all spring to life on these walking tours.

So, insert film into your camera, slip into your walking shoes, put a hat on your head to deflect the semitropical sun, and get ready to embark on a leisurely-paced adventure as you discover some of Florida's venerable architectural and historical treasures.

A Very Brief History of Florida

To appreciate these historic walking tours, it will be helpful for you to know a little bit about Florida history. It began in 1513, when Spanish explorer Ponce de Leon landed near the site of St. Augustine. The mosquito-infested, humid swampland and the threat of attack by native Indians discouraged colonization.

Between 1559 and 1561, explorer Hernando de Soto gave Spain its claim to the vast region called Florida, but a hurricane in 1561 destroyed the Pensacola settlement that had resulted from de Soto's expedition. In 1564, the French established a settlement at Fort Caroline at the mouth of the St. Johns River around St. Augustine.

In 1565, to protect Spanish interests in the area, King Phillip of Spain dispatched Pedro Menendez de Aviles to set sail for Florida. Menendez's land and sea forces destroyed Fort Caroline and ended the French presence. He left 200 Spaniards to establish a settlement at St. Augustine.

The First Spanish Period ended in 1763 when the English gained control of Florida. In 1783, England ceded Florida back to Spain. This marked the beginning of the Second Spanish Period, which lasted until 1821.

The First Seminole War occurred in 1818 when Andrew Jackson invaded Florida to quell Seminole Indian uprisings. In 1821, Spain ceded Florida to the United States. Andrew Jackson became governor of the territory of Florida. A single new capital at Tallahassee was established to replace the capitals of West Florida and East Florida at Pensacola and St. Augustine.

The Second Seminole War (1835–1842) resulted from conflicts between white settlers and the Seminole Indians, who refused to be isolated on Indian reservations.

In 1845, Florida became the seventeenth state in the Union. The United States government issued land grants to volunteers who had enlisted to fight the Seminole Indians. Under the terms of this Armed Occupation Act, 160-acre tracts of land were given out, spurring the development of homesteads throughout Florida.

Florida was a Confederate state during the Civil War, but except for the Battle of Olustee in 1864, which was a victory for the Confederates, Florida remained relatively untouched by the war. After the Civil War, settlers from nearby Southern states filtered into Florida to cultivate cotton and sugar, and to establish communities around river ports where agricultural produce could be transported. Many of the houses were built out of tabby (sand and stone) or coquina (a soft limestone made up of broken sea shells and coral).

By the latter part of the nineteenth century, railroad barons such as Henry Flagler and Henry Plant built opulent hotels and weaved a network of railroad tracks through Florida. The building of the railroads brought new settlers and boosted the economy. The railroads transported wealthy northern vacationers to seaside towns and it contributed to the success of the citrus industry.

Between 1920 and 1925, investors who were attracted to the warm climate swarmed to Florida to buy up land. Land values skyrocketed and bankers became developers. This land boom became a land bust in 1925.

After World War II, Florida experienced a regrowth. The establishment of the Titusville area as a space-probe and missile-testing center brought defense companies and tourists to the area. With the development of theme parks and attractions, most notably Walt Disney World in Orlando, tourism became a year-round, vital component of Florida's economy and it has remained so.

Northwest

NORTHWEST

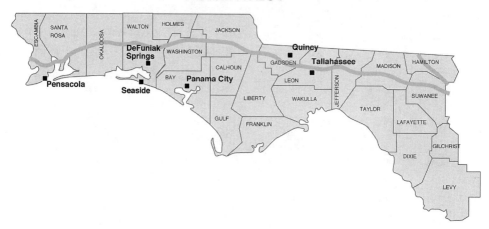

Escambia County

Location

Pensacola is located in southwest Escambia County, the western-most county in Florida, bordering Alabama. To the south is the Gulf of Mexico. Pensacola is the county seat.

History

In the 1500s, Spanish explorers sailed into the deepwater harbor of what they called Panzacola. The king of Spain made it a supply port. In the late 1550s, Spanish conquistador don Tristan de Luna colonized the area, but the settlement was later abandoned.

In 1698, Pensacola was again colonized, this time by don Andres de Ariola and 350 soldiers. They constructed a fort on Pensacola Bay. Their second fort, built in 1719, was Fort Pickens on Pensacola Beach, south of Pensacola. It fell into French hands but the Spanish regained it in 1722. For the next forty years, possession of Pensacola shifted between the French and the Spanish.

In 1763, adhering to the terms of the Treaty of Paris, Spain ceded the area to the British. The British remained in Pensacola from 1763 to 1781, until it was recaptured by Spain. In 1821, Pensacola became part of the United States. Andrew Jackson became territorial governor. It was incorporated in 1822.

Pensacola served as the capital of the territory of West Florida and St. Augustine as the capital of the territory of East Florida until 1823, when the legislature, in need of a central meeting location, designated Tallahassee as the new capital.

During the Civil War, Pensacola was divided between the Union army holding Fort Pickens, located to the southwest of Pensacola in Pensacola Beach, and the Confederate army holding Fort McRee, which was located west of Pensacola on Perdido Key. After the war, the lumber, shipping, and fishing industries boomed, making Pensacola a thriving seaport town. Scottish, French, Spanish, and British settlers lived harmoniously with freed blacks.

Today, Pensacola's architecture melds English, Spanish, French, and Confederate styles. The early Spanish influence is further reflected in many of the street names. Excavations by archaeologists have unearthed artifacts and historic sites that comprise the Pensacola Colonial Archaeological Trail. The Trail has become part of Historic Pensacola Village. A project of the Institute of West Florida Archaeology of the University of West Florida and the Historic Pensacola Preservation Board is being financed by Florida grants to continue unearthing these discoveries.

Walking Tour

This tour is approximately a quarter-mile long and takes about thirty minutes. A detailed walking tour is conducted through the central ticketing office at Historic Pensacola Village, which is part of the Seville Historic District. To get to the Village, take I-10 to Exit 4 (I-110) south to the Garden Street exit, which is U.S. 98 West. Travel to the first traffic light, Tarragona Street, and turn left. Turn left again at Zaragoza Street. Proceed to the Tivoli High House at **205 East Zaragoza Street**. There is parking on the street. Begin the tour at the Ticket and Information Center, which is located in the Tivoli High House.

The Tivoli High House, built in the early 1800s, was a social hall, a boarding house, and a Union barracks during the Civil War.

Exiting the Tivoli House, turn right (east) on Zaragoza. The first building on the right, at **207 East Zaragoza**, is the Weaver's Cottage. This simple house with pyramid-shaped roof was built around 1880 and was moved to its present location when it was threatened with demolition. The Weaver's Cottage presents an exhibit that explains the arts of spinning and weaving. Occasionally, volunteers work on the spinning wheels and looms.

The Dorothy Walton House at **215 East Zaragoza** was the home of the widow of a Georgia signer of the Declaration of Independence. Dorothy's son, George Walton Jr., was the territorial secretary of Florida and a member of Andrew Jackson's staff. He came to Pensacola with his mother in 1821. Ft. Walton was named after him. The house was built in 1810, during the last colonial period in Florida. It is distinguished by its red shutters and red door. It is now occupied by Broadway's Monograms, an apparel and embroidery shop.

Mr. P's Sandwich Shop at **221 East Zaragoza** was once the Moreno Cottage. The shotgun house, so called because the bullet of a gun fired through the front of the house would exit straight out of the rear of the house, was built in 1879 by don Francesco Moreno for his daughter

LaPearle as a wedding gift. The house contained no kitchen since LaPearle and her husband, Octavius Smith, ate meals at her parents' house.

Don Francesco Moreno was the Spanish consul in West Florida when Jackson arrived in 1821. Moreno was married three times and had twenty-seven children and more than one hundred grandchildren. Many of the Morenos listed in the Pensacola phone book are his descendants. The Sandwich Shop menu includes salads, soups, and sandwiches; the shop is open Monday through Saturday for lunch.

At the corner of Zaragoza and Adams Street, turn left (north). You'll pass **Old Christ Church**, which was built in 1832 and is the oldest church bulding in Florida that still stands on its original site. The brick church is believed to have been designed by Sir Christopher Wren. During the Civil War, Union forces used it as a hospital and barracks. During the 1950s, it was used as a public library. In 1960, it became the headquarters for the Pensacola Historical Museum.

Continue walking north on Adams. The Dorr House, on the corner of Church and Adams at **311 South Adams Street**, was built in 1871 by Clara Barclay Dorr. Her husband, a wealthy lumberman, died of fever in 1870. The Dorr house is the last example of Greek revival–style architecture in Pensacola, a style that was popular in the South after the Civil War. Clara had grown up in the Barclay house on the east end of Zaragoza Street. Her father, George Barclay, was a British merchant who married a woman of French descent from New Orleans.

The Dorr House is fully furnished and represents what a woman like Clara Barclay Dorr would have accumulated in a lifetime up to the 1890s. Volunteer guides conduct one-hour tours twice daily, during which they talk about local history.

Continue north on Adams for one block to Government Street. Turn right (east) and walk for one block to Alcaniz Street. Turn left (north) to get to the Quina House at **204 Alcaniz**. This one-and-a-half-story Creole cottage sits on its original foundation. It has a separate kitchen that is attached to the rear of the house. The house was built by Desiderio Quina, an Italian immigrant who came to West Florida in the 1790s with the Spanish military and stayed.

Turn around and walk back on Alcaniz Street, heading south to Church Street. At Church, turn right (west). The LaValle house on **Church, between Adams and Tarragona**, is an example of Creole architecture in early Pensacola.

Charles LaValle was a Creole who was born in Mobile and migrated to Pensacola in the early 1800s. LaValle formed a partnership with a

La Valle House, courtesy of Historic Pensacola Preservation Board

woman of French descent, Marianna Bonifay, who had come to West Florida from the Caribbean Islands with her husband, a Spanish military officer. She owned property, and LaValle knew how to build houses. They built a number of structures in West Florida.

The roof of the LaValle house has a steep pitch. Beams overhang the porches to cast shade on the house. The house is partially furnished with antiques appropriate to the period of the early 1800s. Guides at the house dress in costume representing the clothing of the 1820s. The pale green house has terra cotta–colored exterior trim and features beaded siding, which is purely decorative. Primitive scrollwork on the beams that support the roof eaves and big French-style doors are additional design elements.

Head back on Church Street to Adams Street and turn right. Walk one block to Zaragoza and turn right.

The cream-colored Lear-Rocheblave house at **214 East Zaragoza** was built in 1888 in a folk-Victorian style. This house is also on its original foundation. John and Kate Lear built the house. Lear was a stevedore on the wharf on Pensacola Bay. The house was purchased in 1897 by Benito Rocheblave, who was a tugboat operator. He ran arms to the rebels in Cuba during the Spanish American War. Like Lear, his livelihood depended on the port and the waterfront.

Julee Cottage, at **210 East Zaragoza**, with its pegged framing and beaded ceilings, was probably originally a slave cabin. It was owned by a

Julee Cottage

series of free black women, beginning with Julee Panton, who purchased it in 1805. Today, the house features an exhibit that depicts the experiences of blacks in West Florida dating from the sixteenth century.

The **Museum of Industry** on the corner of Zaragoza is housed in a late-nineteenth-century warehouse and is recognizable by the lumber train with a flatbed car and a caboose that sits outside. The train makes the entrance to Historic Pensacola Village easily identifiable and helps to tell the story of the golden age of the lumber boom in Pensacola.

The **Museum of Commerce** is in the building on the opposite corner of Zaragoza. It looks like a large beige brick warehouse. Inside is a toy store, hardware store, music shop, leather shop, print shop, and a model of a gas station as one would have appeared at the turn of the century.

Cross Tarragona Street. You're actually crossing the railroad tracks. Head right (west) to 320 Jefferson Street. The **T. T. Wentworth Jr. Florida State Museum** is on the corner of Zaragoza and Jefferson.

Originally a city hall, the Italian Renaissance building was erected in 1907 and became a museum in 1988. Theodore Thomas Wentworth Jr. was born in 1898 in Alabama. He was a tax collector for Escambia County. The museum has numerous exhibit galleries that display Wentworth's collections, an eclectic assortment including Coca-Cola memorabilia, old radios, and colonial archaeological artifacts. The collection is the largest an individual has given to the state of Florida.

From the corner of Zaragoza and Jefferson, you can see the **Empire**

T. T. Wentworth Jr. Museum

Building at 226 Palafox Place. It has also been known as Seville Tower. The ten-story bank building was considered the tallest commercial building in Florida when it was built in 1909. The building's ornamental work includes sculpted faces and crests.

Across the way is **Plaza Ferdinand VII**. This area between Zaragoza and Government Streets has been a park since the second Spanish period in the 1500s. The British held drilling exercises here for Indian and black troops during the second Spanish period in 1813. Andrew Jackson formally accepted Florida into the United States in 1821 during a ceremony held in Plaza Ferdinand. Plaza Ferdinand VII is a National Historic Landmark.

From the Wentworth Museum, walk back along Zaragoza, heading east for a short distance to return to Tivoli High House.

Walton County

Location

DeFuniak Springs is the seat of Walton County. It is located in the Florida Panhandle, a little over one hundred miles west of Tallahassee and about forty miles inland from the resort area of Destin.

History

Walton County was incorporated in 1824. It was named for Col. George Walton, who was secretary of West Florida while Andrew Jackson was territorial governor. Between 1846 and 1915, sections of the county were given to Washington, Holmes, and Okaloosa Counties.

From the time it was first settled by the McLendon family from North Carolina, Walton County has been primarily a farming community. The soil was versatile enough to grow everything from vegetables and sugarcane to the grapes that would yield wine from the Chautauqua Winery, Florida's largest. The county's rich supply of pine trees gave way to lumber mills and timber barons.

Soon after the end of the Civil War, a group of ladies rallied to have a Confederate monument erected in Walton County. In 1871, after they raised the necessary $250, a marble monument was erected near Eucheeanna. When DeFuniak Springs became the county seat it was moved there. The monument's three-tiered base is inscribed with the names of ninety-one Walton residents who died in the Civil War. This was the first Confederate monument in Florida.

In 1881, a surveying party for the Louisville and Nashville (L&N) Railroad came upon the area now known as DeFuniak Springs. They named the area for Col. Fred DeFuniak, a prominent official of the L&N Railroad.

The first white residents in DeFuniak Springs were Scots from the Carolinas who were soon joined by friends and relatives from other Southern states. Today descendants of many of those original settlers reside in Defuniak Springs.

With the arrival of the railroad, tourists discovered this bucolic town. In 1884, Dr. A. H. Gillet visited DeFuniak Springs during his search for a suitable site for the winter assembly of the New York Chautauqua, the cultural, social, educational, and philosophical society based in Chautauqua County, New York. Chautauqua is an Indian word for "meeting place."

Chautauqua's objective was to disseminate political, intellectual, and religious ideas, and to spread enjoyment of music, theater, and lectures. The first winter assembly was held in DeFuniak Springs from February to March of 1885. Many of the stately homes that border spring-fed Lake DeFuniak were built by wealthy Chautauqua members and timber barons.

The Chautauqua Auditorium was built in 1909. The dome was dedicated to the soldiers and sailing men of the Republic. The lantern above the dome was dedicated to the Light of Christian Truth.

In 1887, the Walton-DeFuniak Library opened, after a fundraising group named the Ladies' Library Association raised the $578.80 in construction costs. The library was staffed by volunteers. It carries the distinction of being the oldest library in Florida to continually use its original building.

Also in 1887, the State Normal School for white students opened in DeFuniak Springs. It was a school that prepared students for the teaching profession, the only school of its kind in Florida. In 1904, it was moved to Tallahassee to become what is now Florida State University.

In 1907, the DeFuniak buildings that had been used for the Normal School became campus buildings for Palmer College, named for Rev. B. M. Palmer, who was the first moderator of the Presbyterian Church in the United States.

DeFuniak Springs was incorporated in 1901. The library, the Hall of Brotherhood, and many of the turn-of-the-century homes surround Lake DeFuniak, a perfectly round lake. The Victorian town is an Elderhostel site each February.

Walking Tour

This walking tour is approximately one mile, and takes about forty-five minutes. The walking tour encompasses mansions circling Lake DeFuniak, which has a 1.3-mile circumference. The street circling the lake is aptly named Circle Drive. It is where you'll find the Walton County Chamber of Commerce, located inside the **Chautauqua Auditorium**.

To get to the building, take I-10 to the DeFuniak Springs exit. Head north, which puts you onto Highway 331. Proceed to Live Oak Avenue. Turn right. The street will deadend at the library. Turn right. The Chamber of Commerce/Chautauqua Auditorium is on the lake side one block on the left. There is ample street parking. The Auditorium is the starting point for your walking tour.

Chautauqua programs were held in tents around the lake until 1909, when the Chautauqua Auditorium was built at a cost of $28,000. The amphitheater had a seating capacity of four thousand. The Auditorium was known as the Hall of Brotherhood.

The imposing white building has a portico at each end and three more across the facade. The forty columns adorning it are thought to represent either the forty states or forty revered American presidents. The cupola at the top of the building was referred to as The Lantern of Religious Trust.

If you look to the right of the double doors at the entrance to the building, you'll see the ticket booth windows where Chautauqua Society members purchased their tickets to cultural events and lectures.

The Auditorium faces West Avenue. From the Auditorium, walk west on West Avenue for two blocks, to the home of artist Mary Vinson, an award-winning porcelain painter. The Vinson house is on the corner of West and Eleventh Street, at **301 South Eleventh Street**. The huge white folk-Victorian house, built in 1890, has two-story, deep and wide wraparound porches. Vinson converted the servants' quarters behind her house into a studio so that she could hold art classes there.

From the Vinson house, go back onto West and head east in the direction of the Auditorium. When you get back to Circle Drive, turn right

Chautauqua Auditorium/Hall of Brotherhood

(south) and walk to **St. Agatha's Episcopal Church**, at **144 Circle Drive**. Built in 1896, this is the oldest church building in DeFuniak Springs. The church has a square Norman tower and a stained glass window made by Giesler, a student of Tiffany. The window was presented to the church by the Wallace Bruce family. Bruce was an early president of the Chautauqua.

Walk past the red front door and step into the church to see the pipe organ that was handcrafted of African mahogany by acolyte Tom Bartholomew. Father and Mrs. Tom Chesterman live next door to the church in a two-story parish house, which is called Phoenix Hall because it caught fire a few years ago and nearly burned, but instead seemed to rise from the ashes.

The two-story frame house at **168 Circle Drive** was built before 1907 and was owned by a merchant named Charles E. Murray, who passed it down to ensuing generations. The narrow white wood-frame house has gingerbread trim over the side entrance, two-story bay windows on either side, and a porch swing that is often occupied.

The three-story house at **188 Circle Drive** is fun to look at during Halloween. That's when the owners put "Caspar the Friendly Ghost" in the window. Caspar swings back and forth. Built circa 1900 by brothers who were in the lumber business, this Queen Anne–style house, known as the Bullard House, has an inverted cone–shaped pedestal tower with a two-story bay. A beautiful stained glass window can be viewed only from the inside of the house.

The Queen Anne house at **208 West Circle Drive** was built circa 1902 by lumberman Walter Graves. If you look at the right side of the first floor, you can see a diamond-shaped stained glass window. The house features spindled millwork, an intricate fan-shaped pattern under the eave, and a wide, curving balcony. There is a screened sleeping porch upstairs.

At the corner of Circle Drive and Plateau Avenue, you'll see a board-and-batten, folk-Victorian cottage at **234 Circle Drive**. This is known as the Honeymoon Cottage because one of its owners courted his wife for twenty years.

The cottage was built in 1888 and was owned by generations of a banking family. It was, at one time, the only house in DeFuniak Springs to have an indoor toilet. The front of the house has dark green shutters and posts with gingerbread trim on top. The house originally had one room. An upstairs level and downstairs additions have expanded the house to about 2,000 square feet.

Walk past the Honeymoon Cottage and continue south on Circle

Honeymoon Cottage

Drive. At **262 Circle Drive** you will find an authentic folk-Victorian restoration called The Verandas. It was built in 1904. The brick is original to the house, as is the chicken wire–type fence. Mrs. Thorpe, a previous owner, liked to entertain on Chautauqua Saturdays, when she would serve lunch on her verandas. This was important for the ladies because they could not only see everyone walking by, but they could also be seen.

The houses at **294 and 302 Circle Drive** were built as prototypes for homes to be built by a prefab housing company. The company never got off the ground.

Walk to the **corner of Circle Drive and Hubbard Street**. In front of a contemporary house, a majestic magnolia tree gracefully stretches its branches. This is the eighth largest magnolia tree in Florida. The American Forestry Association has a program called Great Trees of America. Program representatives measured this magnolia tree and certified it. It has a spreading crown of seventy-two feet, it is sixty feet high, and its trunk measures twelve-and-a-half feet in circumference.

Cross Hubbard Street and continue on to **404 Circle Drive**, which is known as the Dream Cottage. It was built in a gothic stick style, circa 1888. The chalet-shaped house was built by Wallace Bruce. He was an ambassador to Scotland and an important force behind the formation of the winter Chautauqua. A blue floor echoes the blue ceilings underneath the eaves. Four metal bells hang from the latticed gable. There is a recent addition to the back of the house. The house has had only two owners.

Cross Georgia Street. Twelve beautiful magnolia trees grace the front of the house with green shutters at **470 Circle Drive**, on the corner of Circle and Georgia. The house was built in 1887 by Northerners named Holton. It has fifty-two windows. Considering its large size, the house has a small front porch. As lovely as the magnolia trees are, they cast so much shade that the lawn cannot grow.

The brick Georgian revival with dark green shutters at **504 Circle Drive** is the home of the mayor of DeFuniak Springs.

The brick house at **550 Circle Drive** was built in 1907 for Kenneth Bruce, Wallace Bruce's son. The house was designed to hold the collection of weaponry that is now displayed in the Walton-DeFuniak Library. The diamond-shaped glass enclosure was a later addition to the house. The portico is supported by huge white Doric columns, and the house is surrounded by a colonial-style wrought iron fence. It was here that Bruce entertained celebrities who came to perform at Chautauqua. There was an open door policy here. Visitors were always welcome.

Cross Pine Street. Walk one block and cross Jackson Avenue. Walk to **676 Circle Drive**, on the corner of Circle and Jackson. This white, two-story French colonial–style house was built out of heart pine in 1905 and is known as the McLean House. The house was considered to be ideally situated for viewing the sunsets across the lake. From 1905 until 1992, members of the McLean family continued to occupy the premises. The last McLean owner was Flora Douglas McLean. The private residence is now owned by Mr. and Mrs. Heath.

Cross Bay Avenue and walk to **772 East Circle Drive**. This neoclassical-style house, with red roof tiles and two stone lions flanking the steps, was built in 1901. The lighting over the archway is original to the house. The cameo door panels are repeated on the upstairs balcony. The house has two cantilevered balconies, one at the front and one on the right side.

Stuart Knox Gillis, 772's first owner, was an attorney and owner of an abstract and title business. After his death the house was occupied by the president of Palmer College, a Presbyterian college started by Chautauqua members. The sisters who presently own the house had hoped to turn it into a bed-and-breakfast inn, but were unable to obtain a zoning variance.

Cross College Avenue. The six-columned, green-shuttered corner house at **812 Circle Drive** is known as Tervin's Tara. It was built in 1903 in a neoclassical style. Within its 5,500 square feet are nine fireplaces, twelve rooms, and four baths. The house has a cantilevered stairway inside and a cantilevered balcony. During a Chautauqua session the

Walton-DeFuniak Library

house caught fire. Chautauqua members formed a bucket brigade from the lake across the street and saved the house.

Cross Main Street. Continue on Circle Drive toward the Walton-DeFuniak Library. The house at **14 Circle Drive**, on the southwest corner of Live Oak Avenue, is directly across from the library and was built for the first mayor of DeFuniak Springs. The house has an unusual square-shaped Norman tower. Another unusual feature of the house is its three-story, square bay.

The **Walton-DeFuniak Library, at 100 Circle Drive**, faces Live Oak Avenue. Turn west on Live Oak, heading away from the library. Walk to the intersection of Highway 331 and Live Oak. There is a traffic light at the intersection.

Here, at **30 West Live Oak**, you cannot miss the folk-Victorian house with yellow trim and three-story turret. This is Sunbright Manor, a grand bed-and-breakfast inn that was built circa 1886 and later was home to Sidney J. Catts, who was governor of Florida from 1916 to 1920.

The house was built for J. T. Sherman of Broadhead, Wisconsin, and was used as a winter residence for his family. Governor Catts bought the house in 1924 and lived there until his death in 1936. Catts's campaign slogan reminded backwoods voters that the only three friends a Florida Cracker could trust were Sears Roebuck, the Lord Jesus, and Sidney J. Catts.

Sunbright Manor's tower and porches boast sixteen hundred spindles and thirty-three columns. The house was carefully restored by its present owners, the Mitchells, who serve guests their breakfast on Jewel Tea china.

From Sunbright Manor, turn back on Live Oak so that you are walking east toward Circle Drive and the **Walton-DeFuniak Library**, which has a thirty-thousand-volume collection. When the library opened in 1887, it measured twenty-four by sixteen feet. It has had three expansions.

The library displays a fabulous collection of armor, collected as a hobby by Kenneth Bruce. Some of the weapons are medieval and some are artifacts of the Crusades. They come from Europe, Japan, Persia, Africa, and the United States. Kentucky rifles of the Daniel Boone era are part of the collection.

From the library, walk south on Circle Drive, toward the Chautauqua Auditorium. On the west side of **Circle Drive, at 66**, you can see the Cawthon House, named after merchant Burris Cawthon. The Cawthon House is in a Queen Anne style that is characterized by its octagonal tower with tent-style roof. A generous amount of fish-scale design embellishes the house, which was built in 1907. The front of the house has green and white awnings and a diamond-shaped window. Doric pillars encircle the porch. Return to the Chautauqua Auditorium to end the tour.

SEASIDE

Location

Seaside is located in the Florida Panhandle, on the Gulf coast between Panama City and Destin, on County Road 30A in Walton County. It is one of the Beaches of South Walton. It is eighty miles southeast of Pensacola.

History

An entire eighty-acre town that was built in the early 1980s is not historic in the usual chronological sense, but Seaside is historic in its character and architectural styles. As a replica of an old-fashioned town, there is nothing like it elsewhere in Florida. Purposely planned as a close-knit, walk-to-everything community, its intimate scale has been compared to that of Siena, Italy.

At one time, developer Robert Davis built townhouses in Coconut Grove (Miami). Childhood vacations at the beaches along the Panhandle's Gulf coast fueled his dream to build a town of simple, bungalow-style beach houses.

Davis engaged Miami architects Andres Duany and Elizabeth Plater-Zyberk as Seaside's planners. What has emerged is a town that is as much a place to visit as a neighborhood in which to reside. The cottages overlooking lampposts and brick walkways are largely rented out by their owners.

Tourists have heard and read about the fantasy-like homes with their Cape Cod and Victorian architecture, their turrets and cupolas and widow's walks and porches, their gingerbread trim and decorative detail. Corralled behind white picket fences, these cottages are painted in a palette of pretty pastels — yellow, mint, lilac, powder blue, peach, pink. Some of the older homes wear coats of forest green and matte burgundy, but it is the pastel tones that create the postcard image of Seaside.

Amazingly, Seaside's architectural code dictates that the fence at each house must be different from the fence at every other house, and it must be painted with a specific brand and color number of paint. So although there is uniformity, Seaside is varied. The houses repeatedly conform to basics, yet their very existence, combined with their accessibility to modest shopping, sparkling beaches, and emerald waters, makes for a fascinating walking tour.

Simply put, Seaside was designed as a traditional neighborhood, but it gives visitors a feeling that they have stepped back in time. Not only do the "cottages" evoke a nineteenth-century atmosphere, the Honeymoon Cottages facing the beach were influenced by the architecture of Thomas Jefferson's day. The creation of a town square is also a throwback to yesteryear.

Walking Tour
The walking tour is approximately a quarter of a mile and takes about twenty minutes. To get to the **Central Seaside Square**, take I-10 to Highway 331. Head south to Highway 98. Go east on Highway 98 to C.R. 283 (Seaside/Grayton Beach). Go south on 283 to 30A. Go east on 30A into Seaside and the Central Square. There is parking along 30A.

Begin the tour at the front of the **Hall Building**, in downtown Seaside's Central Square. The front of the Hall Building won a 1992 Design of the Decade Award from *Progressive Architecture* magazine. It houses a series of retail shops on the bottom floor, businesses on the second floor, and eight guest suites above, which have their own terraces and overlook the water. The entire third floor is called Dreamland Heights.

An additional building, with the same concept as the Hall Building, has been constructed in Seaside by Machado and Sylvetti, who are building a park in New York City near the base of the Statue of Liberty. A series of buildings like the Hall Building are planned to be built around Seaside's amphitheater, on the Village Green.

All of the shops in the Hall Building are one-of-a-kind, mom-and-pop operations. There are no franchise outlets here. This is the location of Modica's, the only grocery in town, which is why it's always busy. The grocery sells everything from dry goods, meats, and produce to wine, sundries, and its own brand of spaghetti sauce.

From the Central Square, you can see the beach and the Gulf of Mexico southward across C30A. As you face westward with your back to the Central Square, you'll gaze toward the **Village Green/amphitheater** area, where musical and theatrical events are held. An annual white wine festival and red wine festival are held here. During the summer, sunset serenades and jazz ensembles are welcomed on Tuesday nights. Visitors bring their blankets and picnic dinners. Every Friday night in the summer there are movies and programs for kids.

Josephine's, a bed-and-breakfast inn

The **Seaside Institute** is headquartered at the Village Green. Its mission is to bring arts and culture to northwest Florida. At the heart of the Village Green is the Seaside post office, which may eventually be moved to another location at the front of a library building.

The tiny, free-standing, working **post office**, with its white exterior and its red door, is rumored to be the most photographed post office in the world.

From Center Square, step out to Seaside Avenue, which runs north and south on a slight angle. Head right (north) on Seaside Avenue. You'll pass what is probably the most imposing structure in Seaside. **Josephine's** is a Georgian-looking white bed-and-breakfast inn with big white columns flanking the entrance.

When you get to East Ruskin Street, turn left (west) and walk a very short distance to **Ruskin Place**. This is Seaside's crafts district or artists' colony. It is designed after the SoHo district in New York City, where artists' shops are on the ground floor and their lofts or apartments are above.

The three-story row houses of Ruskin Place are occupied by people involved in varied art forms ranging from woodworking to handmade clothing. The open-air, parklike center of Ruskin Place is an ideal locale for the summertime poetry readings, music ensembles, a cappuccino bar, and strolling visitors.

Head back eastward on East Ruskin Street, to Seaside Avenue. Turn left (north) onto Seaside Avenue to see pretty vegetables all in a row. The only garden in Seaside is behind developer Robert Davis's house, and residents are welcome to pick from the vines.

Seaside Avenue is the main street in the community and is the only street with a median. The homes all have double porches and are all close to the street. That's because Robert Davis felt it was important for residents to be able to walk down the street and say hello to their neighbors without yelling.

You'll notice that all of the houses have the owner's name and hometown posted outside. Two names indicates that two families shared the purchase of the house.

Continue north on Seaside Avenue to reach the **deck pool**, which is one of Seaside's three pools. Turn right on Forest Street and follow the footpath. You'll come to the **Public Works**. Here, you'll wind your way around the second pool, the family pool, the shuffleboard and tennis courts, and what Seaside claims is the only nationally-recognized croquet lawn in all of northwest Florida. A bicycle rental and pro shop are here, as are a family park and playground.

Head back on Forest Street and turn right (south) at Tupelo Street, which leads you to **Tupelo Circle** and a gazebo. During summertime, no cars can get in here. It's a picture-pretty safety zone for children with skateboards and rollerblades. Notice the appealing names owners have given to their houses: Persimmon, Sunnyside, Sandcastle, Dreamweaver, and Brigadoon.

The large, two-story, cream-color house facing Tupelo Circle was built by renowned architect Leon Krier. Architects from around the world come to Seaside to study the Krier house. Prince Charles has twice visited Seaside and has consulted with Krier to build a community like Seaside in the south of Wales. Prince Charles sees Seaside as a visionary model for the future towns he'd like to see built in Great Britain.

Continue south on Tupelo Circle. Cross 30A to the **Tupelo Beach Pavilion**. This pavilion is widely photographed to represent Seaside and Florida's remaining unspoiled beaches.

Each street in Seaside is considered to be a separate neighborhood with a neighborhood association of its own. Each association collects a fee from its neighborhood to keep up the maintenance of the pavilions and the streets. There are changing rooms in the pavilions. The pavilions serve two important purposes. They act as a communal front porch, where neighbors gather and sit during the evenings, and they provide a walkway down to the beach.

Tupelo Beach Pavilion

Leave the Tupelo pavilion and, with your back to the beach, turn left (west). You'll pass the six beachside **Honeymoon Cottages**. While Thomas Jefferson was building his home at Monticello, he and his wife Martha stayed in a guesthouse. The Honeymoon Cottages or Jefferson Cottages are reputed to be replicas of the guesthouse. Six more Honeymoon Cottages are located farther west on 30A.

Look across to the north side of 30A, at the **Information Office**. It's housed in a newer version of a traditional north Florida "dogtrot" house. Dogtrots are houses with rooms separated from each other by breeze-ways for ventilation.

This is the location of an information, sales, and rental office for Seaside's cottages. There is a motor court behind the offices, and a Greek restaurant called Cafe Bouzouki.

Jefferson Honeymoon Cottages

Continue west on the beach side. Directly across from the Village Green, you'll run into **Seaside Square** with its delightful, pastel-colored, open-air marketplace. The pastel shacks with their bazaarlike ambiance make up an outdoor market called **Per.spi.cas.ity**. **Bud & Alley's Restaurant** is next door to the shacks. This is where visitors dine when they're looking for a view of the Gulf while selecting from a menu that includes fresh-caught fish. The restaurant is named after the owners' dog and cat.

From 30A, peer northwestward to Natchez Street. The landmark Seaside water tower was recently removed from this location. Now there is a small park area with a four-foot-tall stone sundial as the focal point. Seaside's third swimming pool, Westside Pool, is located near Natchez Street. Cross 30A to head back to the Central Square.

Gadsden County

Location

Gadsden County is located in northwest Florida's Panhandle along the Georgia border. Quincy, the Gadsden county seat, is twenty-two miles west of Tallahassee. The Gulf coast is less than an hour's drive south.

History

The Gadsden County area was inhabited by Muscogee Indians from the fifteenth to seventeenth centuries, with Seminole and Creek Indians moving into the area between 1500 and 1800. In the late seventeenth century, Spanish missionaries established missions in what is now the town of Chattahoochee.

In the early 1800s, the region was developed into plantations. The most lucrative crops were cotton and tobacco. In 1823, the Florida Territorial Government created Gadsden County, naming it for Andrew Jackson's aide-de-camp, Captain James Gadsden, to recognize his role in the First Seminole Indian War (1818).

Quincy was appointed as the county seat in 1828 and was named in honor of President John Quincy Adams, who was in office at that time. Also in 1828, Dr. Malcolm Nicholson, who had emigrated from Scotland, built a farmhouse on his four-thousand-acre cotton and corn plantation between Quincy and Havana, Florida. Slave labor constructed the house from native pine and bricks that were kilned on the plantation. Wooden pegs were used in lieu of nails.

Four generations of Nicholsons lived in the house. In 1988 Paul Nicholson, Malcolm's great-great-grandson, and Paul's partner Willard Rudd converted the farmhouse and outbuildings into Nicholson's Farmhouse Restaurant. They added two acquired farmhouses, dating from 1890 and 1905, which are now part of the restaurant complex.

During the 1840s and 1850s, plantations in the county prospered, and the tobacco industry grew as Gadsden tobacco was used for cigars. Quincy was the second most highly populated Florida city in 1854. The

Civil War created blockades of Florida ports, and the tobacco industry was temporarily halted. During the war, Quincy served as a medical center and supply commissary for the Confederacy.

By 1887, the tobacco industry was alive again in Quincy. In 1900, local growers discovered that by growing the tobacco under a cloth shade, its color and texture were improved. This discovery catapulted tobacco into a multimillion-dollar-a-year industry and earned the area a reputation as the shade tobacco capital of the world.

Around this time, Mark W. "Pat" Munroe, president of the Quincy State Bank, let local applicants know that their chances of qualifying for a loan would improve if they invested in a particular stock that Munroe favored. This stock was issued by a new company named Coca-Cola. Twenty-four county residents became millionaires, and Quincy became the richest town per capita in the United States. It was "Coke" money that influenced Quincy's architectural appearance, because wealthy stockholders built majestic homes.

By the late 1960s, unable to compete with foreign markets, Gadsden County's shade tobacco industry had nearly died. Today, the county has one of the lowest costs of living in Florida. Quincy's historic district is listed on the National Register of Historic Places and is a Florida Main Street City, a designation given by the Department of State Division of Historic Resources to towns and cities that have restored economic vitality to their downtown areas.

Walking Tour

The walking tour is approximately one mile in length and takes about one hour. To get to the **Quincy Garden Center at 204 East Jefferson Street**, take I-10 west to exit 27 (Quincy). Veer to the right off the exit, onto Highway 90. Continue for about 10 miles. Highway 90 becomes Jefferson Street. The Garden Center is at the corner of Jefferson and Duval Streets, at the first traffic light you'll encounter. Park at the Center or on the street.

The **Garden Center** is in an 1893 house with moldings, porch railings, and stained-glass windows that are typical of the Victorian style. The local Garden Club leases the house from the City of Quincy, the present owner.

The house, which sits at the corner of Jefferson and Duval Streets, was built by Mark W. "Pat" Munroe. When he wasn't playing father to his eighteen children, Munroe was busy serving as president of the Quincy State Bank.

At the corner of Jefferson and Duval, turn right onto Duval and head

Quincy Garden Center, photo by James Gaines, Florida Department of Commerce

up to Washington Street. Then turn right to approach the **Eastern Cemetery** which, along with the **Western Cemetery**, holds the remains of Quincy's oldest settlers. Both cemeteries date to the 1820s.

Many of the headstones reveal interesting facts about people buried here. One reads "Thomas Freeman, son of William and Florence, born in 1876, died in 1898. Here lies the son of a Confederate soldier who died for his country."

Head back west on Washington Street to Love Street. At Love Street, turn right and head up to King Street. Turn right and walk to **305 East King Street**, which is on the south side, the former home of John Lee McFarlin.

McFarlin was a lumberman and tobacco planter who built this house in 1895. It is a left-wing Queen Anne with several sculptured fireplaces, a large, forty-two-pillar veranda, and a left-handed turret. The interior is panelled in curly pine. The beautiful double entrance doors have leaded-glass insets and transom. A lovely one-and-one-half-acre garden that includes a rare Japanese fir tree surrounds the property.

In 1994, the house was bought by Richard and Tina Fauble, who, with Richard's mother Bethany, did extensive, loving restoration work. The Faubles turned the seven-thousand-square-foot house into a lovely bed-and-breakfast inn.

At **306 East King Street**, on the north side of the street, sits the J. E. A. Davidson house. It was built in 1859 in a vernacular Georgian style. Huge Corinthian columns support the semicircular porch, which was added around twenty years later. Davidson was a state senator for

Gadsden County in 1868.

The Underhill-Wedeles house at **318 East King**, with its green shutters and green-and-white-striped awnings, was built in 1905. Max Wedeles was prominent in the tobacco industry.

At the corner of King and Corry Streets, turn left onto Corry. The Old Presbyterian Manse is at **313 Corry**. It was built in 1870 for R. H. M. Davidson.

Continue on Corry Street to East Sharon Street and turn left. Sharon Street loops back around to King Street. There will be a gully on your right. Bear right on King and you'll come upon the George Dismukes Munroe house at **234 East King Street**. George was the brother of Pat Munroe and a founder of the Quincy State Bank. His white, wood-frame Victorian house with yellow shutters was built in 1898 and is most notable for its leaded stained glass windows.

The C. R. Shaw house at **222 King Street** features Corinthian columns and leaded-glass doors. The house was built from 1840 to 1844 by Arthur Foreman, who was involved in the tobacco industry.

At King and North Duval Streets, turn left (south) onto Duval. The blue-shuttered wood-frame house with the three-sided covered porch at **211 Duval Street** was built in 1847 for Isaac R. Harris. It was puchased by William Munroe thirteen years later. There has been only slight alteration to the house.

The living room of the little K. A. MacGowan house at **203 North Duval** was where Dr. Bob Munroe conducted his dental practice around 1890. The house was built in 1884.

The Stockton-Curry house sits at **121 North Duval Street**, at the corner of North Duval and Franklin. This classical revival house was built in 1845. There are two notable changes to the original look of the house. The former semidetached kitchen was incorported into the main house in 1890, and a two-story, semihexagonal bay was added.

Phillip A. Stockton came from the Northeast to Florida in 1836. He carried on his law practice from a small building on the south side of the house. In 1883, the house sold to James E. Broome, who later served as a state senator from Gadsden County. In 1902, the C. H. Curry family bought the house. Curry and his brother-in-law Alexander Shaw pioneered the artificial shade process for growing tobacco.

At the corner of Duval and Franklin Streets, head right (west) on Franklin. Walk to the corner of Franklin and Madison Streets, where you'll find the E. B. Shelfer House at **205 North Madison**. This tan house with white columns and all-copper gutters retains a combination Victorian and neoclassical style, including scroll-and-urn decoration on the veranda's roof pediment. Note the stained-glass windows and the amusing birdhouse that is a miniature replica of the big house. E. B. Shelfer Sr. produced shade tobacco and was a director of the Quincy State Bank and the nearby Havana State Bank.

Turn right (north) on Madison. The A. K. Allison House at **216 North Madison** was designed in the classical revival style with a Georgian, double-parlor floor plan. The house originally rested on pilings. In 1925, the bottom floor was enclosed, so the exterior of the house as it stands today appears quite different from its original plan. Built in 1843, the Allison House has an intriguing history.

A. K. Allison, a general during the wars of Indian removal (1830s), had helped prepare the 1842 resolution requesting statehood for Florida, and he had served as a Gadsden County representative from 1845 to 1862.

In 1865, only eight days before the Civil War ended, Florida Governor John Milton killed himself because he was certain that victorious Union troops would execute all Southern heads of state. At the time Governor Milton committed suicide, Allison was president of the senate. Milton's death propelled Allison into the governorship.

According to the Gadsden County Historic Society booklet, "A Tour

Allison House, circa 1843
Photo by James Gaines, Florida Department of Commerce

of Historic Quincy," Allison traveled to Washington to secure Florida's post-war status as a state. He was arrested by Union troops for this "treason" and imprisoned outside of Savannah. Six months later, he was released. He conducted his law practice in Quincy until his death in 1893.

Allison's house is now a charming bed-and-breakfast inn filled with antique English furniture such as pouting couches, china cabinets, armoires, and vanities. Breakfast is served in Ella's Parlor, which is named for Allison's daughter.

Continue north on Madison Street to the **Owl Cigar Company Warehouse/Shade Leaf Building at 404 North Madison** Street. This red-brick warehouse was built in 1891 by the Owl Cigar Company. Within its thirty-five-thousand square feet, tobacco was cured and packaged under the popular names of White Owl and Robert Burns. In its heyday during the end of the nineteenth century, the Owl Cigar Company employed five hundred people here.

In 1978, Frank DiSalvo and Robert Bischoff bought the building and renovated it into a mixed use complex of apartments, offices, and artists' studios, among them the Bischoff Studios, which specializes in original carved glass commissions.

Turn around and head south on Madison. Walk to King Street and turn right (west) on King. Walk to North Adams Street. At the **northeast corner of Adams and King**, you'll find **Quincy Academy**, a classical revival building that dates to 1851. The private academy educated the children of Gadsden and surrounding counties until 1871. It later was used as a public school, a church meeting room, a vocational school, a library, and, currently, a meeting place for community activities.

Turn right (north) onto Adams Street and walk to **404 Adams Street**, which is the R. K. Shaw/Embry House, an imposing structure with typical Victorian features. The house, surrounded by a decorative wrought iron fence, is owned by antiques dealers.

Turn left (west) on Sharon and walk to the intersection of Sharon and Jackson Streets. Look for a house with a green tile roof, dark green shutters, and white columns at **336 North Jackson Street**. This house was built in 1906 for Meade Love and is still occupied by members of the Love family.

Head left (south) on North Jackson to **320 North Jackson Street**, a two-story, yellow wood house with dark green shutters. It was built in 1890 by Dr. Charles A. Hentz and has been remodeled and expanded.

At the southeast corner of North Jackson and King Streets, the E. C. Love house sits at **219 North Jackson**. The classic Georgian house was

Thomas Munroe House
Photo by James Gaines, Florida Department of Commerce

built around 1831 and purchased in 1874 by Edward C. Love, who was a judge and a mayor of Quincy.

The Thomas Munroe house is at the northwest corner of Jackson and King, at **210 West King**. This white house with dark green shutters was built in 1849 in a classical revival style. The house is still owned by the Munroe family.

Continue south on Jackson and walk to Washington. Turn left (east). At **16 West Washington Street**, you'll find a gray, square building with cobalt-blue trim. It was originally an ice and electric plant that was built in 1899 by a black man named William Harden.

Walk to Duval and turn right. The **Leaf Theatre at 118 East Washington Street**, on the northwest corner of Washington and Duval, was built in 1949 as a motion picture theater. The theater was named after the tobacco leaf and was designed in green and brown, the colors of the leaf. It closed in 1980 but later reopened as a performing arts theater.

Walk to Jefferson to return to the Garden Club/Pat Munroe House.

TALLAHASSEE

Leon County

Location

Tallahassee, Florida's state capital, is located in the Florida Panhandle. It lies twenty miles north of the Gulf of Mexico and fourteen miles south of Georgia, centered between Jacksonville and Pensacola.

History

In 1539, conquistador Hernando de Soto set up a winter encampment in the area now known as Tallahassee. It was the site of the first Christmas mass in America. During the seventeenth century, Spaniards established Franciscan missions among the Apalachee Indians in the area. Creek and Seminole Indians repopulated the region during the last years of the eighteenth century.

In 1823, William Pope DuVal, first civilian governor of the new Territory of Florida, sent an explorer on horseback from St. Augustine, and another explorer by boat from Pensacola, to designate a central location for the legislature to meet. At that time, Florida had two capitals. Before Florida was unified as a United States territory, St. Augustine was the capital of the territory of East Florida, and Pensacola the capital of West Florida.

The two men rendezvoused near a waterfall, an area the Apalachee Indian inhabitants called "tallahassee," or "land of the old fields." This meeting place was declared Florida's capital.

In 1841, Tallahassee was struck by a yellow fever epidemic that raged for eight months, killing as many as four hundred residents. In 1845, Thomas Brown, a Tallahasee hotel operator and former member of the Virginia legislature, represented Leon County in Florida's first House of Representatives. In 1849, he became Florida's only Whig governor.

Tallahassee was a prosperous trade center, and stately homes were built in downtown sections around Calhoun Street and Park Avenue. When the Civil War began, Tallahassee was Florida's wealthiest and most populated city. The area's pre–Civil War landscape was dotted with cotton plantations.

The plantation home called Bellevue was owned by the great-grand-niece of George Washington, who was married to Prince Achille Murat, nephew of Napoleon Bonaparte. Supposedly, he wooed Kate by drinking from her slipper.

Nearby Alfred B. Maclay State Park encompasses 307 acres of floral architecture surrounding reflecting pools and fountains. It is the site of the former winter home of New York financier Alfred B. Maclay .

In March of 1865, Confederate soldiers repelled Union troops at the Battle of Natural Bridge, ten miles from what is now downtown Tallahassee. This victory made Tallahassee the only uncaptured Confederate capital east of the Mississippi. Union forces lost twenty-one men who are believed to be buried in the Old City Cemetery.

In 1892, Florida's first five black college students received their diplomas from the State Normal and Industrial College, now Florida A&M University in Tallahassee.

In 1902, Florida's population had swelled to 530,000, necessitating the enlargement of the 1845 Capitol building from 23,000 square feet to 44,000 square feet. This Old Capitol has been restored and is easily rec-ognizable by its red and white candy-striped awnings and its stained glass dome. The New Capitol, built in 1977, towers over it.

Walking Tour

The walking tour is approximately two miles long and takes about two hours. To get to the **Knott House Museum at 301 East Park Avenue**, take I-10 to Exit 29 (Monroe Street). Follow Monroe to Park Avenue. Turn left onto Park. The Museum will be on your right. There is street parking. The Knott House Museum, constructed by a free black builder in 1843, is located two blocks north and one block east of the State Capitol.

At the end of the Civil War, Union General Edward McCook made his headquarters at the Knott house, and freed the northern Florida slaves by a proclamation read from the front steps on May 20, 1865. The house was the first laboratory for Florida's first black physician, William Gunn, in the 1880s.

Gunn had been born a slave. George Betton, a local physician, had lived in the house after the Civil War. Gunn, who was Betton's buggy dri-ver, expressed an interest in learning medicine. Betton put Gunn through medical school and helped him to become established in Tallahassee.

The house is best known, though, as "The House That Rhymes," because its last owner, Luella Pugh Knott, wrote whimsical poems dedi-

Knott House

Interior of Knott House

cated to her collection of Victorian-era furnishings. Her floor lamps, teapots, chairs, and chests, for instance, were labeled with note cards inscribed with rhymes and attached by satin ribbons. A Victorian chair had this poem attached to it:

Grandmother's chair could have no arms,
For when she sat, she spread.
If she should dare use Grandpa's chair,
Her hoops would hit her head.

Luella authored a book on Christian living, but her best known works were the poems she wrote for her antiques. She published five volumes of poetry.

Luella and her husband, State Treasurer William V. Knott, moved into the house in 1928 and added a colonial revival portico and a side privacy porch. Luella was active in the temperance movement and was instrumental in banning the sale of alcohol in Tallahasee for more than fifty years.

The Knotts' daughter, Mary Bazemore, became the second woman from Florida to earn a medical degree. Their son Charles bequeathed the house and its furnishings to the state in 1986. The house now operates as a museum.

Just east of the Knott house is the Wood house at **311 East Park Avenue**, which was built in 1904 by Henry O. Wood, a lumber merchant. The Wood family used the house as their winter residence. In 1924, the house was taken over by the First Presbyterian Church to be used as a parsonage.

The Murphy house at **317 East Park Avenue** was built circa 1838. It is believed to have been constructed by George Proctor, a free black builder who built a number of homes in the area. In 1850, the house was occupied by Arvah Hopkins, who married Susan Branch, daughter of Florida's last territorial governor, John Branch. It is believed that the gothic revival ornamental woodwork was added around this time. In 1859, Hopkins sold the house to Dr. George Betton, whose offices were in the basement. Subsequent owners were Harry and Irene Murphy, whose descendants still own the house. It is occupied by antiques stores and offices.

The Chittenden house at **323 East Park Avenue** was built in 1849 by Captain R. A. Shine, who had helped to build the 1845 Capitol. Originally a one-story house, it was remodeled when Simon D. Chittenden purchased it in 1894.

The colonial revival house at **403 East Park Avenue** was built in 1913 and owned by a local civic leader and ice company owner named Mr. Lively.

The Queen Anne–style house at **413 East Park Avenue**, known as the Walker-Martin house, was built circa 1896. It was owned by the S. May Walker family. Walker owned a local clothing store.

Turn around and walk west on East Park to Gadsden Street. Turn right, heading north on Gadsden.

The **LeMoyne Art Foundation** at **125 North Gadsden Street** was originally a house built in 1854 for George H. Meginniss, a Maryland native who became a prosperous Tallahassee hardware store owner.

Meginniss had the house built for his bride, Louisa M. Gatlin. When he died in 1895, the house passed on to their daughter Jessie. Jessie, who never married, was a shrewd businesswoman who became wealthy from her real estate deals. When she died in 1935, Jessie left her home and estate to her sister, Maria Theresa Munroe, who passed the home on to her son Ivan.

In 1968, Ivan sold the house to the LeMoyne Art Foundation to be used as an art gallery. The Foundation is named for Jacques LeMoyne, a French artist who traveled through North Florida in 1554, and who captured local scenes in his paintings.

The apartment house at **203 North Gadsden** was built in 1880 for William R. Wilson of Wilson's Department Store. When the house was converted into apartments in the 1940s, it was named the Whitehouse.

Continue northward to the **corner of Gadsden and Virginia Streets**. In 1895, when Edwin Chesley designed this house with its Queen Anne features, he supposedly created a corner entrance so that the address would be either Gadsden Street or Virginia Street. Chesley, a civil engineer, could then choose whichever street address was more impressive. The address is actually **401 Virginia Street**.

The house was built by a local carpenter and cost $3,500. The kitchen was originally detached, but in 1916, with the construction of a breezeway, the kitchen became connected to the main house. Notable architectural details of the house include a wraparound porch with turned posts and brackets, gables with decorative shingles and bargeboards, and ornate hardware. The original doorbell still works. The interior of the house features twelve-foot ceilings and ornate fireplaces.

It is reported that in 1941, the roof of the house caught fire, and Chesley's son Ned was so flustered when he phoned the fire department that he forgot to tell them his name or where the house was, but Ned's voice was recognized because he was a volunteer fireman.

Turn right (east) on Virginia Street and walk to North Meridian Street. On your left, you'll see the Cotten house at **402 North Meridian**. Frederick R. Cotten, a prosperous antebellum plantation owner, acquired this property through an 1869 auction. When he died in 1878, he willed the land to his wife and children. In 1904, his daughter Margaret built a two-and-a-half story house on the property, which she left to her nephew when she died in 1921.

Subsequent owners remodeled the house. At one time, it was converted into apartments. In 1985, John A. Barley, an attorney, bought the property and restored it for use as his law offices.

The impressive classical revival–style Brokaw-McDougall house with Italianate influence at **329 North Meridian** was built between 1856 and 1860, and is now the headquarters of the **Historic Tallahassee Preservation Board**. It was built by livery stable owner Peres Bonney Brokaw, who arrived from New Jersey in 1840 at the age of twenty-six. In 1850, he married Cornelia Tatum. After her death during the Civil War, Brokaw married her sister Elizabeth. After his death in 1875, his daughter Phoebe married Scottish immigrant Alexander McDougall.

Phoebe died in 1883. Alexander married Phoebe's sister Eliza. This marriage produced a son, Peres Brokaw McDougall, who became owner of the property. The State of Florida bought the property in 1973. Outstanding architectural features of the house include its cupola, a one-story porch with six Corinthian columns, and beautiful gardens, including four live oak trees that were planted around 1850.

Turn around and walk back on Virginia Street to North Calhoun Street. Turn right and walk on the east side of the street to the Bradford-Cobb house at **403 North Calhoun**.

This carpenter gothic cottage was built in 1878 by Nancy (Nannie) S. Taylor Bradford, an independently wealthy woman who was married to John R. Bradford, son of a prominent Leon County planter. The traditional story is that she oversaw every nail that went into the construction of the house. When Nannie died in 1904, she left an estate of fine china, furnishings, and jewels. Elizabeth Deberry Cobb purchased the house in 1921 and divided it into two apartments, one of which she rented. She tore down the detached kitchen and converted the back porch into a kitchen. In 1977, Sari and Jerry Wilkey bought the house for $55,000 and remodeled it as their home. Subsequent owners converted the house into offices.

The Georgian-influenced house at **507 North Calhoun** was built circa 1848 for banker Henry Rutgers, formerly of New York. Rutgers died in 1867. Erastus W. Clark, a watchmaker, bought the house in 1893 for

$3,000. Clark's daughters Janie and Minnie Clark inherited the house.

The Rutgers house was designed in a Georgian style with "tripartite," or three-sectioned, front windows. Additional buildings on the property — a detached kitchen, smokehouse, and carriage house — no longer exist. The house was built by George W. Proctor, a free black man whose father, Antonio, was an interpreter for a trading firm. Antonio had been freed by the Spanish government in 1922 for his services during the War of 1812.

George Proctor built a number of houses in Tallahassee and was noted for his master carpentry. He purchased a wife, a slave named Nancy, but was unable to meet payment. Nancy's former owner sued Proctor, who then went to California to seek his fortune by panning for gold. Before he could pay his debt, he died.

Rutgers bought Nancy and her children. Her son John became a schoolteacher after the Civil War and was elected to the Senate from Leon County. John's son Robert became a surgeon. Proctor family members still reside in Tallahassee. In 1954, the Tallahassee Garden Club bought the home for use as their headquarters.

The Towle house at **517 North Calhoun Street** was built in 1847 and occupied by Richard Towle, a Tallahassee mayor. It was expanded between 1856 and 1857 by subsequent owner Richard Whitaker. The house combines classical revival and gothic architectural styles.

Cross over to the west side of Calhoun and turn around to head south.

The Randall-Lewis house at **424 North Calhoun Street** was built between 1843 and 1844 by George Proctor. It is a Georgian-style raised cottage of one-and-a-half stories, built on a high basement to keep the house cool and dry — but dampness was still a problem because the bricks were soft. The house relied upon a windmill to generate running water. This may have been the first house in Tallahassee to have indoor plumbing.

Occupants of the house included Judge Thomas Randall and George Lewis, a banker. Randall was an attorney and a widower with two teenage daughters when he bought the house. In 1864, at the age of seventy-two, he remarried.

The Governor Bloxham house at **410 North Calhoun Street** was built in a Federal style in 1844 by Captain R. A. Shine, a local builder and brick mason. The building plan is called "side hall Georgian." Figg Engineering Group now operates the building.

When William Bloxham was elected governor of Florida in 1880, there was no governor's mansion in Tallahassee. He and his wife Mary lived here during his two terms as governor. Between his terms, he rented the house to Governor Edward A. Perry. In 1885, Bloxham was instrumental in establishing what is now Florida A&M University.

The colonial revival–style house at **318 North Calhoun** ws built in 1906. It was occupied by Dr. R. A. Shine Jr., a dentist and grandson of builder R. A. Shine.

Continue south on Calhoun to East Park Avenue. Turn left. The B. C. Lewis house at **316 East Park Avenue** was built circa 1845 to 1850. Editor Charles E. Dyke owned the property, which he sold to Benjamin Cheever Lewis in 1850 for $1,400. Lewis was a druggist who arrived in Tallahassee from Salem, Massachusetts in 1836. He founded the Lewis State Bank. The Florida Council for Community Mental Health now owns the building, but opens it to the public on a regular basis.

The strip of land in front of the Lewis house is known as Lewis Park. It is a quick walk to the other side of the park, back to the Knott house at 301 East Park Avenue.

HISTORICAL ATTRACTIONS, DINING, AND LODGING

PENSACOLA — *Escambia County*

Suggested Dining and Lodging

Hopkins Boarding House Restaurant
900 North Spring
904-438-3979
Family-style country cooking in a turn-of-the-century house.

Jamie's French Restaurant
424 East Zaragoza Street
904-434-2911
Located in a Victorian house.

Palace Oyster Bar
130 East Government
904-434-6211
Includes the bar from the old Palace Hotel, where the first liquor license in Florida was issued.

Pensacola Grand Hotel
200 East Gregory Street
904-433-3336
The lobby, restaurant and public areas are located in a restored 1912 railroad station

For Information

Historic Pensacola Preservation Board
120 East Church Street
Pensacola, FL 32501
904-444-8905

Pensacola Convention & Visitors Information Center
1401 East Gregory Street
Pensacola, FL 32501
904-434-1234 or 800-874-1234 or 800-343-4321 (Florida).

Other Historic Attractions

For informationa about North Hill Preservation District and Palofax Historic District, contact the Convention and Visitors Information Center.

Fort Pickens
Fort Pickens Road
Pensacola Beach, FL 32561
904-934-2607
Remnants of a nineteenth-century fort erected to protect the city's port. Call for hours. $4 per car.

Historic Pensacola Village
205 East Zaragoza Street
Pensacola, FL 32501
904-444-8905
Open Monday through Saturday. Guided tours at 11:30 A.M. and 1:30 P.M. Adults $5.50, seniors and military $4.50, children $2.50.

National Museum of Naval Aviation
Naval Air Station
Pensacola, FL 32508
904-452-3604
Open daily 9 A.M. to 5 P.M. No admission fee.

T. T. *Wentworth Museum*
320 Jefferson Street
Pensacola, FL
904-444-8586
Open Monday through Saturday 10
A.M. to 4:30 P.M., Sunday 1 P.M. to 4:30
P.M. Adults $5, children $2, senior
citizens $4.

DEFUNIAK SPRINGS — *Walton County*

Suggested Dining and Lodging

Busy Bee Cafe
35 South Seventh Street
DeFuniak Springs, FL
904-892-6700
A replica of an old-fashioned cafe
filled with nostalgic mementos and
antiques. Lunch only. Fabulous fried
green tomato
sandwiches.

H&M Hotdog Stand
43 South Ninth Street
DeFuniak Springs, FL
Built in the 1920s as a shoe stand and
converted to a hot dog stand in 1948.
Workmen pouring cement for the
restaurant floor found hundreds of
shoe soles and heels in the underlying
dirt. H&M stands for Hilda and Mama.

*Sunbright Manor Bed and
Breakfast Inn*
30 West Live Oak
DeFuniak Springs, FL 32433
904-892-0656

For Information

Diane Pickett
Pickett's People Parade
2760 US Highway 331 S.

DeFuniak Springs, FL 32433
904-892-4300

Walton County Chamber of Commerce
P.O. Box 29
DeFuniak Springs, FL 32433
904-892-3191

SEASIDE — *Walton County*

Suggested Dining and Lodging

Bud & Alley's Restaurant
904-231-5900
Located in a turn of-the-century wood-
en sharecropper's shack that was relocated from Panama City.

Josephine's Dining Room
904-231-1939
Located in an antebellum plantation
home.

A Highlands House Bed & Breakfast
10 Bullard Road
Santa Rosa Beach, FL 32459
904-267-0110
Designed to resemble an antebellum
plantation home.

Josephine's Bed and Breakfast Inn
101 Seaside Avenue
Seaside, FL 32459
800-848-1840
An antebellum plantation home.

Seaside Cottage Rental Agency
904-231-1320 or 800-277-TOWN
Rental cottages with a turn-of-the-
century appearance.

Sugar Beach Inn
3501 East 30-A
Seagrove Beach, FL 32459
904-231-1577
Designed to resemble a southern
plantation home.

For Information

Seaside
P.O. Box 4730
Seaside, FL 32459
904-231-4224 or 800-591-8696

South Walton Tourist Development Council
P.O. Box 1248
Santa Rosa Beach, FL 32459
904-267-1216 or 800-822-6877

Other Historic Attractions

Bayou Arts & Antiques
Cessna Park and Highway 393
Santa Rosa Beach, FL 32459
904-267-1404
Local historian Chick Huettel owns Bayou Arts & Antiques, which sits on two former sites: a sugar cane mill and a tiny nineteenth-century chapel where area farmers and fishermen worshipped. Huettel built a replica of the St. Francis Wildlife Chapel on his property and painted the interior wall scenes of fishermen and farmers. Open Tuesday to Saturday 10 A.M. to 4:30 P.M.

Eden State Gardens
P.O. Box 26
Point Washington, FL 32454
904-231-4214
Site of the Wesley mansion, built in the early 1900s by a timber baron. The house was later owned by a female journalist whose extensive antiques collection is on display. Open daily 8 A.M. to sunset. Hourly guided tours of the mansion Thursday through Monday between 9 A.M. and 4 P.M. Tour fee: $1.50.

QUINCY — GADSDEN COUNTY

Suggested Dining and Lodging

Carriage Factory Restaurant
104 East Washington Street
904-875-4660
Housed in a brick, turn-of-the-century, former tobacco warehouse and carriage factory.

Luten's
1214 West Jefferson
904-627-6069
Quincy's oldest continuously-operated family restaurant. Diner-style cafe. Second floor was the local dance hall.

Nicholson's Farmhouse Restaurant
Highway 12 between Quincy and Havana
904-539-5931
Built near Havana in 1828. Several turn-of-the-century buildings have been added to expand the dining facility.

Allison House Inn
215 North Madison Street
Quincy, FL 32351
904-875-2511
Built for Florida's sixth governor.

Gaver's Bed & Breakfast
301 East Sixth Avenue
Havana, FL 32333
904-539-5611
Built in 1907 by Havana's first mayor.

McFarlin House Bed and Breakfast
305 East King Street
Quincy, Fl 32353
904-875-2526

For Information

Gadsden County Chamber of Commerce
P.O. Box 389
Quincy, FL 32353
800-627-9231

Other Historic Attractions

Havana Antiques District
U.S. Highway 27, ten minutes
from I-10, ten minutes north of
Tallahassee.
800-638-9299
Renovated, early-twentieth-century
shops and buildings in Havana, which
was founded in 1916. A major antiques
center.

TALLAHASSEE — *Leon County*

Suggested Dining and Lodging

Carriage Factory Restaurant
104 East Washington Street,
Suite P
Quincy
904-875-4669
The restaurant is located in an 1800s
carriage house.

Nicholson Farmhouse Restaurant
Off S.R. 12 in Havana, twelve
miles north of Tallahassee.
904-539-5931
The restaurant is in several historic
farmhouses. The steaks and atmosphere are worth the drive.

Allison House Bed & Breakfast Inn
215 North Madison Street
Quincy, FL 32351
904-875-2511

McFarlin House Bed & Breakfast Inn
305 East King Street
Quincy, FL 32531
904-875-2526

Reidel House Bed and Breakfast
1412 Fairway Drive
Tallahassee, FL 32301
904-222-8569
An antiques-filled home built in 1937
in a Federal style.

For Information

*Leon County Tourist Development
Council*
200 West College Avenue
P. O. Box 1369
Tallahassee, FL 32302
904-488-3990

Tallahassee Area Chamber of Commerce
P.O. Box 1639
100 North Duval Street
Tallahassee, FL 32302
904-224-8116 FAX 904-561-3860

*Tallahassee Area Convention and
Visitors Bureau*
200 West College Avenue
P.O. Box 1369
Tallahassee, FL 32302
904-681-9200 or 800-628-2866

*Tallahassee Area Visitor Information
Center New Capitol Building,
West Plaza Level*
North Duval Street
Tallahassee, FL 32302
904-681-9200 or 800-628-2866

Other Historic Attractions

*Black Archives Research Center &
Museum*
Carnegie Center
Florida A&M University
Tallahassee, FL 32302
904-599-3020
Exhibits and items relating to African-
Americans in Florida from the colonial
period to the present.
Call the Convention and Visitors
Bureau for information.

Bradley's Country Store
Centerville Road
Tallahassee, FL 32308
904-893-1647
A 1920s country general store on the
National Register of Historic Places. It
is famous for its homemade sausages,
which are cured in the old smokehouse
on the premises.
Open Monday through Friday 9 A.M. to
6 P.M., Saturday 9 A.M. to 5 P.M.

de Soto State Historic Site
1022 de Soto Park Drive
Tallahassee, FL 32301
904-922-6007
Site of Hernando de Soto's 1539
expeditionary force. Call the
Convention and Visitors Bureau for
information.

Florida Governor's Mansion
700 North Adams Street
Tallahassee, FL 32302
904-488-4661
Open in December; March through
May. Thirty-minute free guided tours.

Knott House
301 East Park Avenue
Tallahassee, FL
904-922-2459

Open Wednesday through Friday 1 P.M.
to 4 P.M., Saturday 10 A.M. to 4 P.M.
Families $7, Adults $3, children $1.50.

Maclay State Gardens
3540 Thomasville Road
Tallahassee, FL 32308
904-487-4556
Home, museum, and gardens relating
to New York financier Alfred Maclay,
who developed the gardens and lived
here beginning in 1923.
Open daily 8 A.M. to sunset. $3.25 per
vehicle.

The Old Capitol Building
Monroe Street and Apalachee
Parkway Tallahassee, FL 32399
904-487-1902
Restored 1902 state capitol, easily rec-
ognizable by its red-striped awnings.
Open Monday through Friday 9 A.M. to
4:30 P.M., Saturday 10 A.M. to 4:30 P.M.,
Sunday noon to 4:30 P.M.

*Old City Cemetery and St. John's
Cemetery*
904-891-8712 or 904-222-2636
Two Florida governors are buried here
as well as Civil War soldiers, and
Napoleon's nephew, Prince Achille
Murat, and his wife.

*Tallahassee Museum of History
and Natural Science*
3945 Museum Drive
904-576-2531
Tallahassee, FL 32310
The museum includes an 1880s farm.
Open Monday through Saturday 9 A.M.
to 5 P.M., Sunday 12:30 P.M.. to 5 P.M.
Adults $5, senior citizens $4,
children $3.

Northeast

NORTHEAST

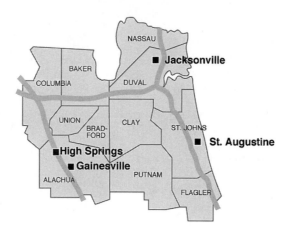

JACKSONVILLE
(RIVERSIDE & AVONDALE)
Duval County

Location

Jacksonville is the county seat of Duval County. It is located in northeast Florida on the St. Johns River.

History

Jacksonville was named for Andrew Jackson, who was the first territorial governor of Florida. In 1801, the Spanish government, eager for new settlers to its East Florida territory, granted eight hundred acres of land to Phillip Dell. In 1868, Boston millionaire John M. Forbes paid $10,000 for five hundred of those acres. He called his platted lots "Riverside." In 1887, Riverside became part of the city of Jacksonville. Less than a decade later, it had become a fashionable residential suburb.

In May of 1901, Jacksonville was devastated by a mammoth fire that destroyed most of the downtown. Shrewd businessmen, architects, and builders flocked to Jacksonville in the realization that the city would need rebuilding. Wealthy families who had lived downtown now built mansions along Riverside Avenue, but the area farther down the river had seen little development.

In 1920, a group of investors headed by Telfair Stockton paid more than $500,000 for a parcel of land that was one mile long and five blocks wide. The land was developed as a desirable residential neighborhood. Stockton named the land Avondale, after a subdivision in Cincinnati.

Houses in Riverside and Avondale were built in the popular styles of the period, beginning with the Victorian style during the last decade of the nineteenth century and continuing with classical revival, bungalow, Tudor revival, and shingle styles during the first decade of the twentieth century. This was probably due to the fact that after the 1901 fire, many young architects, each with his own favorite style of architecture, came to Jacksonville to help design new buildings. Between 1910 and 1920 many houses showed a prairie-style influence, which was followed, from 1920 onward, by the Mediterranean influence. Many of the homes built in Avondale were in the Mediterranean revival style of architecture.

The residents of the Riverside and Avondale Historic District take pride in their community and in the restoration of the grand old homes that characterize this quiet, charming alternative to typical tract house neighborhoods. In 1974, to preserve their architectural and historic heritage, local citizens formed Riverside Avondale Preservation, Inc., a neighborhood improvement organization.

Since 1989, both Riverside and Avondale have been listed as historic districts in the National Register of Historic Places. Collectively they are one of the largest such districts in the southeast to feature mainly early twentieth-century architecture.

Walking Tour

A complete walking tour of the Riverside and Avondale Historic District, which is seven miles long, would encompass too many buildings. The self-guided walking tour of the Riverside neighborhood described here is condensed into a reasonable number of homes and streets. It encompasses approximately one and a half miles and will take about one hour. Riverside in the north end of the historic district is divided from Avondale in the south end by Seminole Road which crosses Riverside Avenue. However, residents frequently do not differentiate between the two sections. They say that they live in Riverside and Avondale.

Begin the tour at the **Cummer Museum of Art and Gardens at 829 Riverside Avenue**. If you are coming from the south on I-95, cross the Fuller Warren Bridge and exit at College Street. Turn left on College, travel to Margaret Street and turn left again. Proceed to Riverside Avenue and turn left. Continue to the Cummer Museum, which has parking across the street. Coming from the north, exit at Riverside Avenue, just before the Fuller Warren Bridge. Turn right onto Riverside and proceed to the Cummer.

The Cummer Museum was built in 1960 on the site of the Tudor revival house of Arthur and Nina Cummer. The house, built in 1902, was a showplace for Nina Cummer's collection of antiques and objects d'art. In 1931, she added a large drawing room to her house. Known as the Tudor Room, it was filled with European antiques.

The house has since been demolished, but the original interior of the Tudor Room is on display in the Cummer Gallery of Art, part of the museum. Nina Cummer's formal English garden with reflecting pools, terraces, sculptures, and 150-year-old oak tree has been preserved.

Walk south on Riverside Avenue to **861 Riverside Avenue**. The Tudor revival–style **Woman's Club of Jacksonville** was built in 1927 at a cost of $60,000. The Woman's Club is in a section that was once called "The Row." It was lined with beautiful mansions, which are now gone except for two. They are on the northeast corner and southeast corner of Riverside Avenue and Lancaster Terrace. Their addresses are **1521 Riverside and 1541 Riverside**.

On the right side of Riverside Avenue, directly across from these two houses, is the **Napier Apartments at 1532–1534 Riverside Avenue**. They were built in 1924 and 1925 and designed by architect H. J. Klutho for developer Leslie Napier Wilkie, who planned to use the building as a four-unit condominium. However, when his partners backed out of the project, he divided the units into smaller apartments.

Henry J. Klutho came to Jacksonville around 1901. Between then and 1914, Klutho designed many of the prominent buildings that were constructed throughout Jacksonville's downtown area. Klutho was a follower of Frank Lloyd Wright's Prairie School of architecture and is widely considered to be one of Florida's two greatest architects. The other, Addison Mizner, designed the Riverside Baptist Church.

Continue around the curve on Riverside Avenue, now heading west. On the right, at **1617–1633 Riverside Avenue**, is the **San Juline Apartments**, which overlooks Memorial Park. The San Juline Apartment building was designed in 1916 by Roy Benjamin. The original construction cost for the building was $85,000. The apartments were advertised as having such modern conveniences as steam heat and gas. Roy Benjamin's reputation throughout the southeastern United States was as a theater architect, although he designed many homes in Riverside and Avondale.

Memorial Park in the 1600 block of Riverside Avenue was built from 1922 to 1924 and was designed by the Olmsted Brothers, landscape architects from Brookline, Massachusetts, and the supervising architectural firm of Benjamin & Greeley. This land was originally used as a picnic ground and occasionally by black church congregations for Sunday baptisms.

Memorial Park was built as a tribute to Florida citizens who died in World War I and is designed in a nineteenth-century romantic style. The focal point of the park is a bronze statue titled "Winged Victory." It was designed by well-known Florida sculptor C. Adrian Pillars and was unveiled on Christmas Day, 1924.

At the corner of Riverside and Margaret Street, turn left onto Margaret and walk one block to the end so that you can get a good view of the **Park Lane Apartments at 1846**. This seventeen-story building, designed by Roy Benjamin, was Riverside's first high-rise. It was constructed in 1926 on a slender strip of land. That land was actually the front yard of a house that until recently stood near the bottom of the apartment building.

Walk back up Margaret Street to Riverside Avenue and turn left. Walk one block and turn left again, onto Goodwin Street. Walk two blocks to the river. On your left, notice the house at **1819 Goodwin**, which was designed by Henrietta C. Dozier, Jacksonville's foremost female architect. The house, comprised of a mixture of architectural styles, was built in 1924 for the family of Charles Welshans at a cost of nearly $20,000.

Also on the left are the **River House Apartments**, circa 1870, which were moved to this site after the turn of the century. The three-story building was constructed in a second empire style. Its original two-tiered veranda is now enclosed.

Turn right onto River Boulevard. Walk one block. On the right, at the corner of Copeland Street, you'll see a brick, prairie style residence at **2165 River Boulevard**, built in 1912 for George F. Bensel, president of Southern States Land & Timber Company.

The house at **1805 Copeland Street** was built in 1919 and 1920 for William Baldwin, vice president of the Baldwin-Lewis Naval Stores Company. The builder and designer was Ransom Buffalow, who built many residences in the prairie style.

Continue west on River Boulevard for one more block until you arrive at the **Cheek Mansion at 2263 River Boulevard**, on the corner of Osceola Street. This castlelike brick mansion was designed by Roy Benjamin for Leon Cheek, who was head of the Cheek-Neal Coffee Company, later known as Maxwell House.

Among the mansion's notable features are its slate roof and an elaborate oriel window that juts out above the front doorway. The window sits on a stone bracket. When it was completed in 1929, the mansion was said to have cost $250,000. It was built in a Jacobethan revival style, with its windows placed in groups and stone trim that frames the arches, corners, and doorways.

Turn right onto Osceola Street and walk north. On the left you'll note the **St. Johns House, at 1718 Osceola**. This two-story house was built in the prairie style and is a bed-and-breakfast inn.

At the corner of Riverside Avenue and Osceola, you'll see a white house with green trim at **1702 Osceola**. It was built in 1914 for lumberman J. D. Sasse. From 1931 to 1946 it was owned by former Jacksonville Mayor John W. Martin, who was governor of Florida from 1925 to 1929. The house was later remodeled.

Leon Cheek Mansion, built 1928-1929

Turn right (east) on Riverside. Walk on the south side of the street. The brick house at **2254 Riverside** was built in 1916 in the prairie style for attorney James A. Yates. Typical of the prairie style are the home's roof overhangs, the horizontal lines, and the band of windows that face the street.

The one-story house at **2237 Riverside Avenue**, with two bay windows and green tile roof, was built around 1937 for the semi-invalid widow of Duncan U. Fletcher. Fletcher was mayor of Jacksonville from 1893 to 1895 and again from 1901 to 1903. He served as a U.S. senator from 1909 to 1937.

At the end of this block note **2201 Riverside**, built in 1912 for William P. Baya Jr., a produce broker. The house is a conglomeration of colonial revival, Queen Anne, bungalow, and stick styles of architecture.

The **Fenimore Apartments at 2200 Riverside Avenue**, at the corner of Riverside Avenue and Copeland Street, was designed by architect Mellen Greeley. Greeley lived on Riverside Avenue from 1880 to 1905 and designed many residences in Riverside and Avondale. He was a former secretary of the Florida State Board of Architecture. When the Fenimore was built in 1922, it was considered to be one of the most luxurious apartment buildings in Jacksonville and served as a first home for many of the city's prominent newlywed couples.

Plantation Manor Inn

Turn left onto Copeland Street. Walk one block to Oak Street. At the corner on the left is a bed-and-breakfast inn, **Plantation Manor Inn, at 1630 Copeland**. Built in a colonial revival style, circa 1906, it has massive white Doric columns and a large veranda. The house was first owned by J. E. Johnson, president of the Realty Title and Trust Company and was bought in 1923 by Augustus Anthony, president of People's Bank.

To the right, on the opposite corner, is "Frogmore," the Arthur Gilkes residence, at **2160 Oak Street**. Gilkes was a prominent architect who designed this Tudor-style house in 1903 for his family. At one time, heavy rains would carry river overflow onto Oak Street, attracting frogs that croaked during the night. They were the inspiration for the whimsical name "Frogmore."

Continue walking east on Oak Street to **2063 Oak**. The Love-McGinnis house is one of the few Mediterranean revival designs by Klutho. It looks almost like a large pentagonal wedding cake. The front of the house has an arcaded porch and columned balcony. The house was built for Dr. James Love and Dr. R. H. McGinnis. They lived on the second floor and had their offices on the first floor.

Continue east on Oak. Cross Margaret and go down narrow Oak Lane to May Street, where you'll turn left. You'll see Col. Cay's carriage house at **1545 May Street**. In 1905, former Confederate colonel Raymond Cay had a stately house built for himself. A subsequent owner was Francis P. Fleming, an attorney whose father was a former governor of Florida. The house later was occupied by the Jacksonville Art Center, but it was eventually demolished. All that is left today is the rear carriage house which is now occupied by a hair studio.

Notice the beautiful brickwork on May Street, only between Riverside Avenue and Lomax Street. The street is paved with brown Augusta paving bricks, and the curbstones of granite are eight to twelve inches high. In 1969, to protest the street's scheduled repaving with asphalt, three women who owned Col. Cay's carriage house, stood in the path of the paving machines. They succeeded in preserving the brick-work.

Continue on May Street, heading north for a few blocks to Post Street. As you turn right on Post Street, look back to your left for a good view of the Queen Victoria at **717 Post**. This yellow and white Queen Anne–style house with tower, spindle work, gingerbread trim, and hand-blown glass windows was built around 1892 for the family of Ernest A. Ricker, a dealer in wines, liquors, coffee, and cigars. The house original-ly sat on Oak Street, but was moved to its present location around 1967, after Mrs. Ricker died at the age of one hundred. The house is now a restaurant called A Tasteful Cafe.

Walk one block to Riverside Avenue. Turn left and head back to the Cummer Museum and Gardens.

If this short walking tour has whetted your taste to see more of the beautiful Riverside and Avondale historic district, you may wish to follow it up with a twenty-minute drive through the heart of the neighborhood. As you exit the Cummer parking lot, turn right (south) on Riverside Avenue. Continue nearly two miles on Riverside Avenue past many ele-gant historic homes, until you reach the stop sign at Ingleside Avenue. Turn left and travel a few blocks to the Avondale Shopping Center, a charming 1920s enclave of restaurants, antique shops, and other stores. Turn left (east) on St. Johns Avenue, which was recently selected as "the Most Beautiful Street in Jacksonville" in a citywide newspaper poll. In about one mile, turn left onto King Street and proceed four blocks to Park Street, where you'll see Addison Mizner's extraordinary Riverside Baptist Church, the end of your driving tour.

ST. AUGUSTINE

St. Johns County

Location

St. Augustine is the county seat of St. Johns County, which is bounded by the St. Johns River to the west and the Atlantic Ocean to the east. St. Augustine is thirty-six miles south of Jacksonville, and fifty miles north of Daytona Beach.

History

Before the Spanish explorers came, the area known today as St. Augustine was inhabited by Timucuan Indians. St. Augustine was founded in 1565, forty-two years before Jamestown was colonized by the English, and fifty-five years before the Pilgrims landed at Plymouth Rock.

In 1513, Juan Ponce de León claimed Florida for Spain and named it La Florida (Land of Flowers). The French established a colony at Ft. Caroline along the St. Johns River in 1564. Because this was a threat to the Spanish treasure fleets that sailed along the Florida coast, King Philip II of Spain sent his most trusted admiral, Don Pedro Menéndez de Aviles, to drive out the French. Menéndez arrived in Florida on the Feast Day of St. Augustine of Hippo in 1565. He came ashore and named the area St. Augustine.

A stone fort eventually was built to protect St. Augustine from foreign invaders. The Castillo de San Marcos fortress was never conquered, and endures as the nation's oldest and only remaining seventeenth-century masonry fort. In 1764, St. Augustine came under British rule until 1784, when the Second Spanish Period began.

In 1821, Florida became an American territory. East and West Florida were united under territorial governor Andrew Jackson. Tallahassee became the territorial capital, thus St. Augustine lost its status as the capital of East Florida. In 1845, Florida was admitted to the Union. Union troops occupied St. Augustine during most of the Civil War. During the last part of the nineteenth century, St. Augustine became a tourist destination, thanks to land developers like Henry Flagler, whose hotels and railroad brought growth to the area.

Because of its unique position as the oldest European settlement in America, 144 blocks of St. Augustine are on the National Register of Historic Places. Anastasia Island and St. Augustine Beach across the Bridge of Lions are the resort areas of St. Augustine, but it is the story of Florida's first colonization that makes historic St. Augustine a magnet for visitors.

Walking Tour

The walking tour is approximately one mile, and can take two to three hours, since it is highly recommended that you visit the buildings that operate as museums. There is parking behind the Lightner Museum.

To get to the **Lightner Museum at 75 King Street**, take I-95 to the S.R. 16 exit (the Outlet Mall exit) and head east. Turn right (south) at U.S. 1. Proceed to King Street and head east. Turn right (south) on Granada and go two blocks to the parking lot. Begin the tour at the entrance to the Lightner Museum.

Across the street and opposite the museum, you'll see **Flagler College**, which was originally the posh Ponce de Leon Hotel, built by Henry Flagler between 1885 and 1887. The building reflects the Spanish Renaissance revival style of architecture and was constructed of poured concrete, a building method Flagler learned from Franklin Smith. Smith's Moorish revival **Zorayda Castle**, designed to resemble the Alhambra in Granada, Spain, is at **83 King Street**.

The former hotel's stained glass windows were created by Louis Tiffany. The Ponce de Leon Hotel was the flagship of Flagler's hotels. During World War II, it served as a Coast Guard training center. In 1968, it was designated a National Historic Landmark, and was converted into the main building of Flagler College.

The Lightner Museum is inside the **St. Augustine City Hall**. This building, constructed in 1888, was originally the Alcazar Hotel, also built by Henry Flagler, although it was not as expensive a hotel as the Ponce de Leon. The building is now used for city offices.

The Alcazar had an indoor swimming pool that was touted as the largest in the world in 1888. The hotel also offered guests Turkish and Russian baths. Sulphur water from an artesian well constantly poured into the pool. The ground-level floor of the swimming pool, which was located in the rear of the building, is now the floor of an antiques mall and the location of the Cafe Alcazar.

Flagler claimed that he had the world's fastest swimmer performing at the Alcazar. The young man would dive from the deep end of the 50 by 120–foot pool, and appear a few seconds later at the shallow end. As the

Flagler College, former Ponce de Leon Hotel, circa 1885

story goes, the young man's twin brother would hide at the shallow end, under the second-floor balcony that extended around the pool. The ceiling that covered the pool area was the third floor. Spectators on the second-floor balcony who peered down into the pool didn't see the hidden twin brother emerging quickly from the shallow end. They believed that they were watching an amazingly fast swimmer.

The statue outside the front of the building is of "don Pedro Menéndez de Aviles, 1519–1574, Governor, Captain General, Conquistador." Menéndez was St. Augustine's founder. The statue is a replica of one that stands in Aviles, Spain.

Next, tour the intriguing **Lightner Museum** inside the City Hall building. Otto C. Lightner, of Chicago, was a collector of antiques who purchased the building in 1947. It had ceased to operate as a hotel as of 1930. Lightner turned the building into a mammoth exhibit hall for his huge and varied collections, which are displayed on three floors. The collections include Victorian period clothes, jewelry, and objects, Tiffany glass, sculptures and paintings, doll houses, buttons, furniture, and more.

After browsing through the Lightner Museum, leave by the back exit, so that you are on Cordova, which is one block east of Granada. Cross to the east side of Cordova Street and turn right onto **Palm Row**. This is an old brick-paved street, developed in 1904 to 1905, with a mix of residential and commercial structures, including some wonderful Victorian-style homes.

You'll come out of Palm Row onto St. George Street. Turn right on St. George. At **234 St. George**, you'll see **Villa Flora**, the coquina and brick building that is used by the Sisters of St. Joseph. Coquina is limestone created by millions of tiny shells. When it was built in 1898 by Rev. O. A. Weenolsen, Villa Flora was used as a winter cottage.

At **250 St. George Street**, on the corner of Bridge Street and St. George, you'll find the **Prince Murat House**, an eighteenth-century coquina house named for Napoleon Bonaparte's nephew, who spent a short period of time in St. Augustine.

At the corner of St. George and St. Francis Street, turn left on St. Francis. Here is where you'll find **St. Francis Park**, which is on the grounds of the Fernandez-Llambias House. The park is approximately fifty-by-seventy-five feet, a small area that is more like a public garden than a park.

The **Fernandez-Llambias House at 31 St. Francis Street** was already extant in 1763, when Spain ceded Florida to Great Britain. Pedro Fernandez owned the one-story, shingle-roofed, coquina stone structure. A subsequent British owner added the loggia.

Two Minorcan brothers, Joseph and Peter Antonio Manucy, owned the house in 1838. They added a second story and balcony. Dona Catalina Llambias, whose name the structure bears, bought it in 1854. She and her family owned it for sixty-five years. The building was designated a National Historic Landmark in 1970. The St. Augustine Historical Society purchased the adjoining corner lot, the park, in 1973 to protect the scenic integrity of the Fernandez-Llambias house.

The **Tovar House at 22 St. Francis Street** was the home of infantryman Jose Tovar in 1763. It was subsequently occupied by a Scottish merchant named John Johnson during St. Augustine's British period.

The **Gonzalez-Alvarez House at 14 St. Francis Street** is known as **The Oldest House**. The house was built after 1715, and was originally a one-story coquina rectangle with two rooms. As times changed with Spanish, British, and American occupations, a wooden second-story off-street porch and other features were added. The Gonzalez family lived here in 1723. Forty years later, unwilling to live under the newly-installed British rule, the family moved to Cuba.

In 1775, South Carolina midwife and widow Mary Evans Fenwick married Joseph Peavett, paymaster for England's East Florida troops. The couple purchased the former Gonzalez house. They expanded the house and turned it into an inn, which was a lucrative venture for them.

In April of 1786, Joseph Peavett died. In November of that year, at the age of fifty-six, Mary Peavett remarried. Her new husband was a twenty-eight-year-old Irishman named John Hudson. Unfortunately, he was a gambler and spendthrift who incurred enough debts to cause Mary's house to be put up for auction. Worse, Hudson was arrested for tearing down a government edict that had been posted in the plaza, and for responding to it with an indecent gesture. At his trial in 1790, Hudson was exiled from St. Augustine. Mary had a plantation north of town, where Hudson remained until he died at the age of thirty-three. Two years later, Mary died.

Geronimo Alvarez was a storekeeper and a baker for the government hospital. He lived in the house with his wife Antonia and their children. Antonia died in 1798 at the age of twenty-five. Geronimo continued to reside in the house with his family.

On the south side of St. Francis, across from the Gonzalez-Alvarez House, you'll see the site of coquina buildings known for years as the **St. Francis Barracks**. They were used as military housing by the British from 1763 to 1783, by the Spanish from 1783 to 1821, and then by the United States. In 1907, the property was leased to the state of Florida for its military headquarters. The main building was gutted by fire in 1915, but the coquina walls were unharmed.

By act of Congress in 1921, the St. Francis Barracks were turned over to the state of Florida. Today, the complex serves as headquarters for the State of Florida Military Department and the state's National Guard.

Face east on St. Francis, looking toward the Intracoastal Waterway, an interior waterway with barrier islands on the ocean side that travels parallel to the coast of Florida. Walk to Avenida Menendez and turn left (north). Walk along the bayfront. Turn left (west) onto Artillery Lane. You'll be in an alleyway that leads to Aviles Street. You'll have crossed Charlotte Street, a pretty little one-way street that has a vintage clothing shop, a French pastry shop, a gallery, boutiques, and restaurants.

Turn right (north) on Aviles Street to the **Spanish Military Hospital at 3 Aviles**. After the Spanish returned to St. Augustine in 1784, this former stable and residence was converted into a Spanish military hospital and pharmacy. You can see the herb garden out back, which was used for medicinal purposes. The restored hospital includes exhibits of hospital memorabilia, including a collection of surgeon-barber instruments.

Amputations were frequently performed at the hospital. The military patient would be seated on a bench where two people would hold him down while his limb was amputated. The surgeon used a large knife or saw and a cauterizing tool.

Among the exhibits are the deathbed in one corner, where a priest would sit with the dying, and a bed with a hole in the center, which is

Charlotte Street

nicknamed the "potty bed." The hospital bed was often just a feather cot, or boards with a straw-filled sack that served as a mattress. Sheets were made of burlap or linen.

When you come out of the Spanish Military Hospital, continue north on Aviles and walk to King Street. At King, turn left (west). Walk to St. George Street and turn right (north). Cross King Street. You'll be looking at the Government House to your left and the **Plaza de la Constitution** to your right. The plaza is named after the monument that stands in the center of the plaza. The Spanish government had ordered the St. Augustinians to put up a plaque on the monument, commemorating the Constitution of 1812. After the plaque was put up, the

Government House, photo courtesy of Jim Donovan

Constitution became invalid, and the St. Augustinians were ordered to remove the plaque and destroy it.

Henry Flagler erected a gazebo in the center of the plaza. Musical bands played there to entertain his hotel guests. On the far end of the plaza is a marketplace where the first system for weights and measures was used in the United States.

Government House is the present-day headquarters for the **Historical St. Augustine Preservation Board and the Museum of St. Augustine History**. Government House was the home of a succession of Spanish and British governors, and later was used as a post office and a United States Customs office. Continue North.

At **143 St. George Street**, you'll see the Pena-Peck House, which Dr. Seth Peck purchased in 1837 and rebuilt. He added the second story. The building's stone walls date from before 1750, when the house was owned by Juan de Pena, the Spanish Royal Treasurer. Governor John Moultrie lived here during the British Period (1763 to 1784).

Dr. Peck's family willed the house to the City of St. Augustine in 1931. Today, it is run by the Women's Exchange, one of the many historic buildings in St. Augustine that are in the charge of a women's organization.

As you continue north on St. George Street, you'll approach the commercial, tourist-beckoning **Restoration Area**. A number of historic buildings are contained within it. The street is open only to pedestrian traffic.

Here you'll encounter the **Genopoly House, or the Oldest Schoolhouse**, circa 1804, touted as the oldest surviving wood-frame building in the United States. It was constructed of red cedar and cypress by a Greek carpenter named Juan Genopoly. The schoolmaster used the downstairs as classrooms and lived upstairs with his wife and children. On display are school-related artifacts and exhibits that show what the pupils and the school itself were like. Visitors receive a complimentary diploma.

Continue walking north on St. George until you come to Orange Street. Turn left (west) onto Orange. At Cordova Street, turn left (south) to see, at 31 Orange Street, an unusual corner drugstore. This is **Speissegger Drug**, the Old Drug Store. It was built in the Italianate style in 1739 by Antonio Gomaas and was used as a trading post and a general store. In 1875, it became a pharmacy under its new owner, T. W. Speissegger, a pharmacist who bought it from descendants of Gomaas.

As you continue on Cordova Street, you'll see fence-enclosed **Tolomato Cemetery** on the west side of the street. During the First Spanish Period prior to 1763, this was the site of the Christian Indian village of Tolomato. Franciscan missionaries officiated over a chapel and burying grounds. Around 1777, this cemetery was established. The first bishop of St. Augustine, who died in 1876, is buried in the mortuary chapel at the rear of the cemetery. The last burial took place in 1892.

At this point, if you continue walking south on Cordova Street, you'll soon return to Flagler College at King Street, but on your way, you might want to make a quick stop at **70 Cuna Street**, to see **Carriage Way Bed & Breakfast**. It is only a short distance from Tolomato Cemetery.

The romantic Carriage Way Bed & Breakfast is located at the corner of Cuna and Cordova. This is one of many bed-and-breakfast inns around

Old Drug Store, built circa 1739

St. Augustine. The Victorian frame vernacular house was built from 1883 to 1885 by Edward and Rosalie Masters. During the 1940s, it was used as an apartment building. In 1984 it was beautifully restored. It is now under the ownership of former Oklahomans Bill and Diane Johnson, who serve guests a full breakfast, and who have filled the nine guest rooms with charming period furnishings and antiques.

Alachua County

Location

High Springs is located between Gainesville and Lake City. It is twenty-two miles northwest of Gainesville, which is the county seat of Alachua County in north central Florida.

History

High Springs is named for a spring situated on a hill near the city. It provided a dependable source of water for the Indians who first occupied the area and for the settlers who began to arrive in the 1840s.

Surrounded by abundant timberland and fertile soil, the High Springs landscape was dotted with farms, saw mills, and cattle ranches. Cotton was an important crop. When phosphate was discovered in the area in 1889, High Springs became a mining town centered around the Savannah, Florida, and Western Railroad, which cut through the town.

In addition to several fires that gutted many wood-frame buildings, a tornado blew through High Springs in 1896, destroying much of the town. It was quickly rebuilt, with sturdy brick buildings replacing those that had burned. High Springs was incorporated in 1892. Four years later, Henry Plant's railroad tracks stretched into town, making it a railroad service hub and beckoning hundreds of men who wanted to work on the railroad.

High Springs developed a reputation as a roughneck, lawless town. Its commercial and economic growth continued until World War I, when shipments of phosphate to its main overseas customer, Germany, were blocked. During the 1920s, the Florida land boom seeped into High Springs and, thanks to the construction of two highways, the town became a tourist attraction, luring visitors to its surrounding springs.

High Springs' economy declined in the 1930s, partly because of the Great Depression, but more because diesel engines replaced steam engines, and the railroad shops prevalent in the town were geared toward servicing and repairing steam locomotives.

High Springs attracted tourists for two reasons. Outdoor lovers came here to swim, tube, and dive in the springs, and to fish, kayak, and canoe in the Santa Fe, Ichetucknee, and Suwanee Rivers. The downtown area of High Springs became a destination for antiques collectors. Many of the houses on North Main Street and the surrounding streets were converted into charming galleries and shops with names like Wisteria Corner, Greentree Pottery Studio, Country Emporium, and Miniature Attic.

High Springs has been for many years a bedroom community for many people who work for the University of Florida and other business-es in nearby Gainesville. The restored railroad depot serves as a railroad museum offering exhibits, displays, and artifacts, and oral histories focusing on America's railroad heritage.

Walking Tour

This walking tour is approximately half a mile long and takes about thir-ty minutes. To get to the **Grady House at 420 Northwest First Avenue**, take I-75 to exit 79. Head west for five miles on S.R. 236, which becomes Main Street. You'll pass a traffic light. Travel to the second traffic light and turn right. Go four blocks to the Grady House. There is street parking.

The Grady House Bed and Breakfast Inn, a Craftsman-style wood-frame home, built circa 1917 is distinguished by its huge square piers. Local materials were used to build the house, and everything used is vis-ible, such as the knee braces that are part of the design.

The Nisi Bakery was located in this house. Around 1917, it became a boarding house and then an apartment house, which explains its expansion to two full stories. The house was owned by a prominent busi-nessman named Mack L. Grady, who later was mayor of High Springs. Mack didn't live in the house but his son George did. George's daughter Georgeann also lived there. At varying times through the years, four High Springs mayors occupied Grady House, including Georgeann, who is principal of nearby Newberry Elementary School.

Around 1991, lifelong High Springs resident Diane Linch-Shupe and her husband Ed Shupe purchased the Grady House and slowly and meticulously transformed it into a charming bed-and-breakfast inn with comfortable amenities, period furnishings, and photos and scrapbooks reflecting High Springs' past. The Shupes live in one part of the house and accommodate guests in another section. The inn features a honey-moon suite and three guest suites with sitting rooms.

If you face the Grady House, the Easterlin house at **410 Northwest First Avenue** will be to your right. This light green wooden Victorian house with antique white trim was built circa 1896 and was most recently occupied by octogenarian Juanita Easterlin, nicknamed Skeet.

There are several stories that have emerged through the years that cast Skeet as a colorful character. She was born in this house in 1910. Her mother Ada would stand on the balcony and point a telescope toward Emily's Dress Shop on Main Street to see if the shop was having any sales. But Skeet was an independent nonconformist who preferred wearing pants to dresses. She is said to have owned a restaurant, run a gas station, and become involved with a moonshine ring. She never married.

When Ada Easterlin was a young woman she became engaged to High Springs railroad engineer James S. Roach. He wanted to marry Ada and have her move to another house, but Ada wouldn't budge from her own home. Roach borrowed the plans to Ada's house from her father, and in 1897, painstakingly built an identical house (Roach-Rawls house), which you'll come to later on the tour. When Ada still refused to move, he married her and they lived together in her home until his sudden death in 1901 at the age of thirty-four. He was killed when his train hit a log that had been placed on the railroad tracks.

According to a story that has circulated in High Springs for many years, a disgruntled man had put the log onto the track. When Roach's train hit the log, all the coal tumbled from the coal tender and pinned Roach against the engine boiler. The man was found and hanged. Ada later married a merchant named George W. Easterlin, whose family members were among High Springs' earliest residents. Easterlin died in 1912 when Skeet was two years old. Ada died in 1963 at the age of eighty-seven. Skeet now lives in a nursing home and the Easterlin house is unoccupied.

Continue walking east and cross North West Second Street. On the corner, at **105 Northwest Second Street**, you'll see **St. Bartholomew's Episcopal Church**. Built circa 1898 by carpenters from the railroad company, this is one of north Florida's oldest Episcopal churches.

In 1896, a hurricane swept through town, destroying many buildings. This was the only church to survive. It was constructed of heart pine. The High Springs area was covered with pine trees, so carpenters used the available lumber. They trimmed off the outside of the tree and left the extremely durable heart, which, like amber, seems to get stronger as it ages. The style of the church is carpenter gothic, which was a popular style for country churches.

The **High Springs Woman's Club at 30 Northwest First Avenue** was built in 1912. The clubhouse was constructed of concrete block, a popular building material common to many of the buildings in High

The High Springs Woman's Club

Springs. The clubhouse was built in a Craftsman style, with exposed knee braces and open gable entrance. The windows are original. The Woman's Club was important in the community because it was the women who organized the library, encouraged the planting of trees, and formed garden clubs.

At **Northwest First Avenue and North Main Street**, you'll encounter the **Pan Am Station**. Mack L. Grady, for whom the Grady House is named, was involved in several businesses in town. He built this brick filling station in the 1930s in a cottage style. It is now occupied by a real estate company.

Turn left on North Main Street, heading north. The **High Springs Presbyterian Church at 205 North Main** was rebuilt after the 1896 storm destroyed the original building.

The Will Godwin House at **215 North Main Street** was built circa 1890 by railroad worker Will Godwin. It features triple gables and an enclosed front porch. It is easily recognizable by its purple awning. The house is now occupied by Main Street Gallery. The Godwins were a large family, and there are several Godwin homes in the area.

The J. A. Stevens House at **225 North Main Street** was occupied by pharmacist J. A. Stevens. It was constructed in a classical style with symmetrical facade and front gable. The interior beaded ceiling is original to the house. When the 3,500 square foot house was built in 1911, it cost $1,275. The house is now an antiques store, The Wisteria Corner.

J. A. *Stevens house*

Walk back to the corner of Main Street and Northeast Second Avenue. Cross Second Avenue and walk to Northeast First Avenue. Turn left onto Northeast First Avenue and walk to Northeast First Street.

The Elias Godwin House is at **30 Northeast First Avenue**, on the corner of First Street and First Avenue. This yellow Queen Anne house with elaborate detailing was built in the 1890s by Will Godwin's brother Elias Godwin who was a Justice of the Peace. It is currently the location of First Street Antiques.

Turn around and head back on Northeast First Avenue toward Main Street. The High Springs Opera House (Great Outdoors Trading Company) is at **65 North Main**. This brick building with Romanesque arches was erected in 1896. The bottom floor housed a variety of mercantile firms and on the top floor stage shows, dances, and silent movies were presented.

The Theatre of Memory is now located upstairs. It features an array of ancient, antique, and contemporary artifacts and documents. The Great Outdoors Trading Company Cafe & Inn is located downstairs.

Head south on Main Street toward Railroad Avenue. Cross Railroad Avenue and walk to the Thomas Apartments at **115 South Main Street**. Originally, this building was a boarding house built in the late 1890s by Saul Thomas, who owned the Palace Saloon. His daughter, Maude Renfro, later converted the house into apartments.

The Tyre house at **120 South Main Street** was built in the 1920s by

Elias Godwin house

a physican, Dr. Tyre, and features knee braces and heavy battered piers, elements of its bungalow style.

The Priest-Cone house at **205 South Main Street** is notable for its eyebrow dormer and its porch columns. In 1918, the cottage was occupied by W. J. Priest, who owned the Priest Motor Company. Louise Cone, Mrs. Priest's sister, was another longtime occupant.

The Pfifer House (The Spring House) at **215 South Main Street** was built by Samuel Pfifer in 1912. Pfifer owned a lumber supply company. The house has fine woodworking, diamond pane windows, a wraparound porch, and combines Queen Anne, classical, and Victorian styles. It is now a bed-and-breakfast inn whose owners and restorers named it Spring House because they dive in the nearby springs. Many of their guests come to dive in the underground spring caverns.

At Southwest Third Avenue and South Main turn right (west) and walk to the corner of Southwest First Street to the Roach-Rawls house at **220 Southwest First**. James Roach, who built this house circa 1897, was an engineer with the Plant Railroad system. He built this house for his wife Ada as a replica of her own home, but he and Ada never occupied it. The only difference between the two houses is that the upper veranda of this one is longer.

When Roach's wife Ada wouldn't move into the house, he sold it to the Rawls family. Burton Rawls was a state legislator. The house has a classical Southern colonial look, but also Victorian elements such as decorative railings and bannisters on the porches. The up-and-down porches allowed the owner to open the windows upstairs to come out onto the veranda.

Walk north on Southwest First Street, across Railroad Avenue, to **15 Northwest First Street**, the location of the **Priest Theater**. This brick building was built in 1929 as an auto showroom but was never used for that purpose. Shortly afterward, it was converted into a movie theater. The first movie that appeared there starred Al Jolson as "The Singing Fool." Bobby and Janice Sheffield purchased the theater in 1985 and refurbished it. The entire Sheffield family works at the theater, from collecting tickets to manning the concession stand. Ticket prices range from $1 to $3.

Head north to Northwest First Avenue and turn left (west). This will bring you back to the Grady House. There are two additional houses near the Grady House that you may want to add to your walking tour.

The Cole-Cothron house at 525 **Northwest First Avenue** was built just prior to the turn of the century, by railroad superintendent G. C. Cole. The house is a Queen Anne–style with decorative shingle work in the gable. A pretty gazebo corner flanks either side of the front porch. Notice the carving and turned wood posts on the porch.

The Cole family sold the house to the Cothron family in the 1940s. The Cothrons were also railroad people. Hidden from view is a balcony at the side of the house. It's possible that family members used it to keep an eye on the incoming trains, so they would know when to put dinner on the table.

The Day house at **505 Northwest First Avenue** was built in 1898 by railroad man John Day. This yellow house with white picket fence is a four-square with a high peaked hip roof. The six-post porch wraps around all four sides.

GAINESVILLE

Alachua County

Location

Gainesville sits in the center of Alachua County, which is located in north central Florida. Gainesville is the county seat.

History

Alachua County was created in 1824, three years after Florida became a U.S. territory. By 1845, when Florida had achieved statehood, the county had experienced heavy growth thanks to planters and farmers who settled in the area. Gainesville was founded in 1853 and named in honor of Seminole Indian War Gen. Edmund P. Gaines. By 1860, Gainesville had more than 250 residents.

During the Civil War, Gainesville became the site of a Confederate storehouse. A skirmish and battle were fought here. After the war freed slaves settled into the western and southwestern sections. In 1867, the county's first black school, the Union Academy, began operation. It was located in the Pleasant Street Historic District, the oldest black residential area in Gainesville. Many of this neighborhood's settlers were from South Carolina and were skilled workers who helped to establish a thriving community.

By 1882, Gainesville's population had climbed to two thousand, and the town had become a prime cotton-shipping center. Citrus and vegetables were major agricultural crops. Ten years later, after freezes destroyed citrus crops, phosphate and lumbering industries developed importance. Gainesville became one of Florida's largest phosphate producers. In the early 1900s, the northeastern section of Gainesville became an elite residential area. Gainesville experienced continuing prosperity when, in 1906, the University of Florida opened.

After World War II and the expansion of businesses into Gainesville, the northeast residential area was threatened with the demolition of homes that had deteriorated. To prevent this, and to preserve and protect the neighborhood, residents of the northeast section banded together in 1972 to form Historic Gainesville, Inc. The Northeast

Residential Historic District was listed on the National Register of Historic Places in 1980.

Walking Tour

The walking tour takes about thirty minutes and is approximately half a mile. To get to the **Thomas Center at 302 Northeast Sixth Avenue**, take I-75 to exit 76. Go east on S.R. 26 to Main Street. Turn left. Go six blocks to Sixth Avenue. Turn right. Continue for three blocks. There is parking at the Center.

Begin at the Thomas Center. In 1906, what is now Gainesville's cultural center began as a private home for Charles W. Chase, the president of a phosphate company. When he died, only the exterior walls and the roof had been completed.

Business executive William Reuben Thomas bought the six acres of property and completed the house. On the day in 1910 when he and his wife moved into their new home, their fifth child, Margaret Omerea, was born in one of the bedrooms.

The wood-frame, shingle-covered Thomas residence was opulent. It encompassed fifteen thousand square feet. The rooms opened onto a sunken atrium. The house contained twenty-one rooms, seven bathrooms and twelve fireplaces. There was also a gymnasium, a gardener's cottage, a barn, and a garage.

Thomas Center

Between 1928 and 1968, the house was renovated to become a hotel. The first floor was altered to provide three dining rooms, a lobby, a lounge, and a multipurpose room. The hotel, although predominantly Mediterranean revival, incorporated Renaissance decorative elements including shell motifs, garlands, and "wave" motifs similar to those designed by Michaelangelo for a library in Florence. Helen Keller and Robert Frost were two of the hotel's celebrated guests.

After World War II, vacationers flocked to Florida's beach areas rather than to inland cities, and the popularity of the hotel declined. The Thomas family leased the hotel to Santa Fe Community College for use as its east campus.

In the early 1970s, the site was added to the National Register of Historic Places and purchased by the City of Gainesville. Today, as Gainesville's Cultural Center, the Thomas Center contains art galleries, period rooms, performance space, and local history exhibits.

Visitors are welcome to browse through the Thomas Center, where Thomas family mementos are displayed, including a cameo dating from around 1880 that was a gift from Maj. Thomas to his wife Katie and passed down to their daughter Margaret. It is carved from the white lava of Mt. Vesuvius.

When you come out of the Thomas Center, walk south, away from the Center. You are in the Northeast Historic District, which is largely residential. Cross Northeast Sixth Avenue and walk south down Northeast Third Street. The streets originally had names but were changed to numbers in the 1950s. Most of the houses in the area were built between the 1880s and the 1930s and have since been restored. Between 1910 and 1950, four University of Florida presidents lived in the district. Some faculty members still live here. This was the first area in Alachua County to be designated as a Historic District. Many of the houses have plaques to identify them.

Cross Northeast Fifth Avenue. At Northeast Fourth Avenue, turn left (east). The Gracy house at **314 Northeast Fourth Avenue** was built in 1904 in a colonial revival–style by Luther C. Gracy, a lumberman and turpentine dealer. The hand-picked lumber used to build the house came from Gracy's lumber mill. The interior of the mansion features leaded glass windows, cherry paneling and marble fireplaces. Gracy was a prohibitionist who is said to have entertained Cary Nation at his house. This house was restored in 1992 and is now the residence of a local physician.

The Newell house at **404 Northeast Fourth Avenue** was built in 1887 in a colonial revival–style. The olive-green house was expanded with each new owner. From 1920 until the 1970s, the house was owned by Dr. Wilmon Newell, a noted entomologist who was instrumental in eradicating the Mediterranean fruit fly in the United States.

The Denham house at **405 Northeast Fourth Avenue** was built in 1898 for Capt. W. B. Denham and his wife Carrie. The Queen Anne–style house has a wraparound porch and double bay windows. The house is surrounded by a low stone wall and a curbside carriage block, both of which are original. The carriage step made it convenient for women to step out of a horse-drawn carriage. Maj. W. R. Thomas and his family lived here from 1900 to 1909, while awaiting the completion of the house that is now the Thomas Center.

The Gillis-Eaton house at **414 Northeast Fourth Avenue** is a Victorian cottage that was built circa 1884 and has remained in the Eaton family. This pretty white house looks like a little Victorian dollhouse. It has a steeply gabled roof and an ornate bay window. Ruth Eaton and her husband Sinclair Eaton, who owns an insurance agency, have been long-time occupants.

The McArthur-Graham house at **417 Northeast Fourth Avenue** was built in 1897 for Gainesville's fire chief, A. J. McArthur. The shingle house has Romanesque features and decorative iron fencing. The entrance door is a four-foot-wide Dutch door. In 1917, the house was purchased by Klein Graham, who was the University of Florida's first business manager. In 1972, a new owner restored the house.

At the corner of Northeast Fourth Avenue and Northeast Fifth Street, turn left, heading north. The H. L. Phifer house at **420 Northeast Fifth Street** was built in 1897 for Henry Phifer and his bride, Mary Ridenhour. Henry and his two brothers were prominent business and civic leaders in Gainesville. They owned Wilson's Department Store and they ran the Phifer State Bank. This white Queen Anne cottage features turned spindles, a wagon wheel design above the portico, and sunburst designs in the peaks of the gables.

Cross Northeast Fifth Avenue and turn east toward the duck pond. You'll pass the W. B. Phifer house at **506 Northeast Fifth Avenue**. This colonial revival house was built in 1903 for H. L. Phifer's brother William. The porch columns are constructed of solid cypress.

This section of the historic district was a housing development called The Highlands. Through it ran Sweetwater Branch, a creek which at this area was controlledby a retention pond. The pond was soon inhabited by ducks. Eventually, the whole historic community became known as the "Duck Pond."

Continue east on Northeast Fifth Avenue to the Thomas house at **540 Northeast Fifth Avenue**. This brick colonial revival house was built

Duck Pond

in 1932 for longtime Gainesville physician Dr. William C. Thomas, who lived here until his death forty-two years later. The house at **608 Northeast Fifth Avenue** was built in 1904 for H. E. Taylor, a First National Bank president. The house features a huge front gable with a fish-scale shingle pattern and a large wraparound porch. Its last owner added an ornamental English garden to the property.

Turn around and walk west on Northeast Fifth Avenue, to Northeast Boulevard, commonly referred to as "The Boulevard." Turn right (north). The Gehan house at **531 Northeast Boulevard** was built in 1939. It was designed in a Cape Cod style by architect Sanford Goin, who designed the local high school, many local buildings, and number of attractive cottages.

A distinguishing feature of the house is the exterior molding, which depicts maidens picking flowers and youths playing musical instruments. For many years, the house was the home of Clara Gehan and her family. She was the first female graduate of the University of Florida Law School and a revered local attorney.

Across from the duck pond, at **532 Northeast Boulevard**, you'll see a red brick Georgian revival home with white shutters and three dormers. It was built as a duplex in 1937 by Hattie Roebuck. In 1942, the house was purchased by Myrtle Geiger, who owned a women's apparel store. In 1989, the new owner converted the house into a single-family residence.

Continue to Northeast Sixth Avenue and turn left (west) to return to the Thomas Center.

NORTHEAST FLORIDA
HISTORICAL ATTRACTIONS, DINING, AND LODGING

JACKSONVILLE — *Duval County*

Suggested Dining and Lodging

A Tasteful Cafe
717 Post Street
904-642-7506

Partner's Restaurant
3585 St. Johns Avenue
904-387-3585
Housed in a 1940s building that exudes Old World charm.

The House on Cherry Street Bed and Breakfast Inn
1844 Cherry Street
Jacksonville, FL 32205
904-384-1999
Located on the St. Johns River, the two-story inn is full of antiques and collectibles.

Plantation Manor Inn
1630 Copeland Street
Jacksonville, FL 32206
904-384-4630
Built in 1905, this three-story manor house has Greek revival architectural details.

The St. Johns House Bed and Breakfast Inn
1718 Osceola Street
Jacksonville, FL 32204
904-384-3724
Prairie-style house built in 1914.

The Willows on the St. Johns River
1849 Willow Branch Terrace
Jacksonville, FL 32204
904-387-9152

For Information

Riverside and Avondale Preservation, Inc.
2623 Herschel Street
Jacksonville, FL 32204
904-389-2449
They provide a map and self-guided walking tour brochure.

Other Historic Attractions

Cummer Gallery of Art
829 Riverside Avenue
Jacksonville, FL 32204
904-356-6857
Open Tuesday 10 A.M. to 9:30 P.M., Wednesday through Friday 10 P.M. to 4 P.M., Saturday noon to 5 P.M., Sunday 2 P.M. to 5 P.M. Adults $5, seniors and students $3.

Kingsley Plantation
11676 Palmetto Avenue
(Ft. George Island off highway A1A) Jacksonville, FL 32226
904-251-3537
Purchased in 1817 by Zephaniah Kingsley and his African wife. The house and the slave cabins still stand. The plantation is on the National Park Service Timucuan Ecological and Historic Preserve. Open daily 9 A.M. to 5 P.M. Guided tours available.

ST. AUGUSTINE — St. Johns County

Suggested Dining and Lodging

Columbia Restaurant
98 St. George Street
904-824-3341
Great Spanish cuisine in an Old World Mediterranean setting. Touted as the oldest restaurant in the United States.

Courtyard Deli
75 King Street
904-823-DELI
In the Alcazar-Lightner Building.

O. C. *White's Seafood & Spirits*
118 Avenida Menendez
904-824-0808
Located in General William Jenkins Worth's house, built circa 1790. Ft. Worth, Texas, is named for General Worth.

Raintree Restaurant
102 San Marco Avenue
904-824-7211
Located in a restored 110-year-old house.

Casablanca Inn on the Bay
24 Avenida Menendez
St. Augustine, FL 32084
904-829-0928
A restored 1914 Mediterranean revival home.

Carriage Way Bed & Breakfast
70 Cuna Street
St. Augustine, FL 32084
904-829-2467

Castle Garden Inn
15 Shenandoah Street
St. Augustine, FL 32084
904-829-3839
This building was constructed in the 1890s in a Moorish revival style.

Cedar House Inn Bed and Breakfast
79 Cedar Street
St. Augustine, FL 32084
904-829-0079 or 800-233-2746

The Old Mansion Inn Bed and Breakfast
14 Joyner Street
St. Augustine, FL 32084
904-824-1975
A three-story mansion built in 1872.

St. Francis Inn
279 St. George Street
St. Augustine, FL 32084
904-824-6068 or 800-824-6062
Built of coquina in 1791, this was originally the home of a Spanish soldier.

Westcott House Guest House
146 Avenida Menendez
St. Augustine, FL 32084
904-824-4301

For Information

Sandy Craig
Tour St. Augustine
P.O. Box 860094
St. Augustine, FL 32086
904-471-9010 or 800-797-3778

Historic St. Augustine Preservation Board, Division of Historical Resources, Florida Department of State P.O. Box 1987
St. Augustine, FL 32085
904-825-5033

St. Augustine Historical Society
271 Charlotte Street
St. Augustine, FL 32084
904-824-2872

St. Augustine Tourism/ St. Johns
County Tourist Development
Council/Chamber of Commerce
1 Riberia Street
St. Augustine, FL 32084
904-829-5681 or 800-OLD-CITY.

Other Historic Attractions

Fountain of Youth Archaeological Park
155 Magnolia Avenue
St. Augustine, FL 32084
800-356-8222
Explores the lifestyles of sixteenth-
century Indians and explorers, and the
sailing techniques of Ponce de Leon.
Open daily 9 A.M. to 5 P.M. Admission:
Adults $4.75.

Lighthouse Museum of St. Augustine
81 Lighthouse Avenue
St. Augustine, FL 32084
904-829-0745
A maritime museum featuring
Lighthouse artifacts. Open daily 9:30
A.M. to 5 P.M. Admission: $2.

Lightner Museum
75 King Street
St. Augustine, FL 32084
904-824-2874
Open daily 9 A.M. to 5 P.M.
Admission: $5.

Old Jail
167 San Marco Avenue
St. Augustine, FL 32084
904-829-3800
Built in 1891, the jail exhibits old
weapons.
Open daily 8:30 A.M. to 5 P.M.
Admission: Adults $4.25.

Zorayda Castle
83 King Street
St. Augustine, FL 32084
904-824-3097
Treasures depicting how Moorish kings
lived and entertained. The castle is a
replica of the Alhambra in Granada.
Open daily 9 A.M. to 5 P.M. Admission:
Adults $5.

HIGH SPRINGS — Alachua County

Suggested Dining and Lodging

Great Outdoors Trading Company
65 North Main Street
904-454-2900

Harry's Seafood Bar and Grille
110 South East First Street
Gainesville
352-372-1555
Located in an 1880s opera house.

Sovereign Restaurant
12 South East Second Avenue
Gainesville
352-378-6307
Beautiful New Orleans-style atmosphere. A former carriage house in the
historic downtown area.

Grady House Bed & Breakfast Inn
420 North West First Avenue
Post Office Box 205
High Springs, FL 32655
904-454-2206

Rustic Inn
5105 South Main Street
P.O. Box 387
High Springs, FL 32655
904-454-1223

High Springs Country Inn
520 North West Santa Fe
Boulevard
High Springs, FL 32655
904-454-1565

The Spring House Bed & Breakfast Inn
211 South Main Street
P.O. Box 2257
High Springs, FL 32655
904-454-8571

For Information

Alachua County Visitors and
Convention Bureau
30 East University Avenue
Gainesville, FL 32601
352-374-5260

High Springs Chamber of Commerce
P.O. Box 863
High Springs, FL 32655
904-454-3120

Other Attractions

High Springs Railroad Museum
20 North West Railroad Avenue
High Springs, FL 32655
904-I-LIKE-RR
Open Wednesday through Saturday
10 A.M. to 5 P.M., Sunday noon to 5 P.M.
Admission: $3.

GAINESVILLE — Alachua County

Suggested Dining and Lodging

Harry's Seafood Bar and Grille
110 Southeast First Street
352-372-1555
Located in an 1880s opera house in
downtown Gainesville.

Sovereign Restaurant
12 Southeast Second Avenue
352-378-6307
Excellent Continental cuisine in a New
Orleans-style setting in a former carriage house in the historic downtown
area.

Herlong Mansion Bed and Breakfast
Cholokka Boulevard
Micanopy, FL 32667
352-466-3322

Magnolia Plantation Bed and
Breakfast
309 South East Seventh Street
Gainesville, FL 32601
352-375-6653
Restored second-empire mansion built
circa 1885.

Shady Oak Bed and Breakfast
203 Cholokka Boulevard
Micanopy, FL 32667
352-466-3476

Sweetwater Branch Inn
625 East University Avenue
Gainesville, FL 32601
352-373-6760 or 800-451-7111
A restored Victorian inn built circa
1885.

For Information

Gainesville Area Chamber of Commerce
300 East University Avenue
Gainesville, FL 32601
352-334-7100

Alachua County Visitors and
Convention Bureau
30 East University Avenue
Gainesville, FL 32601
352-374-5231

Other Historic Attractions

Marjorie Kinnan Rawlings State Historic Site
Cross Creek, FL 32640
352-466-3672
Located twenty-one miles southeast of Gainesville on Highway 325. This is the former home and farm of the author of *The Yearling*.
Open Thursday through Sunday 10 A.M. to 11 P.M., 1 P.M. to 4 P.M.
Admission: $1.

Matheson Historical Center
513 East University Avenue
Gainesville, FL 32601
352-378-2280
Housed in a restored American Legion building, the Center exhibits items relevant to Florida and Alachua County history. Tuesday through Friday 9 A.M. to 1 P.M., Sunday 1 P.M. to 5 P.M. Adults $2, seniors $1, children 50 cents, students $1.

Thomas Center
306 North East Sixth Avenue
P.O. Box 490
Gainesville, FL 32602
352-334-2197
Open Monday through Friday 8 A.M. to 5 P.M., weekends 1 P.M. to 4 P.M.

Central

CENTRAL

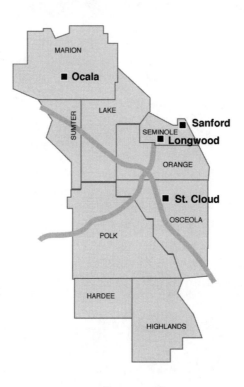

OCALA

Marion County

Location

Ocala, in Marion County, is located in north central Florida, southeast of Gainesville. It is situated almost exactly in the geographic center of the state. Just to the east of it are the Ocklawaha River, Silver Springs, and Ocala National Forest.

History

With an area of 1,039,360 square miles, Marion County is one of Florida's largest counties. It was named for Francis Marion, the Revolutionary War hero nicknamed "The Swamp Fox." Prior to the 1820s, the land that is now Marion County was occupied by Timucuan and Seminole Indians. During the 1820s, under Andrew Jackson's governorship of the Florida territory, the Seminole Indians were ordered out of Florida and onto lands west of the Mississippi.

Under the leadership of Osceola, the Seminole Wars ensued. Ft. King, about three miles east of present-day Ocala, had been built in 1827, and during the wars it remained an important military post.

When Florida gained statehood in 1845, there were fewer than fifteen hundred people living in Marion County. During the 1850s, settlers who farmed the land discovered that the soil was fertile for producing corn, sugarcane and cotton. Many settlers became ranchers who raised livestock, particularly horses.

During and after the Civil War, there was little growth or development in Marion County. Ocala's primary industries were citrus growing and phosphate mining. With the arrival of the railroad in the 1880s, the county became a center for tourism. Tourists flocked to Silver Springs.

Silver Springs is Florida's oldest tourist attraction. Located one mile east of Ocala, the attraction includes the world's largest artesian well, and seven springs that surround the headwaters of the Silver River, which joins the Ocklawaha River, the western border of Ocala National Forest. Glass-bottom boats were developed here in 1878.

Ocala was incorporated in 1868. It was named for Ocali, a Seminole

Indian chief who once lived in the area. On Thanksgiving Day in 1883, a fire swept through the city's downtown area, destroying the wooden buildings. They were rebuilt out of brick the following year, earning Ocala the nickname of "The Brick City." The city's Historic District extends for approximately fifty-five blocks and was Ocala's most desirable residential area between 1890 and 1930. The Garys were one of Ocala's earliest and most prominent families.

In 1855, S. M. G. Gary and his bride Fannie cruised down the Silver River to honeymoon in Ocala. They were smitten with the town and decided to live there. Gary opened a law practice. He and Fannie built a house on what is now Silver Springs Boulevard, but fire destroyed it in 1908.

In 1857, Gary's brother Thomas, a physician, relocated his medical practice to Ocala. S. M. G. Gary turned his attention to politics and land brokerage. During the Civil War, he served as a Confederate captain. Thomas served as a surgeon. In 1866, S. M .G. Gary became Ocala's first mayor, a position also held by Thomas during the 1870s.

In 1925, Ocala's Ritz Hotel was completed. Designed in a Spanish style, it became Ocala's premiere place to stay. It has been restored, and is listed on the National Register of Historic Places.

Ocala is often referred to as "horse country," because of its hundreds of horse farms. The county ranks with Kentucky and California as a prime producer of thoroughbreds. In 1978, Marion County gained national attention when Affirmed won the triple crown in the Kentucky Derby.

Walking Tour

The walking tour stretches along both sides of Southeast Ft. King Street, which runs east and west, parallel to Silver Springs Boulevard. To get to the **Dunn House at 416 Southeast Ft. King Street**, the starting point of the tour, take I-75 to the Silver Springs Boulevard exit (S.R.40) and head east to Ninth Avenue. Turn right on Ninth Avenue and go to Ft. King Street. Turn right on Ft. King. There is street parking. The tour covers approximately four blocks and takes about twenty minutes.

The gray house at 416 Southeast Ft. King Street was built circa 1888 and was occupied by John F. Dunn, a prominent attorney who founded Ocala's first bank in 1882. In 1875, the Marion County courthouse, jail, and public square were auctioned off. Dunn bought them, but later deeded the property back to the county.

Walk east to the W. R. Bryant house at **712 Southeast Ft. King**, which was built circa 1895 in a Victorian style, with some gothic details.

William Anderson, an Ocala dentist, was the first owner of the white house at **728 Southeast Ft. King**. It was built circa 1891 in a classical revival style and was later owned by state legislator Marcus Frank.

The house at **740 Southeast Ft. King Street** was built circa 1891, and was occupied by S. R. Birdsey, founder of a hardware company. Notable features of this white Victorian house are its beveled glass front doors, and eleven Doric columns on the wraparound porch.

The Bullock house at **808 Southeast Ft. King** was built circa 1891 in a Victorian frame vernacular style with touches of carpenter gothic. Notable design features are the balustrades, lathework columns, and stained glass windows. The house was owned by W. S. Bullock, who became mayor of Ocala around the turn of the century. He was also a circuit court judge. His father was Civil War Gen. Robert Bullock. The house now serves as the law offices of Richard and Blinn.

The former G. S. Scott house at **820 Southeast Ft. King** is easily recognizable from the sign, **7 Sisters Inn**, in front of the house. The three-story Queen Anne house began in 1888 as the residence of G. S. Scott, who owned Scott and Sons Insurance. The dusty-blue painted house with its baluster porch, cupola, and turret, is now owned by former Braniff pilot Bonnie Morehardt and her partner, United Airlines pilot Ken Oden. Morehardt is one of the few women to pilot a C-130 heavy cargo transport aircraft.

In 1990, Morehardt bought the house from the woman who had previously owned it and who had converted it into a bed-and-breakfast inn with seven guest rooms named for her daughters.

Fireplaces, Victorian soaking tubs, wicker and gingham-covered chairs, four-poster canopy beds, and a French Monet breakfast room lend charm and comfort to this immaculate inn. The full-breakfast specialties are three-cheese stuffed French Toast and baked puffed pancakes with glazed fruit.

Continue to cigar maker Charles Rheinauer's former house at **828**. This carpenter gothic–style two-and-a-half-story house with wavy porch rails was built circa 1895. The original kitchen was in a separate building to the rear. Rheinauer was an early mayor of Ocala.

The Jewett house at **850 Southeast Ft. King** was built circa 1912 in a Victorian gothic style. The slate-blue house with white trim and black shutters was the home of Miss M. J. Jewett, whose family had a phosphate mine and a bookkeeping business.

The white house with black shutters at **906** was built in a classical revival style circa 1906. It has Ionic columns on the veranda and a wedding cake design at the top of the porch. It was the home of businessman

William G. Marshall. The two-story wood frame house with hip roof at **916 Southeast Ft. King** was built circa 1921 and occupied by J. Phillips. It is now a law office.George Taylor owned a printing company in Ocala, and was a building contractor. He lived in the Bungalow-style house at **936 Southeast Ft. King**.

Cross over to the north side of Southeast Ft. King Street and walk west, heading back toward the Dunn house.

Ocala attorney Robert A. Burford lived in the house at **943 Southeast Ft. King**, which was built circa 1893 in a Queen Anne revival style. The iron fencing was made in Canton, Ohio, in the 1800s and is said to have originally circled the old courthouse.

Until 1927, Edward Tucker, a civil engineer, lived in the house at **931 Southeast Ft. King**, which was built circa 1924. The beige stucco walls and barrel tile roof are typical of its Mediterranean–revival style.

The carpenter gothic–style house at **743** was built circa 1891. This house, painted light blue, with five posts around the porch, was occupied by Z. C. Chambliss, who was vice president of the Monroe and Chambliss Bank, which was founded in 1897. Notice the fish scale design on the exterior.

Edward Holder, owner of a phosphate mine, lived in the house at **733 Southeast Ft. King**, which was built circa 1906 in a frame vernacular style with Victorian influences. Notice the high step up to the sidewalk. This was a convenience for ladies when they emerged from horse-drawn carriages. There was a carriage house to the rear.

Edward Holder house

The Fanny Clark house at **711–713 Southeast Ft. King** was built circa 1912 in a Victorian frame vernacular style. Clark was a teacher at Ocala High School.

Dr. J. W. Hood, an early Ocala physician, lived in the house at **613 Southeast Ft. King**, which was built circa 1912 in a Victorian frame vernacular style. The house is now the office of attorney Ray Gill. Note the diamond-shaped window on the second-story balcony, the fish scale shingles, the old-fashioned mail slot in the front door, and the old-fashioned doorbell.

In 1887, county legislator Daniel Miller moved into a Victorian house at **521 Ft. King Street** that was built on property he purchased from Fannie Gary. In 1911, Fannie's son W. T. Gary paid $5,500 to buy the house. Members of the Gary family continued to occupy the house until 1978. W. T. Gary was valedictorian of the second graduating class of Ocala High School in 1893. In 1914 he was co-owner of the Ocala Telephone Company. Like his father, he served as a mayor of Ocala. He later became a Florida state senator.

Patricia's Antiques and Gifts is now located in the Gary House. The gray house with burgundy trim is recognizable from the red flag on the front lawn. The house was built in a Victorian stick style with gothic influences. In 1989, Perry Lovell purchased the Gary house as a birthday gift for his wife Patricia, and began a lengthy restoration project. The house

W. T. *Gary house*

has six gables and nine fireplaces with their original mantels. The double front doors are ten feet high and have stained glass windows. The ceilings are thirteen feet high. The house has front and back stairs.

Auntie's Attic Antiques, a shop featuring antiques, gifts, and collectibles, is located at **507 Southeast Ft. King**. This Victorian frame vernacular house with some gingerbread detail was built circa 1888.

The building at **409 Southeast Ft. King** was built circa 1901 in a frame vernacular style with Victorian influences. The First Presbyterian Church, which was built in the 1890s, sat on the corner. The manse (which housed the ministers) was at 409. It eventually became "Mrs. McLean's Boarding House." Mrs. McLean is said to have tried to match up the girls from the local telephone company with the flyboys from the local flying school during World War II.

Cross to the other side of King Street to return to the Dunn House.

SANFORD

Location

Sanford is located in central Florida's Seminole County, a few minutes north of downtown Orlando. It sits on the shore of Lake Monroe. Sanford is the southern terminus for the Amtrak Auto Train.

History

After the United States acquired Florida from Spain in 1823, an army post named Camp Monroe was built along Lake Monroe to keep the Seminole Indians in check. In 1837, Capt. Charles Mellon was killed during the Second Seminole War. In his honor, the fort was renamed Fort Mellon. Settlers migrated to the area, which they named Mellonville.

In the 1840s, with the arrival of commercial steamboats, the county became a thriving trade center and port. In 1870, Henry S. Sanford purchased 12,548 acres of land west of Mellonville. Sanford was a distinguished lawyer and diplomat. He was born in Connecticut in 1823. At the age of eighteen, he inherited his father's fortune.

While serving as minister to Belgium, a position appointed to him in 1861 by President Lincoln, Sanford met an American socialite named Gertrude Dupuy, who he married. They had seven children. Sanford's plan was to build a city named after himself, which would serve as the center of all transportation to southern Florida.

In 1877, the city of Sanford became incorporated, and in September of 1877, a bakery caught fire, spreading quickly and destroying the eastern part of what had become a prosperous town. The wooden buildings that had burned were rebuilt out of brick. In 1883, Mellonville was annexed to Sanford.

Two disastrous citrus freezes, one in 1894 and one in 1895, dealt a devastating blow to Sanford's prosperous citrus industry, prompting many of the residents to leave the area. Yet, by the first decade of the twentieth century, Sanford was one of the largest vegetable-shipping centers in the United States, and had earned the nickname of Celery City.

In 1913, Seminole County was established, and Sanford became the county seat. Sanford retains its pristine, turn-of-the-century charm, which is evident in the Victorian, Queen Anne, and Cracker-style architecture.

Sanford is a Main Street city, a designation given by the Florida Department of State, Division of Historical Resources to towns and cities that have restored economic vitality to their downtown area. The large brick commercial buildings from 1887 are still in use, and comprise one of two districts in Sanford that are on the National Register of Historic Places. Thirty-four thousand permanent residents and fifteen hundred winter residents live within Sanford's thirteen square miles. It has developed a reputation as an antiques center.

Walking Tour

The walking tour is approximately one mile long and takes about one hour. Sanford Avenue runs north and south. First Street runs east and west and becomes Route 46, which leads to I-4.

To get to the **four-faced black clock** located on **First Street at Magnolia Square**, take I-4 to Exit 51 (Sanford/Mt. Dora exit, C.R. 46). Travel south on C.R. 46, which becomes First Street and which will take you to the clock, the starting point of this tour.

The clock originally hung from the exterior of the First National Bank building on First Street and Park Avenue. In 1923, the bank moved to a new location, and the clock was put into storage. In 1930, it was donated to the city of Sanford, and placed at the intersection of First and Park.

The clock was crowned with a traffic signal, but as automobiles began to congest the road, the clock seemed to get in the way of traffic flow, and it was again relegated to storage. In 1985, after being refurbished and having new works installed, the clock was put into its present location.

Stand under the clock with your back to it and face First Street. Turn right and walk east on First Street to the first corner, which is Palmetto. Cross over to the north side of First Street. Palmetto Avenue was a section of the historic district that burned during the 1887 fire. Nearly all of the wood buildings were leveled and replaced. In effect, Sanford became a brick city.

The commercial buildings within the historic district are commonly called "Blocks." **The Bishop Block** is on the southeast corner of First and Palmetto, at **301–309 East First Street**. The two-story red brick building was constructed between 1887 and 1888. It was designed in a Romanesque revival style, featuring a flat roof with parapet, rectangular columns, ornamental brackets, decorative carvings and moldings, and a first-floor marquee. The city hall was located in the building during the early part of the twentieth century. It continues to be occupied by various shops and businesses.

The **Hester and Shepard Block** is located next door at **109 South Palmetto Avenue**. It is easily identifiable by its green striped awnings and the "rising sun" design at the center of the pediment above the second-story windows. The building, constructed of brick and stucco, is in the architectural style of beaux arts classicism. Notice the decorative horizontal course of brick set into the wall.

In 1890, three years after the Hester and Shepard Block was built, the firehouse was located here, where it remained for eighty-four years. The city hall and the police station and jail have also been located here. It is presently a private residence.

To the right of the former firehouse is the **E. E. Brady Livery Stable Building at 113 South Palmetto Avenue**. It was built circa 1890 and was occupied by a blacksmith and wagon shop. Between 1910 and 1914, E. E. Brady, a celery grower, operated a livery here. The building has also been the headquarters of the Seminole County Jail and the County Health Department. Today, it is part of Sanford Cleaners.

The Bishop Block, the Hester and Shepard Block, and the E. E. Brady Livery Stable are on the southeast corner of Palmetto and First. **The Hotchkiss Block, at 213 East First**, is on the southwest corner of Palmetto and First. The Romanesque revival–style Hotchkiss Block was built in 1886, but was not completely destroyed by the 1887 fire. It was rebuilt right after the fire and has been occupied by various stores and businesses, including Manuel Jacobsons Department Store.

The old post office at **230 East First Street** sits on the northwest corner of First and Palmetto, and is now a **Seminole County Library** office. The front of the red pressed-brick building is flanked by two pillars and was built in a classical revival style in 1917. It served as a post office for forty-four years before becoming part of the library system.

The **People's Bank Building and Block at 201–203 East First Street** is on the southeast corner of First Street and Magnolia Avenue. The four-faced clock sits on Magnolia Street in front of Magnolia Square. The red brick bank building with blue awnings was built out of sand brick in 1906. The Peoples Bank Block was completed in 1910 in the beaux arts classical style. It has been occupied by a variety of shops and businesses.

As you walk back toward the four-faced clock, you'll notice a building with a beige brick facade and green awnings, located on the south side of First Street at **121 East First**. This is the **DeForest Block**, which sits to the right of the clock. No doubt because it was constructed of brick, this building, one of Sanford's oldest, survived the fire of 1887.

The building was constructed in a beaux arts classical style for Henry DeForest, a young Connecticut cousin of Henry Sanford. In 1917, the building was occupied by the Seminole County Bank. At that time, changes were made to the appearance of the building. In 1933, W. C. Touchton bought the building to serve as Touchton's Drugs, which operated at that location for some sixty years.

Walk to the corner of Park Avenue. Cross North Park Avenue. Now turn around and face eastward on First Street. On the southeast corner of Park and First, you will see the **First National Bank Building Number Two, at 101 East First**, and the **First National Bank Building Number One** on the southwest corner at **101 West First**.

Bank Number One was built in a neoclassical style. The white stucco partially hides a brick foundation and a marble facade. It is the oldest brick building in the historic district. It originated as the Lyman Bank. By 1908 it was the First National Bank. The First National Bank Number Two was built by the George Fuller Company in the early 1920s. At six stories, it was touted as Sanford's first "skyscraper." The building is still occupied by a bank.

The **Brumley-Puleston Building at 100 East First Street** was completed in 1923. In its day, the four-story beige brick, artificial stone, stucco, and tile building was also considered to be a skyscraper. It was built for Dr. L. A. Brumley and Dr. Samuel Puleston, and its first tenant was a drugstore. George A. Fuller was the contractor. He also built the Lincoln Memorial in Washington, D.C., and the Biltmore Hotel in New York City.

Walk west on First Street for one block, to Oak Avenue. Cross to the other side of Oak Avenue and turn around to face east on First Street. Look to the left, or northeast side of First Street, toward the **PICO Block Restaurant and Stores and the PICO Hotel**.

The brick and stucco PICO Block Restaurant and Stores building was intended as an office building for Henry Plant's railroad and hotel company. PICO is an acronym for Plant Investment Company. There is a carriageway on the side of the building which is still distinguishable behind the wrought iron gate. During the 1920s, the building was used as an apartment building. It is now an office and retail building.

Facing east on First Street, walk left (north) on Oak Avenue for one block to the intersection of Oak and Commercial. Looming above you will be the PICO Hotel. Henry Plant had the hotel built in 1887 to

PICO *Hotel*

resemble his Tampa Bay Hotel. The hotel was a terminus for Plant's railroad and the steamers that served Sanford.

The brick hotel was built in a Turkish style and has horseshoe arches over the windows. Its resemblance to a Turkish mosque extended to a tower capped with an onion-shaped dome, which was later removed.

Continue down to Commercial, and turn right (east). Walk to Park Avenue and turn right (south) to First Street. Cross over to the south side of First.

Facing east, look to your left toward the **Rand Building**, the **N. P. Yowell** and **Garner-Woodruff Buildings**, and the **Meisch Building**. They face the four-faced clock, and they are located at **108 East First Street, 200–208 East First Street, and 224 East First Street**.

The red brick Rand Building was constructed in a beaux arts classical style in 1887. It is banded with a metal cornice at the roof. Frederic H. Rand was general manager and attorney for the Florida Land and Colonization Company formed in 1880 by Henry Sanford. The city of Sanford's first newspaper operated out of this building. It is now occupied by various shops.

An Orlando merchant named N. P. Yowell hired a Jacksonville architect to design a building which would house a dry goods store. When completed in 1910, it was known as the N. P. Yowell building.

The building next door, designed by the same architect, went up at the same time. It was built for two local real estate agents named N. H. Garner and F. L. Woodruff. Various shops now operate in both buildings.

Sanford Herald Building

The Meisch Building was constructed in early-twentieth-century commercial style, as were the N. P. Yowell and the Garner-Woodruff Buildings directly west of it. It was built in 1923 of concrete surfaced with brick, stone, and stucco for John Meisch, the president of the Sanford Investment Company. A Piggly-Wiggly Grocery, a clothing store, and a cafeteria were among the building's first tenants. Some of its architectural features include copper windows trimmed with a marble base, terra-cotta tile on the facade wall, and a marquee covering the exterior ground floor level.

Walk to the four-faced clock on Magnolia Avenue and First Street. Facing the clock, walk south on Magnolia. The Meisch Building will be behind you. You will be walking along Magnolia Square.

At **107 South Magnolia Avenue** on your left, you'll see the two-story **Sanford Herald Building**, built in 1910 of white rusticated concrete block. It now houses the IOOF (Independent Order of Odd Fellows). The former **Imperial Opera House** at **119 South Magnolia Avenue** was built in a Florentine palazzo style and first opened in 1910.

You may wish to end your tour here by returning to the clock at Magnolia and First Street. However, many of the homes that surround the historic commercial district of Sanford have been restored as they have been acquired by new owners. You may want to stroll through this old-fashioned, countrified neighborhood of pristine old houses. Certainly the most notable restoration is Higgins House, which is worth

Higgins House

walking to. The hospitable owners who operate the house as a bed-and breakfast inn will be glad to show you around.

To proceed, walk to Second Street and turn right (west). Walk to Park Avenue, cross to the other side of Park, and turn left (south). Continue on Park. Cross Third Street and walk up to Fourth Street. At Fourth Street, walk to Oak Avenue and turn left (south). Walk to the corners of Oak and West Fifth Street.

The **Higgins House, at 420 South Oak Avenue**, is at the northwest corner of Fifth and Oak. This blue, two-story Queen Anne home with a cheerful red door was built in 1894 for James Cochran Higgins, who was superintendent of the railroad in Sanford. In 1989, Walter and Roberta Padgett sold their Miami home, bought this house, and restored it, converting three of the eleven rooms into charming and immaculate bed-and-breakfast guestrooms.

The Queen Anne room overlooks a Victorian box garden.The other two rooms are the Wicker Room and the Victorian Country Room. The latter features an antique brass bed, a stenciled wood floor and a cedar ceiling. Also on the property is Cochran's Cottage, which offers guests two bedrooms, two baths, a living room, porch, and complete kitchen. From the upstairs veranda, you can see Sanford's earliest church, Holy Cross Episcopal. Higgins House has a gift and antique shop and serves guests a Continental breakfast.

The **Cultural Arts Center on the southeast corner of Oak and**

Fifth was formerly a library. The mint-green stucco building was designed in a Mediterranean revival style in the 1920s by Elton Moughton, a prominent local architect.

To return to the historic commercial district, head north on Oak Avenue, crossing Fourth, Third, and Second Streets. At First Street, turn right (east) and walk to the four-faced clock, the originating point of the tour.

It is worthwhile to add another destination to the walking tour. When you reach the clock, continue east on First Street for several blocks. Shortly after you pass the Chamber of Commerce Building, you'll arrive at the **Sanford Museum at 520 East First Street**.

This one-story peach-colored building houses books, furniture and other memorabilia that belonged to General Sanford. The museum opened in 1957 and has twice been expanded in size and scope to include photographs and exhibits depicting the life of General Sanford and the history of Sanford itself.

LONGWOOD

Seminole County

Location

Longwood is located in central Florida's Seminole County, which is just minutes north of downtown Orlando. Seminole County's eastern boundary is on the St. Johns River. Lake Monroe forms the northern boundary.

History

Seminole County encompasses 344 square miles, which makes it one of Florida's smallest counties. The county is comprised of seven principal cities: Altamonte Springs, Lake Mary, Casselberry, Longwood, Sanford, Oviedo, and Winter Springs.

Longwood is Seminole County's oldest city. Its founder, Edward Henck, was a surveyor and Civil War veteran who came to the area in 1873 and gave it the name of Longwood, after a subdivision in Boston that he had helped to survey. With a population exceeding one thousand, Longwood was the third largest city in Orange County (after Orlando and Sanford) during the 1880s. In 1913, it became part of Seminole County.

Longwood was primarily a mill town. One of its most important residents was Josiah Clouser, a carpenter who built many of Longwood's oldest structures. Residents were a mixture of mill workers, farmers, local merchants, and sea captains.

In 1893 and 1894, two freezes took their toll on the citrus industry and prompted an exodus from Longwood that left only 325 people in the town, according to the 1900 census. During the land boom years in the 1920s, Longwood thrived, just as many small towns did. But development came to a halt when the depression swept the country. By 1940, the city's population was only 406.

In the 1950s and later, with the growth of central Florida and the building of nearby theme parks and regional malls, Longwood developed into a conveniently-located bedroom community. It has remained a quiet residential neighborhood intent upon preserving its past. In 1995 the City of Longwood Historic Commission adopted a Wilma Street Brick Paving Project, encouraging people to buy a custom-inscribed brick for $15 and leave their mark on Longwood's history. The bricks are on sale at shops within the historic district.

The historic district, which comprises the walking tour, is full of lovely gift shops inside old houses. The shops offer gourmet foods, creative wearables, country furnishings, and gifts and novelties.

Walking Tour

To get to the **Bradlee-McIntyre House at 130 Warren Avenue**, take I-4 to the Longwood/Winter Springs exit and travel east on S.R. 434 to C.R. 427. Turn left at C.R. 427. Cross the railroad. At Warren Avenue, turn left.

A more detailed description of this walking tour can be found by following the Historic Old Longwood Village Walking Tour Guide, available from the city hall. This walking tour takes about forty-five minutes and encompasses approximately half a mile. There is ample street parking.

Begin the tour at the Bradlee-McIntyre House. The octagonal tower, steep pitched roof, decorative shingles, and gingerbread porch details are indicative of the Queen Anne style of this house. The three-story house was designed circa 1885 by a Boston architect named Nathaniel Bradlee who used it as his winter home. It was originally located in nearby Altamonte Springs on the grounds of the Altamonte Hotel and was moved to its present site in the 1970s.

Bradlee enjoyed great success in Boston as an architect and civil engineer and as an astute businessman. He came from an illustrious family, including a great-grandfather who was the first speaker of the Massachusetts House of Representatives. Bradlee died in 1888.

The house had two or three owners before it was purchased in 1904 by S. Maxwell McIntyre, who was born in Philadelphia in 1844. He and his wife Annie had no children. Annie continued to live in the house until her death in 1946, after which time the house fell into disuse. In 1971, the Central Florida Society for Historic Preservation purchased the house for $1 with the stipulation that it would move the house to Longwood and restore it. The house is open for tours at specified hours. Call the city hall for more information.

Although the house is elaborately restored, the only remaining furniture from the McIntyres' occupancy is Mrs. McIntyre's bed. Also original is the grand salon's cypress fireplace mantel. The salon is separated from the stairway by three gingerbread arches. The staircase was probably built by Josiah Clouser, an important craftsman in Longwood.

Bradlee-McIntyre House

The house has no kitchen, since the Bradlees ate at the nearby hotel or had their meals sent over to the house. The second floor hallways, which lead to four bedrooms, are large enough to have served as sitting rooms. The three bedrooms on the third floor were sometimes occupied by servants.

With your back to the Bradlee-McIntyre House, turn left and walk to the corner of Warren Avenue and Wilma Street. Turn right on Wilma and walk to Church Avenue. At Church, turn left.

The **Clouser Cottage at 218 Church Avenue** is a simple pioneer house constructed of vertical board-and-batten siding nailed directly to the interior paneling without structural stud framing.

Josiah Clouser was enticed by an advertisement in his Pennsylvania newspaper. The proposed Longwood Hotel was in need of a master carpenter. When Clouser and his family arrived in Longwood, they were provided with a flea-infested house that Mrs. Clouser deemed unsuitable. Hastily, Josiah gathered salvaged lumber and built the cottage in 1881. The family resided here for two years until Clouser built a more suitable house on Warren Avenue. The cottage was later used as an animal shed, storage space, and a rental property. In the mid-1980s, Clouser's great-grandsons Fred and John Bistline renovated the house for use as a gift shop. The glass enclosure was once an open porch. The **Apple Basket Gift Shop** is located here.

Clouser Cottage, built in 1881

Inside-Outside House

Turn around and head east on Church Avenue. **Christ Episcopal Church, at 151 Chuch Avenue**, is on the north side of the street. It was built circa 1881. With its square bell tower, symmetrical plan, and board-and-batten siding, the simplicity of the design is typical of an early pioneer church. The interior of the church retains its original dark hardwood, old-fashioned pews, stained glass, and altar.

The **Inside-Outside House at 141 Church Avenue** was so named because the framing structure was placed outside the exterior siding to form panels which were then bolted together in shiplap fashion. The house may be one of the oldest prefabricated houses in the United States. It was built around 1870 in Boston by a sea captain named W. Pierce.

In 1873, the house was disassembled and transported by steamship to Jacksonville. A river barge then moved it to Sanford, There it was met by a mule cart to take it to Altamonte Springs, where it was reassembled. For five years the house was used as a way station for federal soldiers. Then Capt. Pierce retired to become a cabinet maker. He lived on the second floor and used the main floor as his woodworking shop.

An outside staircase provided access between the two floors until Pierce built an interior staircase, which he crafted to resemble a ship's ladder. For many years after Pierce's death the house was occupied by Dr. J. R. Christy, an entomologist who was a pioneer nematologist for the U.S. Department of Agriculture. In 1973, the house was moved to Longwood and restored. The Central Florida Society for Historic Preservation leases it to a gift shop.

The **Civic League Women's Club at 150 Church Avenue** was originally a one-room structure built circa 1880. The center section of this white wood-frame building may be the oldest structure in Longwood. It was first used as a community center and as a schoolhouse under the instruction of a traveling teacher named Professor Lynch.

Walk to the corner of Church and C.R. 427. Turn left on C.R. 427, heading north. At the next corner, turn left onto West Jessup Avenue.

The gray bungalow-style house at **138 West Jessup Avenue** was built circa 1920 for L. R. Tucker. The center portion of the house is flanked by a wing on either side. The windows are three-over-one double-hung. The lower portion of the house has piers and wide steps. The house looks much as it did when it was built. The original garage stands to the rear of the house.

Go back out to C.R. 427 and turn left. Keep walking until the road seems to fork left and right. Bear left onto Freeman Street. At **288 Freeman Street** at the southwest corner of Freeman and West Magnolia

Avenue, you'll find the house that Charles Entzminger built for his daughter circa 1926. The residence was later purchased by C. C. Jackson, a food market proprietor whose descendants still own the house.

Typical of the bungalow style that was prevalent during Florida's boom period (1920–1927), the house has tapered wood columns on masonry piers, a low, pitched roof, and exposed rafters and beams.

Turn left onto West Magnolia Avenue. The white building at **110 West Magnolia**, with its pretty red flowers in window boxes, was also constructed by Charles Entzminger circa 1926. It was a garage apartment. The second floor is covered with vertical board-and-batten siding.

Walk back out to **Freeman Street** to the beige house at **346**. Known as the Fitch House, it was built circa 1888 for an alderman and early Longwood settler named J. C. Fitch. In the early 1890s, it was the home of G. W. Hardaway, the minister of the Longwood Congregational Church. After World War I, the house was bought by Charles Entzminger. Because of additions to the house, it does not resemble its earlier form.

Continue up **Freeman Street** to **398**, the Edward Henck house, which was owned by a founder of Longwood who came to the area in 1873. It was built circa 1886 by Josiah Clouser. From 1896 to 1914, Henck lived in New Jersey, but he continued to own the house. He returned to it in 1914 and lived in it for the next sixteen years, until his death. Turn around and head back on Freeman Street to Church Avenue.

Turn left and walk to C.R. 427. Cross 427 to the other side of Church, which is East Church Avenue.

The **Payne Building at 107 East Church Avenue** was constructed by Lester Payne and S. R. Long, a local carpenter. It was built in a masonry vernacular style. The building is constructed of rusticated concrete blocks and features a stepped parapet wall on the front facade and a cantilevered sleeping porch. Lester Payne and his wife Blanche operated a hardware store here. They lived on the second floor.

The building next door, at **117 East Church Avenue**, was built circa 1910 and was later owned by the Paynes. It served as the Longwood Post Office from 1932 to 1946, with Blanche acting as postmistress.

Go back up to the corner of C.R. 427 and East Church Avenue. **101–159 South C.R. 427**, on the southeast corner, is the address of the Henck-Tinker Building, constructed around 1925 by Edward Henck and Baseball-Hall-of-Famer Joe Tinker, a shortstop for the Chicago Cubs. The Longwood State Bank operated out of the building's north end, and a drugstore, a grocery and a barbershop operated out of the south end. Hit by the Depression, the bank folded in 1932, but its vault is still inside the building. The Henck-Tinker Building is constructed of brick and false-brick stucco.

Turn left on C.R. 427 and walk to **West Warren Avenue**, to the **Longwood Hotel**, which is now an office building. The hotel faces the Henck-Tinker building across 427, but the south side of the hotel faces the Bradlee-McIntyre house across Warren Street. This wood-frame vernacular-style building with Italianate details has a varied history.

In 1883, E. W. Henck commissioned Josiah Clouser to build the hotel. When it was completed in 1888, it was called The Waltham, but the name was changed to the Longwood Hotel in 1893. Disastrous citrus freezes in 1893 and 1894 forced the hotel to close its doors. In 1910, Charles Entzminger bought the hotel. In 1922 it was purchased by George E. Clark, who renamed it the St. George Hotel.

A year later, Clark died. The hotel reopened as the Orange and Black Hotel, a gambling house. It had two subsequent owners until 1952, when it was used for the George Barr Umpire School. Five years later, it had a new owner. In 1966, *Johnny Tiger* was filmed at the Longwood Hotel. It starred Chad Everett as a half-breed Seminole influenced by a schoolteacher played by Robert Taylor. In 1979, Cornell University used the building for a hotel operation school. In the 1980s, it was renovated for office use.

Continue west on **West Warren**, to **211**, which is the wood-frame vernacular-style house with tin roof that was built by Josiah Clouser, circa 1885, as a permanent home for himself and his family. Clouser's craftsmanship is keenly visible in the Chinese Chippendale–style handrail and the spindle work on the porch. The house was subsequently used as an antiques store and is now the **Family Birthing Center**.

The **R. Entzminger House** is at **241 West Warren Avenue**. The two-story bungalow-style house was built circa 1925 and owned by Charles Entzminger's cousin Robert.

Turn around and walk east on West Warren to Wilma Street. Turn right on Wilma. Walk to West Bay Avenue and turn right onto West Bay. The beige wood vernacular-style structure with brown trim at 211 West **Bay Avenue** was built as a garage apartment circa 1925.

The brown and beige bungalow at **241 West Bay Avenue** was built around 1920 and is known by locals as Miss Dolly's house, after the retired woman who lived there in the 1920s and 1930s. Except for the porch, which is now enclosed, the stucco-on-wood frame house retains its bungalow characteristics, including tapered wood porch columns on brick mansonry piers and a gabled roof with a wide overhang.

Turn around and head back on **West Bay to 212**, which is known as the Arnett House. It was built circa 1920 in a vernacular style, but with bungalow-style characteristics, including the tapered wood columns on brick piers and exposed roof rafters. During the 1920s and 1930s, the house was occupied by Lossie Arnett Cramer and her daughter Hettie, a Longwood schoolteacher. It remains faithful to its original construction.

The gray stucco house on the southwest corner of Wilma and **West Bay**, at **204**, is known as the Menick House. It was built circa 1920 for Longwood Mayor J. Henry Menick, who was a novelties manufacturer.

Turn right onto **Wilma Steet** and walk to **390**. This was the **Old Longwood School**, built circa 1885. The two-room schoolhouse was in use until 1924. For the next thirty years it served as Longwood City Hall and Fire House. It was renovated to its original form in the 1980s.

Turn around and walk back north to Bay Avenue. Turn right on Bay, heading east. Walk to **133 West Bay Avenue**, the LeRue house. Shaped like a T, this yellow house was built circa 1885 by staircase-builder and blacksmith, J. S. LeRue. The decorative details on the house are indicative of LeRue's craftsmanship. For many years the building was used as a boarding house.

The Slade house, surrounded by a white picket fence, is at **117 West Bay**. It was built circa 1885 and purchased in the 1920s by Frederick Slade, who was J. Henry Menick's partner in their manufacturing business. The house is now covered with aluminum siding. Due to additions and changes, the house little resembles its original appearance.

Walk to C.R. 427 and turn left (north). At the next block, which is Warren Avenue, turn left. You're now back at the Bradlee-McIntyre House. But before you end your tour, continue west for a very short distance on Warren so that you can view three final houses.

The **Lewis House at 152 Warren Avenue** was occupied by Tunis Lewis and his mother. Lewis was a local notary and telephone operator. The frame vernacular house was built circa 1915.

The white house at **172 Warren** was built circa 1885. Kate Beesley's millinery shop was located here in 1887. The house was sold in 1916 to a family whose descendants still own it. During the 1920s, the house was remodeled to include a second story and a porch.

The house at **192 West Warren** was built circa 1889 by Josiah Clouser and his son-in-law Frederick Niemeyer (married to Clouser's daughter Frances). Niemeyer served on Longwood's city council during the 1890s and was a Longwood postmaster until 1924. A Victorian-style second story and porch were added onto the house in 1905.

The three houses described above are across the street from Longwood City Hall.

ST. CLOUD

Osceola County

Location

The Kissimmee-St. Cloud area is located in central Florida in Osceola County, which lies just south of Orange County and Orlando's theme parks. St. Cloud is situated on East Lake Tohopekaliga.

History

During much of the 1800s, the area now known as Kissimmee-St. Cloud was largely a swampy wilderness, inhabited by tribes of Caloosa, Creek, and Seminole Indians. The few settlers who existed here were fruit farmers. When hurricanes destroyed their crops, they turned to cattle ranching. One of those ranchers was E. L. D. Overstreet, grandfather of Irlo Bronson. A local highway bears Bronson's name.

In the 1870s, a Philadelphia businessman named Hamilton Disston, who was president of Keystone Saw, Tool, Steel and File Works, made fishing trips to Florida and decided to develop four million acres of land that he purchased at 25¢ an acre. He named the area Kissimmee, the Caloosa word for "Heaven's Place."

Disston's Atlantic & Gulf Coast Canal & Okeechobee Land Company dredged the lake so that he could ship sugar from his sugarcane plantation. Kissimmee became a busy boatbuilding port. With the arrival of the railroad in 1882, Kissimmee became a center of commerce in central Florida and vacation destination.Osceola County was formed from parts of Orange County and Brevard County in 1887. Kissimmee was the county seat.

Disston's sugar plantation was the start of the Florida Sugar Manufacturing Company. When Disston died the company failed, and the plantation was sold to the Seminole Land and Investment Company, which divided the property into lots. The investment company was formed by the Grand Army of the Republic (GAR) and the *National Tribune*, its official newspaper, to establish St. Cloud as a home for Union veterans of the Civil War.

Each lot cost $50 and included a free five-acre tract. In May of 1909 the first veteran, Albert Hantsch, arrived from Chicago with his household goods and pitched a tent while he waited for his home to be built. By September of that year, the St. Cloud Hotel opened for business, a postmaster had been appointed, and Dr. George Penn, a descendant of Philadelphia's famous William Penn, had arrived with his wife and son to build a two-story house. St. Cloud was incorporated in 1911.

There is speculation about how St. Cloud got its name. One story is that the principal of the Kissimmee High School suggested the name, after the city in Minnesota. Another story is that it was named for the ancient French city of St. Cloud, which had sugar refineries.

By 1910, eighty-six charter members organized St. Cloud's *Lucian L. Mitchell Post, No. 4,* GAR *Department of Florida*, which was named in honor of the first veteran to die in St. Cloud. Mitchell died five weeks after arriving from Arkansas with his wife and five chldren.

By the late 1920s, St. Cloud had prospered from the Florida land boom. Several banks and churches flourished, and businesses in the Hunter Arms Building were thriving.

In 1933, the former Palm Theater in the Conn building was rechristened The Granada, thanks to two students who shared a $5 first prize in a name-the-theater contest. The theater's first talking pictures shown were *Hidden Gold*, starring Tom Mix, scheduled for the afternoon, and a grand opening double feature, Lee Tracy in *Private Jones* and Eddie Cantor in a Ziegfeld Follies film.

Walking Tour

The walking tour of historic downtown St. Cloud's antiques district takes about half an hour. It encompasses approximately four blocks running east and west and approximately four blocks running north and south. Streets with names of states run north and south, and numbered streets run east and west.

To get to St. Cloud, take I-4 west to the Highway 192 exit. Head east to New York Avenue and turn left. Or take I-95 to Highway 192. Head west to New York Avenue and turn right. Or take the Florida Turnpike south to Exit 244 (Highway 192) and head east for three miles to New York Avenue. Turn left. There is ample street parking.

Begin the tour at the **Chamber of Commerce building at 1200 New York Avenue**. When it was built, circa 1910, to serve as the First National Bank Building, columns at the front of this masonry vernacular building were round and fluted. They have since been replaced with square, straight columns. The sand-colored brick building was used as a dry cleaning operation, an apartment house, a Spanish American War Veterans Post, and a Golden Age Club before it became the headquarters of the local chamber of commerce. The Museum of Early St. Cloud History is located inside the building. The museum includes documents and artifacts relating to the area's development.

The Chamber of Commerce building faces east. It stands on the corner of New York Avenue and Twelfth Street. When you come out of the Chamber, walk to the corner to your left, and continue left (west) on Twelfth Street to the next corner, which is Massachusetts Avenue.

On the south side of **Massachusetts Avenue**, you'll notice a corner two-story gray wood house on your left, at **1205**. This was the G. W. Penn residence, built in 1909. The family was related to William Penn, Pennsylvania's founding father. The house features a stacked front porch and an exterior wooden staircase that leads to the second-floor porch on the south side of the house.

Turn right on **Massachusetts Avenue** and cross Twelfth Street. A majestic moss-draped tree faces the entrance to **1117**, a corner white brick building with black trim and black shutters. Constructed in 1909 as a post office, the building was formerly St. Cloud City Hall, a boarding-house, and a nursing home. It is now a retirement home called **The Homestead**.

G. W. *Penn House*

The **Fisk Funeral Home and Chapel** is at **1107–1111 Massachusetts Avenue**. Built in 1909 in a masonry vernacular style, it was the home and hospital of Dr. C. S. Cooper. Additions to the building were made in 1925, including Moorish style arches. In 1972, the brick front was added.

A former Baptist church built in 1911 sits on the corner of **Massachusetts** and Eleventh Street, at **1100–1102**. The two-and-a-half-story church was built in a masonry vernacular style. A dance center occupies the building.

Memorial Hall, at 1101 Massachusetts, was the Grand Army of the Republic (GAR) building, built circa 1914. The brick building, which faces the former Baptist church, still has its original pine floors and tin ceiling. The building's cornerstone was opened in 1995 and the contents were put on display upstairs. They include old newspaper clips and a $10 stock certificate dated 1914.

At one time, the upstairs was used as a Masonic Hall, and as the Palm Theater, which showed silent films. Bob Fisk, who owns the Fisk Funeral Home next door, remembers how, as a youngster, he could peer out of the funeral parlor's upstairs window into the window of the theater, where he could watch the screen.

Millar's Money Saving Store, a two-story gray building at **1022**, on the corners of **Massachusetts Avenue** and Eleventh Street, was built in 1911 from axed-frame concrete block. Bob Fisk and his wife lived in one of the upstairs apartments when they were first married fifty years ago.

Next door to the apartment building, the former War Veterans Memorial Library at **1014 Massachusetts** is today occupied by the **American Cancer Society Boutique** and the **Women's Club**. The stucco building was constructed circa 1923 by P. E. Morgan. It was designed in a simple Grecian style by architects Ida Annah Ryan and Isabel Roberts of Orlando.

The beige brick building with red and blue trim at the corner of **Tenth Street and Massachusetts Avenue** was once a garage. It is now a hardware store.

Turn right on Tenth Street and walk eastward toward New York Avenue. The original **St. Cloud Hotel, at 1002 New York Avenue**, was built circa 1909, but burned in a 1909 fire. It was rebuilt with sand brick the following year.

Cross Tenth Street to the other side of New York Avenue. Here you can look across to the beige and brown **People's Bank Building at 920–924 New York Avenue**, which was built circa 1925 and now houses shops and offices.

The **Police Unit** building faces the old People's Bank. At one time, the clock on the building hung from a decorative exterior arm of the People's Bank. The clock was relocated to the Police Unit building in the 1970s.

Next door to the People's Bank, the red brick **Antiques Mall at 918 New York Avenue** was once Makinson Hardware. The building was constructed in 1914. The Antiques Mall is open daily.

A red brick train depot, built in a prairie style in 1917, sits on the east side of New York Avenue. It was the former depot for the Atlantic Coast Line Railroad. The **Veterans of Foreign Wars** (VFW) owns the building now and uses it to hold their meetings.

Turn around and retrace your steps so that you are heading south on New York Avenue. On the left (east) side of New York Avenue, the blonde-brick bank building with pale green trim was built in 1910 and is now a clothing store.

The northwest corner of New York Avenue and Eleventh Street, at 1036, was the site of the Seminole Hotel, circa 1910, a familiar St. Cloud landmark for twenty-five years. A strip of shops and businesses is now located on the site.

St. Cloud's historic antiques strip was built between circa 1910 and 1912. The buildings in which the antiques shops now flourish were once occupied by a variety of businesses. The ceramics store was once a clothing store. The real estate office was formerly a bookstore.

The **Hunter Arms Building at 1029 New York Avenue** was built circa 1925. The pink and green–trimmed stucco, Mediterranean revival–style building, which extends to the corner of New York Avenue and Eleventh Street, was known as the Hunter Arms Hotel. The hotel declined and was shut down for many years, until it was purchased, restored, and reopened in 1995 by two ambitious young mothers, who learned that operating a forty-room bed-and-breakfast inn is much easier than running three Orlando-area daycare centers.

The hotel's restaurant serves full breakfasts to guests and walk-ins. An off-to-the-side lobby area functions as a small wedding chapel, which can accommodate wedding parties of up to 150 people.

At the corner of New York Avenue and Eleventh Street, turn left onto Eleventh Street, heading east toward the next corner, which is Pennsylvania Avenue. At Pennsylvania Avenue, turn left. As you walk the avenue, you'll pass by several antiques shops. These buildings were formerly occupied by a justice of the peace, a furniture store, a pool hall and feed store, and an electronics store.

Hunter Arms Hotel, Cafe and Arcade

Young's Apartments

Young's Apartments stands at the corner of **Pennsylvania Avenue** and Tenth Street, at **1124**. The white building with green trim was built circa 1915 and was called Conn's Apartments, after St. Cloud's mayor. Zimmerman's Clothing was located downstairs.

Next door, at **1120 Pennsylvania**, the gray brick building with blue trim was known as the Pennsylvania Hotel. It was actually constructed as a theater in 1917.

Turn left (west) on Tenth Street. Walk one block to New York Avenue and turn left (south), which will bring you back to the strip and to the Chamber of Commerce. You have the option of returning to the Chamber, or turning right (north) and strolling several blocks past some of the charming old homes in the neighborhood. Some of these homes are owned by proprietors of the shops in the antiques district.

If you choose to stroll past the homes on **New York Avenue**, note the pretty blue Craftsman-style house with a tin roof at **813**. This home was built circa 1919. The charming bungalow-style house next door, at **809**, was built circa 1914 and was occupied by Rev. William and Helen Landiss. These two houses are typical of the earlier homes built in St. Cloud.

When you reach the intersection of New York Avenue and Lakeshore Boulevard, you'll arrive at East Lake Tohopekaliga, which was developed in 1935. This is a popular area for fishing. It's also the site of a boat basin, a lovely beach area with picnic and playground facilities, and a bike and walking path.

You will immediately notice a charmingly-landscaped, beautifully-restored blue and white house facing the boat basin. There is a sign in the front yard that says, "**Graff Gregory House**, 1908." The present owner, who has lived there for more than twenty-five years, claims that this is the oldest house in St. Cloud.

CENTRAL FLORIDA
HISTORICAL ATTRACTIONS, DINING, AND LODGING

OCALA — *Marion County*

Suggested Lodging

The Ritz Hotel
1205 East Silver Springs Boulevard
Ocala, FL 32670
904-867-7700

Seven Sisters Inn Bed & Breakfast
820 South East Ft. King Street
Ocala, FL 34471
904-867-1170

For Information

Historic Downtown Ocala
151 Southeast Osceola Avenue
Ocala, FL 34471
904-629-8423

Historic Ocala Preservation Society
P.O. Box 3123
Ocala, FL 34478
904-351-1861

Ocala/Marion County Chamber of Commerce
110 East Silver Springs Boulevard
P.O. Box 1210
Ocala, FL 32678
904-629-8051

SANFORD – *Seminole County*

Suggested Dining and Lodging
The Rose Cottage
1301 Park Avenue
407-321-4356

Has the atmosphere of a European Victorian-era tea shop.

The Higgins House Bed and Breakfast
420 South Oak Avenue
Sanford, FL 32771
407-324-9238

For Information

Greater Sanford Chamber of Commerce
400 East First Street
Sanford, FL 32771
407-322-2212

Sanford Main Street Welcome Center
101 West First Street, Suite B
Sanford, FL 32771
407-328-8393

Seminole County Convention & Visitors Bureau
P.O. Box 160816
Altamonte Springs, FL 32716-0816
800-800-7832

Other Historic Attractions

Museum of Seminole County
Highway 17-92
(across from Flea World)
407-321-2489
Highlights the history and lifestyle of Seminole County. Housed in the former "Old Folks Home" built in 1926. Open Tuesday through Saturday noon to 5 P.M.

Sanford Museum
520 East First Street
Sanford, FL 32771
407-330-5698
Open Tuesday to Friday 11 A.M. to
4 P.M., Saturday 1 P.M. to 4 P.M.

LONGWOOD — Seminole County

For Information

Central Florida Society for Historic
Preservation
P.O. Box 520500
Longwood, FL 32752

Historic City of Longwood, City Hall
175 West Warren Avenue
Longwood, FL 32750
407-260-3440

Seminole County Convention &
Visitors Bureau
P.O. Box 160816
Altamonte Springs, FL 32716-
0816 1-800-800-7832

Other Historic Attractions

Bradlee-McIntyre House
130 Warren Avenue
Longwood, FL 32752
407-260-3440
Open the second and fourth
Wednesday of the month, 11 A.M. to
4 P.M., second and fourth Sunday of
the month, 1 P.M. to 4 P.M. Admission:
$2 donation.

ST. CLOUD — Osceola County

Suggested Dining and Lodging

Caruso's Palace
8986 International Drive
407-363-7110
The interior resembles a sixteenth-
century opera house.

Chimento's
1002 New York Avenue
407-957-8771
Italian restaurant located in the historic St. Cloud Hotel.

Hunter Arms Bed and Breakfast
1029 New York Avenue
St. Cloud, FL 34769
407-892-5505

Unicorn Inn English Bed & Breakfast
8 South Orlando Avenue
Kissimmee, FL 34741
407-846-1200
A beautifully-restored 1901 colonial-
style house whose furnishings and
decor reflect the Yorkshire, England,
background of the present owners,
Don and Fran Williamson. Fran is
famous for her confections.

For Information

Kissimmee-St. Cloud Convention &
Visitors Bureau
P.O. Box 22007
Kissimmee, FL 34742-2007
407-847-5000 or 800-327-9159

St. Cloud Area Chamber of Commerce
1200 New York Avenue
St. Cloud, FL 34769
407-892-3671

Other Historic Attractions

Flying Tigers Warbird Air Museum
231 North Hoagland Boulevard
Kissimmee, FL 34741
407-933-1942
A World War II aircraft restoration
facility displaying a collection of historic planes and artifacts.

Open daily 9 A.M. to 5:30 P.M. Adults $6, senior citizens $5.

Old Town Shipping (Dining and Entertainment Attraction)
5770 West Irlo Bronson Memorial Highway Kissimmee, FL 34746
407-396-4888
The attraction resembles turn-of-the-century shops and restaurants and includes a 1927 Big Eli Ferris Wheel.

Spence-Lanier Pioneer Center
750 North Bass Road
Kissimmee, FL 34741
407-396-8644
A circa 1900 store, museum, and smokehouse typifying rural Florida life. Open daily 10 A.M. to 4 P.M. Adults $2.

Central East

CENTRAL EAST

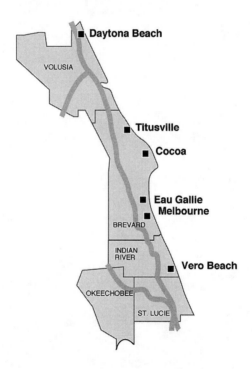

Volusia County

Location
The Daytona Beach area is located in Florida's central east coast region. Daytona Beach is the largest municipality in Volusia County.

History
The earliest known inhabitants of the region known as Daytona Beach were the Timucuan Indians. In the 1600s, Spanish families were given land grants and settled there. In 1768, fourteen hundred Greek and Minorcan colonists, led by Dr. Andrew Turnbull, founded a farming colony some twenty miles away in New Smyrna Beach. The colony failed after ten years. By the early 1800s, many indigo, cotton, sugarcane, and rice plantations were thriving. However, most of them were ruined during a Seminole uprising in 1836.

Further growth and development slowed in the area until after the Civil War. In 1870, Mathias Day came to Florida from Mansfield, Ohio, to invest in Florida land. Attracted to the acreage that was an old sugar plantation, he purchased the property and laid out the town of Daytona. It was incorporated in 1876.

In 1890, Henry Flagler took ownership of the Ormond Hotel in nearby Ormond Beach. He built a steel railroad bridge over the St. Johns River, and he brought his Florida East Coast Railroad into Daytona. It was the arrival of the railroad that made Daytona a destination for wealthy Northern vacationers. The Ormond Hotel hosted such prominent figures as John D. Rockefeller and car manufacturer R. E. Olds.

In 1902, while staying at the Ormond Hotel, R. E. Olds and Alexander Winton participated in a contest to see whose automobile could travel faster across Daytona's hard-sand beach. They tied at fifty-seven miles per hour. In 1903, Winton won with a speed of sixty-eight miles per hour, and the Florida East Coast Automobile Assocation was established to foster local beach racing. The beach, with its packed sand, became well known because it was used as a proving ground for developing the automobile engine. Today, there are eighteen miles of beach on which car traffic is permitted. Daytona continues to be a racing mecca.

Daytona Beach was home to two influential women, both of whom were born in the mid-1870s. Mary McLeod Bethune founded Bethune-Cookman College for black students. The fifteenth child of freed slaves, she was an advisor to Franklin Delano Roosevelt and four other presidents. Her two-story frame house was built in 1914 and is one of the buildings on the college campus. She lived there until her death in 1955.

Josie Rogers was the daughter of Daytona pioneers. She was the first female physician in Daytona Beach. She used a bicycle or horse-and-buggy to make her house calls. In 1922, she became Daytona Beach's first woman mayor.

Walking Tour

To get to the **Live Oak Inn at 444–448 South Beach Street**, take I-95 to the International Speedway Boulevard exit (U.S. 92) and head east to Beach Street. Turn right. Go four blocks to the corner of Loomis Street and Beach Streets. This walking tour is approximately three-quarters of a mile and takes about thirty minutes. There is parking at the inn or on the street.

Live Oak Inn

The Live Oak Inn is comprised of two houses that are next door to each other and that sit on the ruins of an orange grove plantation destroyed during the Seminole Wars. The property belonged to Mathias Day, who sold it to Riley Peck in 1871. Peck, from upstate New York, was an early settler in Daytona Beach. In 1871, he built a five-room house on part of the property and sold part of the lot to his brother Myron ten years later.

Riley's house at 444 South Beach Street is the oldest building in Daytona Beach. In 1881, Myron Peck built the two-and-a-half-story wood frame vernacular house next door at 448 South Beach Street. It was built on a coquina foundation.

Long before the house at 448 was converted into an inn by a local resident named Dr. Vinton Fisher, it was occupied by Maria Huston Davidson Brower Pope, who was the first white child born in Daytona. In 1900, Maria married Charles Brower of Cincinnati. Later, widowed and with two children, Maria moved back to Daytona Beach. She bought the house at 448 South Beach Street. She remarried and was again widowed. Maria continued to live in the house. She was in her nineties when she died.

A few years ago, Dr. Fisher purchased both houses and converted them into a bed-and-breakfast inn. Later, ownership returned to Mr. and Mrs. Del Glock. The thirteen-room Live Oak Inn is now overseen by a manager. The restaurant at the inn is open for dinner and is being leased by a local chef named Tom Papa.

Walk north on **South Beach Street** to **440**. On this site in 1880 there was a private boarding school. The present colonial revival house was built circa 1904 on a coquina foundation. The house was constructed for Peter Siems, who built the Northern Pacific Railroad. It was later owned by a violinist and then by Dr. J. E. Rawlings, whose widow donated the property to Volusia County. For a while the house was used as a courthouse annex.

The two-story wood-frame vernacular house at **432 South Beach Street** was built in 1883 by Calvin Day, a relative of Mathias Day. It was built for Lawrence and Mary Thompson, who paid $300 for the lot. The house has had several owners, including W. Wright Esch, the founder of WESH-TV. It now houses law offices.

Next door, the house at **426 South Beach Street** was the Thompson Brothers' general store. The store itself was on the first floor, and meetings and religious services were held on the second floor. Just before the turn of the century, the house was purchased by the Rhodes family, who made additions to it so that it could be used as a residence.

Thompson house, built in 1883

Harrison Garfield Rhodes lived and worked in the house. He was a prolific writer, a Harvard graduate, and a friend of author Sloan Wilson. The present owner, Dr. William Doremus, has lived in the house for more than forty years. According to Dr. Doremus, his lawyer was handling the Rhodes estate, and said, "Bill, I want to tell my boss that I at least have a bid on the house. You're a friend of mine. Give me a bid. Any bid." Dr. Doremus says he gave a figure "off the top of my head." Two weeks later his lawyer called him to announce, "You own a house in Daytona Beach."

The **YWCA at 344 South Beach Street** is in a prairie-style stucco building that was known as the Thomas H. White winter home, which White built in 1910 for his wife. White manufactured sewing machines and bicycles and owned White Trucks. What began as a bungalow was enlarged by Richard H. Edmonds, editor of *Manufacturer's Record*, who bought the house from White's widow in 1919. The YWCA took it over in 1937.

At Orange Avenue, turn left and walk to **St. Mary's Episcopal Church at 216 Orange**. The church was built in 1883 in a gothic revival style, and has twenty-eight stained glass windows. On April 25, 1883, parishoners of St. Mark's Mission of Daytona gathered at the church to see the new cornerstone laid. The cornerstone had been engraved incorrectly with a *y* instead of a *k*, making the church St. Mary's instead of St. Mark's. The Church has been called St. Mary's ever since.

Walk back to South Beach Street and turn left (north) to the Merchants Bank at **252 South Beach Street**, which now houses the **Halifax Historical Society**. It was designed in a beaux arts style by Jacksonville architect W. B. Talley and built of brick and masonry in 1910. A victim of the Great Depression, the bank closed in 1929. The building was used by the Florida Bank & Trust Company in 1936, and then as a gift shop and a restaurant. In 1984, the Halifax Historical Society headquartered here, and since has used the building as a regional museum providing exhibits and displays that chronicle the history of the area.

Across the street, on the east side of Beach Street, you can see part of the **Jackie Robinson Memorial Baseball Park**. In 1946, Robinson played here for the Brooklyn Dodgers farm team, the Montreal Royals, making the ballpark the site of the first racially-integrated spring training game.

Turn left (west) on Magnolia Avenue, and walk to **220–224 Magnolia**, known as the Amos H. Kling House, which was built around 1907. In 1891, Florence Kling, Amos's daughter, married an Ohio senator named Warren Gameliel Harding. He was elected President of the United States in 1920. Because of the famous couple's frequent visits to the house, it became known as the winter residence of Warren G. Harding.

Continue to Ridgewood and turn left (south). Walk to the corner of Live Oak and Ridgewood. Here, at **390 South Ridgewood**, you'll find Olds Hall, named for the automobile manufacturer who was a yearly winter visitor to Daytona Beach. The building was built in 1923 as a Mediterranean-style apartment complex. It was built by Julian Arroyo who was Franklin Delano Roosevelt's law partner. In the 1940s, the building was purchased by R. E. Olds and used as offices. In the 1970s, it was occupied by the Evangelical Lutheran Good Samaritan Society. Today it is a nursing home.

Turn east on Live Oak Avenue and walk to Palmetto Avenue. Turn right (south). **The Coquina Inn Bed and Breakfast at 544 South Palmetto Avenue** was built in 1912. It was designed by S. H. Gove, the same architect who designed the Thomas White winter residence and the Peter Siems house. Charles Nichols, a fur and hide trader from Colorado, lived here in the 1920s. It later served as offices for the director of the Volusia County Health Unit and then was used as a residence for ministers of the First United Methodist Church.

In 1990, Jerry and Susan Jerzykowski purchased the residence and restored it, converting it into a charming four-unit bed-and-breakfast inn with Victorian soaking tubs, canopy beds, and a pretty garden patio.

At Loomis Avenue, turn left and walk to Beach Street. Just before you reach Beach Street, you'll see the Queen Anne home of Cynthia Lindsay, built circa 1900. Craft demonstrations are held on the grounds of the house.

At Beach Street, turn left to return to the Live Oak Inn. You'll see the Halifax Harbor Marina on the east side of Beach. **The Halifax River Yacht Club, at 356 South Beach Street**, was incorporated in 1896. In 1897, when the original clubhouse was built, it cost $1,367. Warren G. Harding enjoyed playing card games here.

You might want to cross Beach Street to the Yacht Club side and walk across the street from the Club to **Riverfront Park** to see an unusual and poignant sight. In the park, red flowers surround a granite gravestone embedded in the grass. The stone covers the grave of a stray dog who wandered into Daytona Beach in 1940 and was adopted by the local residents.

Brownie, as the dog was called, wandered around Beach Street for fifteen years, making daily visits to the merchants, and enjoying the attention and food handouts he received from shoppers and school children. Donations toward Brownie's food and veterinary bills were put into a bank account. When the dog died, a funeral was held. Seventy-five people attended, including the mayor, who proclaimed that Brownie was a good dog. The bank account paid for the dog's grave and headstone on which is engraved, "Brownie. A Good Dog. 1940–1955."

Coquina Inn, built in 1912

Location

Titusville is located in Brevard County along Florida's Atlantic coast approximately thirty-five miles east of Orlando. It is part of Florida's "Space Coast."

History

During the 1500s, Brevard County was occupied mostly by Indian tribes. During the 1700s, the Indian population was largely replaced by European settlers. Several years after Florida was admitted to the Union in 1845, a lighthouse was erected at what is now Cape Canaveral.

After the Civil War, settlers from surrounding Southern states moved to the area. By the 1880s, hundreds of people were living in Melbourne, Rockledge, Cocoa, and Titusville.

In the 1860s, Mary Hopkins, the daughter of a Georgia planter, owned a small piece of land in Sand Point, Florida. Her husband, Col. Henry Titus, suffered from rheumatism, so he moved his family from Kansas to Sand Point. Titus opened the Titus House Hotel in 1870 along the Indian River. With daily hotel rates of $3 and menu entrees of fresh fish and vegetables, the hotel proved successful.

Legend has it that in 1873 Titus competed with a friend in a game of dominoes in which the winner would have the right to change the name of Sand Point. Titus won, and Sand Point became Titusville.

Titus campaigned to have Titusville declared the Brevard County seat. In 1879, Titus's efforts were rewarded. He had amassed considerable land in Titusville, much of which he donated to the city. Government buildings and St. Gabriel's Episcopal Church were later built on the land.

Titus was crippled by rheumatism. He died in 1881 and was buried in LaGrange Cemetery in North Titusville near Mims. Hopkins Avenue in Titusville is named in honor of Henry Titus's wife, Mary Hopkins.

In 1887, Titusville was incorporated. The population was four hundred. Around 1895, the coming of Henry Flagler's railway swelled the population of Titusville, which had become a popular stop for winter visitors. Titusville benefited from the land boom of the 1920s, but fell into economic depression after the land bust in 1927.

Titusville's modern era began in 1940 with the opening of the Banana River Naval Air Station, today known as Patrick Air Force Base. During World War II, construction of hundreds of military boats took place here. When Kennedy Space Center was built here in the 1950s, Titusville, known largely as an agricultural area, emerged as a high technology research and development center and an enormously popular tourist destination.

The buildings in the downtown historic district comprise a variety of architectural styles including beaux arts, mission, masonry, and frame vernacular. They date from 1895 to 1926. With twenty-four historic buildings, the downtown area of Titusville has been designated as a Main Street City. The program is administered by the Florida Department of State, Division of Historical Resources. It has generated tourism and economically revitalized Titusville's "old downtown." The district is on the National Register of Historic Places.

Walking Tour

The walking tour is approximately half a mile in length and takes about forty-five minutes. To get to the **North Brevard Historical Museum**, your starting point, take I-95 to Exit 79 (S.R. 50) and head east until you come to a dead end, which is U.S. 1.

Hopkins Avenue is U.S. 1 South, and Washington Avenue is U.S. 1 North. Turn north on Washington and continue for approximately two miles to the museum at **301 South Washington**. There is street parking, and there is a municipal parking lot behind the museum.

The North Brevard Historical Museum, which is operated by the Historical Society of North Brevard, contains carefully collected and exhibited memorabilia about Titusville's history, businesses, and people. Bob Hudson, a journalist who dresses up as Col. Henry Titus when he conducts walking tours of the area, created a pictorial "Panorama of Titusville" that is on display. Some of the interesting artifacts in the museum are the handprints of six of the seven original Mercury astronauts, a black family's Bible dating from circa 1800, an 1870 trousseau, a solid oak wheelchair from the 1920s, an 1881 typewriter, and a jury chair from the Brevard County Circuit Court, circa 1898.

The building next door to the museum, at **303 South Washington**, was the location of a Western Union telegraph relay station between Jacksonville and Miami in 1910.

Walk to the corner of Washington Avenue and Main Street and turn

Stewart's Cash Store, built in 1913

right (east) on North Main. **Badcock Furniture** is located at **21 Main Street**. The building was the former home of the Van Croix Theater, which opened in 1926 and could seat a thousand people. It showed silent films. In the 1940s, the abandoned building became a high school basketball gym and community center. If you walk to the rear of the furniture store, you can see the old wood gym floor.

The shops and businesses in the **Gaslight Mall at 13 Main Street** are located in the former lobby of the Titusville Post Office, which opened at this location in 1926. The antiques store at **106 Main Street** was Stewart's Cash Store, which opened in 1913.

Walk back to Washington Avenue and turn left (south). The Spanish-style structure with arched arcade, at **302 South Washington**, is now used for commercial purposes but was built in 1924 as the Walker Apartments. Notice the carved sailing ship above the entry.

Step inside the children's resale shop at **305 South Washington** and you'll see the original tin ceiling, heart pine floor, and display shelves that were built for the Titusville Hardware Store that sat on this site in 1910.

The Spanish-style building erected in 1910 at **307–311 South Washington** had the distinction of having the first elevator in Titusville. Through the years various retail stores have operated here.

The one-story masonry vernacular building at **315 South Washington** opened in 1910 and continues to operate as a real estate office.

The beige brick building with green trim at **317–319 South Washington** was constructed in 1912 by J. C. Spell, M.D. who served as Titusville's first licensed pharmacist and operated a pharmacy here. The Bank of Titusville was located here between 1912 and 1924. It was followed by the citrus-packing firm of Nevins Fruit Company.

The **O.K. Barber Shop at 322-1/2 South Washington** opened in 1937. The barber chairs, sinks, cash register, and shoe-shine stand are originals.

In 1890, Capt. James Pritchard built his Pritchard and Son Hardware Store at **327 South Washington**. You can still see reminders of the store, such as the tiled entry, the tin ceiling, and the original floors and walls.

The masonry vernacular–style building at **337 South Washington** was built in 1890 to house the Denham Department Store. In 1990 it became the home of Kloiber's Cobbler & Eatery, a charming, casual restaurant that retains the building's original brick walls, beams, and skylight. Among the eclectic memorabilia at Kloiber's are an old Coca-Cola sign and the first traffic light in Titusville. There is a mantel in the waiting area of the restaurant that was carved from one of the original floor joists. More of the history of the building is available from Kloiber's owners, Joe and Pixie Kloiber. Ask for their information sheet.

The Alpine Hotel and Saloon opened circa 1888 in the mission-style building at **338–340 South Washington**. It was later occupied by a bar and a jewelry store.

The two-story, wood-frame house at **424 South Washington**, with its decorative woodwork and trim, is considered Titusville's premier example of Queen Anne architecture. It was built in 1891 by Captain James Pritchard for his wife Mary.

Fifteen years earlier, Pritchard, a former Civil War officer, arrived in Titusville from St. Louis. He served as president of the Indian River State Bank, which he helped to organize, and he owned a hardware store in town. The house has continuously passed on to Pritchard's descendants, who still occupy it.

At the corner of Washington Avenue and Pine Street, turn right (west) on Pine. Cross U.S. 1 South, which is Hopkins Avenue, and continue on Pine to 414.

St. Gabriel's Episcopal Church, built in 1887, is Titusville's oldest church. The land on which it sits was donated by Mary Evalina Titus, the widow of Col. Henry Theodore Titus, the founder of Titusville. The church is constructed in the carpenter gothic style and is visually noteworthy for two reasons. Its Victorian stained glass was made in England and com-

Pritchard house

pleted in New York, at Tiffany's and Gorham's. The steeple bell, which is reputed to be the largest in Titusville, was installed in 1892.

Walk back to U.S. 1/Hopkins and turn left (north). Walk to Julia Street. The building at **301 Julia Street** was built in 1905, partly as a hotel and apartments and partly as a saloon and pool hall. It was remodeled and became the first silent movie theater in Titusville. In the 1950s it was known as the Florida Theater. After another remodeling, it reopened as a playhouse.

At U.S. 1/Hopkins and Julia Street, you'll come to a Spanish-style stucco building which was built in 1925 by fruit grower Mr. Duren and is now occupied by an antiques shop.

Turn right (east) on Julia Street and walk to U.S. 1/Washington Avenue. Turn left (north) on Washington Avenue and head back to the North Brevard Historical Museum at 301 South Washington.

COCOA
(COCOA VILLAGE)
Brevard County

Location

Cocoa Village, on S.R. 520 east of I-95, overlooks the Indian River. It is in the city of Cocoa, north of Melbourne and south of Titusville in Brevard County on Florida's central east coast.

History

Prior to the late 1800s, the area around Cocoa was inhabited by Indians. It was a wilderness thick with forests, sticky with humidity, and plagued with mosquitoes. The Seminole Wars were another factor in deterring settlers.

In 1875, the LaRoche, Sams and Porcher families settled on the northern part of Merritt Island east of Cocoa. They had come from Charleston, South Carolina where their homes and plantations had been ravaged by the Civil War. It wasn't until the 1880s that settlements increased around the Indian River area.

In 1881, the Willard brothers built a trading post along the river. In 1882, a post office was established about two miles north of Cocoa. In 1883, Edward Porcher built a warehouse in Cocoa, where he packed the citrus he transported by riverboat from his citrus groves on Merritt Island. In 1884, Delmonico's restaurant opened in Cocoa.

By 1888, Travis Hardware was operating on Delannoy Avenue, St. Mark's Episcopal Church had been built and a daily steamship from Titusville was transporting local farmers' citrus products to northern markets. Cocoa's population was approximately four hundred. The community had a weekly newspaper called the Indian River Sun. In 1889, homesteader Albert Taylor founded a bank across from his house. It was the first bank in Brevard.

Blacks were among Cocoa's first settlers. By 1885, they were working in orchards, as servants for wealthy summer vacationers, or on the building of tracks that the Jacksonville, Tampa and Key West Railroad was extending into nearby Titusville.

In 1886, Melissa Moore, a black resident of Cocoa, was instrumental in establishing the Mount Moriah A.M.E. Church. Moore had come to Cocoa in 1885 with the Travis family when they relocated from Sanford. In 1890, she opened a restaurant that is said to have been frequented by Henry Flagler whenever he came to town.

The Great Freeze of 1894-1895 was devastating to citrus growers, many of whom sought new occupations. Nevertheless, by 1900, Cocoa handled much of the state's processing and production of citrus, which had made Brevard primarily a citrus-producing county. By 1915, Cocoa's population had stretched to one thousand.

During the land boom years of 1919 to 1926, Gus Edwards came to Cocoa from Georgia and became the town attorney. Through developing and promoting oceanfront land east of Cocoa, he attracted investors to a peninsula he called Cocoa Beach. Two bridges were built to connect the mainland to Cocoa Beach, which was incorporated in 1925.

By 1926, the land boom had busted. Building activity greatly slowed. The 1940s gave birth to Brevard County's nickname, "The Space Coast," thanks to the building of Patrick Air Force Base just south of Cocoa Beach and a missile-testing program at Cape Canaveral. Flocks of tourists and scientists in need of housing revitalized the Cocoa area.

In 1975, the City of Cocoa decided to recreate the old downtown area as it looked many years ago. The result is Olde Cocoa Village, a quaint collection of charming shops and eateries along oak-shaded brick sidewalks and cobblestone streets.

Walking Tour

This walking tour encompasses approximately four blocks and takes about thirty minutes. To get to the **Porcher House**, which is your starting point, take I-95 to Exit 520 east into Cocoa Village. Cross U.S. 1. Turn right just before you reach the Humphrey Bridge. Travel one block south. On your right, you'll see the parking lot at the rear of the Porcher House. After you park, enter the house from the rear or walk around the block to the front entrance on Delannoy Avenue.

The imposing **Porcher House at 434 Delannoy Avenue**, with its coquina stone and four white columns, is a historic landmark. It was built in 1916 by Edward Porcher and his wife Byrnina Peck Porcher. Edward Porcher, a South Carolina Huguenot, became a prominent grove owner. An inventor of citrus-handling equipment, he is credited with being the first to wash, inspect, and grade fruit. His wife Byrnina, formerly of Atlanta, was the daughter of William Henry Peck, author of seventy-four historic novels.

Playing a game of bridge was Byrnina Porcher's favorite pasttime.

Porcher House

She was so fond of the card game that she had workers carve a spade, club, heart, and diamond into the coquina stone on the front of the house.

The house was built in a classical revival style. The front has a two-story, Ionic-style portico. A grand wooden staircase ascends from the entrance foyer and winds left and right beneath a large crystal chandelier as it leads to the upstairs rooms.

The house has served as a family residence, a hotel, a city hall, and a home for orphaned boys. It is now owned and operated by the City of Cocoa. Walking tours of Cocoa Village can be arranged at Porcher House. The house is rented out for weddings, teas, parties, and other special events.

If you stand on Delannoy, looking toward the front of the Porcher House, you'll be facing east. Turn right and walk south on Delannoy to the **corner of Delannoy and Church Street**, the site of **St. Mark's Episcopal Church**.

This first church building in Cocoa was built in 1886 in the Florida gothic style of frame and clapboard construction. The church was enlarged in 1926. The exterior was redone in a Spanish style.

Walk back toward, then past the Porcher House. At **415**, on the west side of **Delannoy**, you'll see a Florida gothic house that was built in 1890.

Miss Julia's millinery and dress shop

The white, wood house with slate blue trim was the home, millinery, and dress shop of Miss Julia Roberts O'Brian, known as "dressmaker for the ladies of Cocoa." The house is now an art studio.

The building next door to Miss Julia's was owned by a widow who operated it as a boardinghouse. She showed moving pictures behind her house in what was known as the Victor Theater. The Victor entertained audiences during the silent movie era and ceased operating in 1924. The front of the building was occupied by a jewelry shop.

On the right (east) side of Delannoy, you'll come upon the **Travis Hardware** store. The same family has owned this business for more than 100 years. In 1888, S. F. Travis bought a one-story building at **300 Delannoy** that had been built in 1885. It was here that he ran his business. In 1907, the Travis family expanded the business and added an adjoining brick building.

Today, Travis Hardware consists of the original building, the 1907 addition, and four adjoining buildings that were added through the

The Arcade

years. When you step inside the store, you will see the sliding ladders, the tin ceiling and the skylights from the 1885 building. Notice the mix of tin patterns on the ceilings.

At the corner of Delannoy and King Street, turn left (west) onto King. Walk to the corner of Brevard Avenue and King Street and turn left (south) onto Brevard. This will lead you to a courtyardlike area known as **The Arcade**, which dates to 1925. The stone and stucco, Moorish-design shops and galleries are topped by pineapple designs on the roof. The pineapple was a symbol of hospitality in the South. **The Cocoa Village Playhouse**, built in 1924, sits next to The Arcade. It is on the National Register of Historic Places.

The three-story building on the west side of Brevard is called the **Village Tower**. It was built in 1919 as a Masonic Temple. The building has been the site of a post office, a bank, and small businesses.

Number **401 Brevard** was once the site of Mrs. James's Cottage. She served meals to travelers up and down the Indian River and is credited with naming Cocoa after the Baker's chocolate powder that was sold locally.

This walking tour follows a horseshoelike path. Continue on Brevard to Church Street and turn left on Church, which leads you back to Delannoy.

EAU GALLIE

Brevard County

Location

Eau Gallie is a northern section of Melbourne in Brevard County on Florida's central east coast, south of Daytona Beach. Because Kennedy Space Center is in Brevard County, the area is also known as the Space Coast.

History

Following the Civil War, black freedmen came to what was known as Crane Creek and became the first families to settle there. Among them were two men: Wright Brothers and Peter Wright. In 1877, the family of Richard Goode, from Illinois, became one of the first white families to settle in the area. In 1878, Cornthwaite John Hector bought land from Peter Wright near the harbor. On the land, he built a rooming house, part of which he used as a store and post office.

It was Hector, formerly of Melbourne, Australia, who chose the name Melbourne for the post office. Peter Wright was the first postman. Twice a week he sailed his boat up to Titusville to gather the mail and bring it down to Melbourne.

Indians were the first to inhabit Eau Gallie, the small community north of Crane Creek (Melbourne). The first white settler there was John Houston, who arrived in 1859 with his cattle and slaves. In 1871, William H. Gleason bought 16,000 acres of land along the central east coast of Florida, part of which he settled on in 1882.

Between 1874 and 1878, Eau Gallie was the county seat of Brevard County. In the 1880s, boat building and boat servicing were thriving businesses in Eau Gallie, because boats were the main means of transportation. In 1893, the construction of the Florida East Coast Railway transformed Eau Gallie from a sleepy town to a busy one, thanks to the arrival of railroad workers and their families. New banks, stores, and businesses sprang up.

In the early 1920s, the Florida land boom hit Eau Gallie, just as it had caused real estate prices to spiral upward in other parts of the state.

With the land bust that followed came failed businesses and folded banks. The Depression didn't help. In 1939, the area began to recover, and continued to do so as a result of activity created by the building of the Banana Naval Air Base, which is now Patrick Air Force Base. All of Melbourne, and the rest of Brevard experienced a tremendous growth in population after the Space boom in 1950. Kennedy Space Center has become the dominant tourist attraction in the county.

Walking Tour

The walking tour is approximately three-fourths of a mile and takes about one hour. To get to St. John's Episcopal Church, take I-95 to the Eau Gallie Boulevard exit. Head east to Water Street. Turn right (south) on Water Street and take it to Young Street. At Young Street, turn right to get to the church, which has a parking lot. This walking tour of Eau Gallie will take you along tree-shaded country streets and through a charming, tranquil neighborhood. It is one of the most pleasant walking tours you're likely to encounter.

Begin your tour at **St. John's Episcopal Church at 610 Young Street**. The church, built in 1897, was designed after a church in Canada that was attended by Alex, Henry, and John Hodgson, three brothers who were early white settlers in Eau Gallie. Although in colonial times congregants had to buy a pew seat, the Hodgsons declared that all seats in the church should be free to those who wished to worship. One of the stained glass windows in the church was installed within the past thirty years and has a space program theme. If you study it carefully, you'll see that part of it depicts a rocket taking off. The overhead beams in the church resemble an inverted ark.

The church faces southward toward the yacht basin across the street. With your back to the church entrance, turn left (east) on Young Street. Along the tour you will encounter historical markers that explain the significance of the houses or sites that you are viewing.

Stop at the two-story house on the **southwest corner of Young and Houston**. John Hodgson remarried after the death of his first wife. His second wife was a medical doctor, an uncommon profession for a woman in the early twentieth century. This house was built around 1910 by John and Dr. Sarah Hodgson. Her offices and examining rooms were located upstairs. The first floor was a pharmacy. Florence Hodgson, a niece, later remodeled the house as her retirement home. There had been a large drugstore window overlooking Young Street, which she removed along with the heavy doors that led into the drugstore.

Turn right (south) on Houston, and walk down to the tranquil, pic-

Hodgson house, built circa 1910

turesque deepwater harbor. Here, **facing the Eau Gallie River**, the large house **on the east side of Houston** that was once the meeting place of the local yacht club is now a private residence. Across the street, on the west side of Houston, is the site where the Hodgson families founded their mercantile business during the 1890s. They also operated a machine shop and a small steamboat, and they owned an orange grove on the south side of the Eau Gallie River.

Walk back up Houston to Young Street and turn right (east) onto Young. Walk until you get to **Sunny Point Drive**. On the **north side** of the street, the white wood-frame house with green shutters was built circa 1900 and bacame the home of Gen. John Castleman, who died in 1918. Castleman was a Civil War general from Louisville, Kentucky, who also fought in the Spanish American War. He was one of the founders of the yacht club. Castleman's house is recognizable by the immense tree in front of it.

Walk to the right (south) on **Sunny Point Drive** until you reach a **cul-de-sac**. Here, set back behind oak trees, is Mrs. Sunny Ballard's former home, which she christened Sunny Point. The house was built in 1915 at a cost of $40,000 for the S. T. Ballard family, owners of Ballard Flour Company. The house, with yellow siding and black shutters, is now an apartment house. The Ballards, who hailed from Kentucky, used it as a winter home. In the 1880s, the land it sits on was owned by John

Deepwater harbor of Eau Gallie River

Sunny Ballard home, Sunny Point

Houston, Eau Gallie's first settler. He was a cousin of Sam Houston. It was in this area that John Houston had a sugar mill and grew rice.

Walk back on Sunny Point Drive to the corner of Young and turn left on Young. When you get to Houston again, turn right (north). As you walk up Houston, you'll come to a cozy-looking lavender cottage with four white columns. The house is not historic, but the site is. It is the site of the first Houston family homestead. John Houston had come here in 1859 with ten slaves and some of his six sons in order to build a large hickory log cabin for his family.

During the Seminole Indian Wars, Houston served in the U.S. Army and was stationed at an army fort in Enterprise, Florida. When his log cabin was completed, Houston went back to Enterprise to get his family and bring them to Eau Gallie. It took three weeks to drive their covered wagons, cattle, and horses from Enterprise to Eau Gallie.

Houston had an amicable relationship with the Seminole Indians who lived in the area. He gave them sugar and coffee, and they gave him animal hides. The Houstons built a small fishing boat, but they had no tackle. They would light a torch, and pole around in the creek. Attracted to the light, the fish would jump into the boat.

Front view of James Rossetter house

As you continue walking north on **Houston**, you'll arrive at **1296**, a gray cottage that was home to Thruston Morton, a Kentucky politican.

At Houston and Old Oak Streets, turn left (west) on Old Oak. On the northeast side of the street, on land once owned by the Houstons, is a side view of the wood-frame James Wadsworth Rossetter home, which sits behind a low black wrought iron gate. Rossetter came to Eau Gallie in 1902. Rossetter was a citrus grove owner and had an interest in the Standard Oil Company.

The exact year in which the house was built is uncertain. Rossetter bought the property in 1902 and built the front part of the house around 1908. It is possible that the older, rear part of the house, which was supposedly the Houston family's slave quarters, dates to Civil War days.

Walk up to the **corner of Old Oak and Highland Avenue** and turn right (north), so that you are walking past the front of the Rossetter house for a better view of the two-story veranda that is enclosed by a balustrade. The entrance features a transom window and sidelights. The ceilings and walls inside the house are constructed of small pieces of heart pine set in intricate patterns, an apparent design whim of the ship-building carpenter.

From the street, you can get only a glimpse of the garden behind the Rossetter house. The garden is lush with birds of paradise, fishtail palms, cactus, confederate jasmine, angel trumpet, fruit trees, and sugarcane mill remnants. Rossetter's two daughters donated the house to the Florida Historical Society, which hopes to turn it into a museum.

Across the street and facing the Rossetter House is the William Roesch House at **1320 Highland Avenue**. The frame vernacular house, built circa 1901, has shiplap siding, fishscale ornamentation, and two-over-two, double-hung sash windows. Roesch was an early pioneer and the first mayor of Eau Gallie. He was editor of the Eau Gallie newspaper.

One of James Rossetter's daughters purchased the house in 1945 to store family furnishings and belongings. In 1992 she donated it to the Florida Historical Society. It now serves as statewide headquarters for the Society.

Facing the front of the Rossetter house, turn right (south) on Highland. Cross Old Oak and continue on Highland to a small park, **Rossetter Park**, on your left.

Just past the park is the **Houston family cemetery**. The first burial in the cemetery was that of Samuel Houston, a son of the original pioneers John and Virginia Houston. Samuel died at the age of twenty-seven.

Across the street from the cemetery, and surrounded by a chain link fence, there is a white wood-frame house with a screened porch. The house is appropriately called **Twin Oaks**, because of the huge twin oak trees on the property.

The former owner of the house, a Mrs. Glen, had a niece named Jean Faircloth, who was an occasional visitor to Twin Oaks during her later teenage years. Some of Eau Gallie's longtime residents remember Jean because she became the second wife of Gen. Douglas MacArthur in 1937.

From the cemetery, continue south on Highland to the corner of Highland and Young. Turn right on Young to return to St. John's Episcopal Church.

VERO BEACH

Indian River County

Location
Vero Beach in Indian River County is located on the east coast of Florida between St. Lucie and Brevard Counties. It is south of Daytona Beach and north of West Palm Beach.

History
Indian River County's earliest white settlements were situated along the Indian and Sebastian Rivers. The first white settlers were fishermen. The proliferation of mosquitoes was a deterrent to settlement, but the eventual large-scale drainage of swampland eased the problem.

In 1891, settler Henry Gifford established a post office in his home. This was the Vero Post Office. Vero later became Vero Beach. It was part of St. Lucie County until the 1925 incorporation of Indian River County.

The Indian River provided the primary means of transportation until the railroad was extended down the east coast in 1893. The railroad was a boon to the farming and citrus industries in the area, as well as to tourism.

Once the Indian River Farms Company was established in the early 1900s, farmers from the Midwest and the North moved to the area, bringing their cattle with them. The cattle were shipped aboard the railroad trains, and the cattle industry in the county was on its way.

In 1914, Indiana tillery machinery salesman Waldo Sexton visited Vero Beach. He was so impressed with the area that he bought and developed oceanfront and westerly acreage. In 1920, Sexton built a citrus packinghouse, considered to be the oldest operating packinghouse on the East Coast. He is most famous, though, for the Driftwood Resort on Ocean Drive, which began as the beach house he built for his family. The lumber for the house was obtained from a demolished cow barn and from ocean-washed wood. Carpenters didn't work from plans. Instead, Sexton shouted directions and instructions at them.

With his penchant for collecting, Sexton's large house became an eclectic treasure trove of artifacts, antiques and other objects. Sexton salvaged stained glass, Spanish and Italian tile, wrought-iron gates, religious statuary, and other items from torn-down buildings that had been designed by famed architect Addison Mizner. Bells from cathedrals, ships, and locomotives, solid bronze boiler heads, centuries-old paintings, sixteenth- and seventeenth-century furniture, and ship cannons added to his collection. This rather outlandish conglomeration of displayed items attracted so many curious people to Sexton's home that he turned it into a hotel.

Today, the Driftwood's restaurant and its two-story C-shaped breezeway are on the National Register of Historic Places, and the name of Waldo Sexton lends some levity to the history of otherwise conservative Vero Beach, a community of quiet residential neighborhoods and upscale shopping.

Walking Tour

The walking tour encompasses a small section of Vero Beach, but it centers on a downtown area that was the hub of activity for early Vero residents. This walking tour covers approximately five blocks and takes about thirty minutes. To get to the Heritage Center, take I-95 Exit 68 (Vero Beach/Lake Wales) and head east to Fourteenth Avenue. Turn left (north) at Fourteenth Avenue and continue for two blocks to the Citrus Museum/Heritage Center. There is ample street parking.

Begin at the **Heritage Center**, on the east side of **Fourteenth Avenue**, at **2140**. Built in 1925, part of this long, white, green-roofed building was originally a rest room facility that served visitors to the park on the site where the Center now sits. Due to an increasing residential and tourist population, an addition was built to provide meeting rooms, a stage, and a kitchen for visitors and local clubs. Completed in 1935, at a cost of $5,000, this addition became the community center. During World War II, the Naval Air Station came to Vero. The community building gave military personnel a place to socialize, so a north wing was added in 1943 to provide a men's lounge and rest room which included a dressing area and showers. The wing now houses the Indian River Citrus Museum. If you use the rest room in the museum, you'll notice the old-fashioned white porcelain shower faucets on the wall, although the showers are long gone. The plaster-and-lath and heart-of-pine building is listed on the National Register of Historic Places.

Be sure to browse through the Citrus Museum as part of your walking tour, to learn about the development of the citrus industry and its importance to Indian River County, the Florida economy, and the world. The exhibits include historic photogaphs, old farm tools, collectible

138

antique citrus labels, original harvesting equipment, and memorabilia of the pioneers of Indian River citrus territory.

On the grounds of the Heritage Center a plaque has been erected in memory of William Jennings Bryan, who delivered a public address from a platform erected at that spot. He was the honored guest and orator on July 2, 1925, to celebrate the incorporation of Indian River County.

Look directly across the street to the **west side of Fourteenth Avenue**. The **old Indian River County Courthouse** dominates the street as it faces the Heritage Center. The courthouse was completed as a WPA project in 1937 and is a typical example of the stark, Depression-era architectural style. The old courthouse presently sits empty. A newer courthouse was built several blocks westward.

With your back to the Citrus Museum and Heritage Center, turn right (north) to continue up Fourteenth Avenue. Next to the Museum and Center is the playground area of **Pocahontas Park**, the site of social gatherings during the 1920s, 1930s, and 1940s. The Indian River Farm Corporation, developers of the downtown area, deeded the park to the city of Vero in 1921. The park had a small zoo, a wading pool, and children's play equiment. Today, it accommodates a colorful playground and shuffleboard and tennis courts.

Just north of the park is the old train station, once used for passenger and freight service on Henry Flagler's Florida and East Coast (FEC) Railway. The station was built in 1903. Indoor plumbing was added in 1936. In 1984, the **Indian River Historical Society** bought the station for one dollar from the railway company and moved it to its present location from the south side of town. The Historical Society, located inside the train station, serves as an exhibition center to tell the story of Vero Beach and Indian River County.

Train station

139

Pocahontas Building

Walk back past the Citrus Museum. At the corner of Fourteenth Avenue and Twenty-first Street, turn right, crossing to the west side of Fourteenth Avenue. At **1414 Twenty-first Street**, you'll see the beige Pocahontas Building on the corner and the image of Pocahontas on the beige stucco facade. Notice the decorative eave work. The Mediterranean revival–style building, completed in 1926, houses retail stores and apartments.

If you walk upstairs to the second floor, you'll find yourself in an open parlor, where, a half century ago, residents could gather to sit, rest, and chat. The nostalgia continues. Notice the transoms over the apartment doors? The glass doorknobs? The louvre-and-screen doors? The little black doors along the bottom of the hallway walls? Those small doors, close to the hallway floor, open into the apartment kitchens underneath the sinks; they functioned as a passageway for the milkman to deliver milk to tenants.

Continue south on Fourteenth Avenue to **Theater Plaza**, home of the former Florida Theater. It is a mixed-use complex, with commercial space and upstairs apartments. The skylights, once covered up, were exposed after they were discovered during restoration work. The theater, built in 1924, is not currently in use.

The **Pueblo Arcade** has been restored to accommodate various shops. There is a huge old bank safe in the entrance to the arcade, and on the floor are the typical 1920s small black-and-white tiles.

At the **corner of Fourteenth Avenue and Twentieth Streets**, turn right onto Twentieth. Here you'll see the white, two-story former Citrus Bank building, with its arched windows and mission-style roof line. It is now the **Vero Furniture Mart**.

You'll also see the beige Maher Building, built in 1919 for W. J. Maher's dry goods, shoes, and furnishings. The building burned in a fire that year but was immediately rebuilt. It is fronted by six archways and a pediment on top of the building and is now occupied by apartments and businesses.

At Twentieth Street and Fifteenth Avenue, turn right onto Fifteenth and walk north one block to Twenty-first Street. Turn left onto **Twenty-first Street** and walk to **1534**. This brown vernacular cottage, built in 1915, served as the county's library from 1916 to 1962 and has always housed the **Vero Beach Woman's Club**. The building still has its original wooden doors.

Facing the Woman's Club, turn right, heading east to Fourteenth Avenue. At Fourteenth Avenue, turn left, which will bring you back to the Heritage Center/Citrus Museum.

CENTRAL EAST FLORIDA
HISTORICAL ATTRACTIONS, DINING,
AND LODGING

DAYTONA BEACH — *Volusia County*

Suggested Dining and Lodging

Live Oak Inn Restaurant
448 South Beach Street
904-252-4667
Located in an 1880s house built by a pioneer family.

Coquina Inn Bed and Breakfast
544 South Palmetto Avenue
Daytona Beach, FL 32114
904-254-4969 or 800 727-0678

Indian River Inn
1210 South Riverside Drive
New Smyrna Beach, FL 32168
904-428-2491 or 800-541-4529
Built in 1916. Supposedly frequented by Al Capone.

Live Oak Inn
448 South Beach Street
Daytona Beach, FL 32114
904-252-4667

Riverview Hotel
103 Flagler Avenue
New Smyrna Beach, FL 32169
904-428-5858 or 800-945-7416
1885 former bridgetender's house.

The 1888 House
124 North Clara Avenue
Deland, FL 32720
904-822-4647
Former boarding house originally built in 1888 and remodeled in a classical revival style.

For Information

Daytona Beach Area Convention & Visitors Bureau
126 East Orange Avenue
Daytona Beach, FL 32114
904-255-0415 or 800-544-0415

Halifax Historical Society
252 South Beach Street
Daytona Beach, FL 32114
904-255-6976

Other Historic Attractions

Mary McLeod Bethune Home
631 Pearl Street
Daytona Beach, FL 32014
904-255-1401
Located on the Bethune-Cookman College campus, this former home of the famous black educator is on the National Register of Historic Places. Call for information.

The Casements
25 Riverside Drive
Ormond Beach, FL 32074
904-673-4701
Built in 1912, this former winter home of John D. Rockefeller is now a cultural center.
Open Monday through Thursday 9 A.M. to 9 P.M., Friday 9 A.M. to 5 P.M., Saturday 9 A.M. to noon.

TITUSVILLE — *Brevard County*

Suggested Dining

Alexandria's
2543 North U.S. 1

Mims, FL 32754
407-264-1134
Located in a restored Victorian home.

Kloiber's Cobbler & Eatery
337 South Washington Avenue
Titusville, FL 32796
407-383-0689

For Information

Historical Society of North Brevard
301 South Washington Avenue
Titusville, FL 32796
407-269-3658

Space Coast Office of Tourism
P.O. Box 1969
Cocoa, FL 32923
407-633-2110 or 800-936-2326

Titusville Area Chamber of Commerce
P.O. Drawer 2767
Titusville, FL 32781-2767
407-267-3036

Other Historic Attractions

North Brevard Historical Museum
301 South Washington Avenue
Titusville, FL 32796
407-269-3658
Open Tuesday through Saturday 10
A.M. to 2 P.M.

Valiant Air Command Warbird Museum
6600 Tico Road
Titusville, FL 32780
407-268-1941
Educational institution that exhibits
vintage war planes. Open daily 10 A.M.
to 6 P.M. Adults $6, children $4.

COCOA — *Brevard County*

Suggested Dining and Lodging

Cafe Margaux
220 Brevard Avenue
Cocoa Village
407-639-8343
Classic French cuisine in an old
Village building.

The Inn at Cocoa Beach
4300 Ocean Beach Boulevard
Cocoa Beach, FL 32931
407-799-3460 or 800-343-5307
Luxurious bed-and-breakfast inn, formerly a hotel, with European
ambiance. Breakfast in a country
French dining room.

For Information

Cocoa Beach Chamber of Commerce
400 Fortenberry Road
Merritt Island, FL 32952
407-459-2200

Florida's Space Coast Office of Tourism
2725 St. Johns Street
Melbourne, FL 32940
407-633-2110 or 800-USA-1969

Historic Cocoa Village Association
274 Brevard Avenue, D6
Cocoa, FL 32922
407-631-9075

Other Historic Attractions

*Brevard Museum of History and
Natural Science*
2201 Michigan Avenue
Cocoa, FL 32926
407-632-1830
The museum offers walking tours of
historic Cocoa Village. Items on display chronicle the history of Brevard

County. Open Tuesday through Saturday 10 A.M. to 4 P.M., Sunday 1 P.M. to 4 P.M. Adults $3, children $1.50.

Grant Historical House
5795 U.S.1
Grant, FL 32949
407-723-8543
A wood frame, cracker house built in 1916 by Atley Bensen for his wife Clara. The Bensens were pioneers in the commercial fishing industry in the area.
Open Tuesday through Friday 10 A.M. to 4 P.M. Donation requested.

The Henegar Center
625 East New Haven Avenue
Melbourne, FL 32901
407-723-8698
A small cultural center housed inside the seventy-year-old Ruth Henegar School, the oldest public building in Brevard County.
Call for information.

EAU GALLIE — *Brevard County*

Suggested Dining

Dr. Joe's Intracoastal Restaurant
531 West Eau Gallie Boulevard
Melbourne, FL
407-255-2446
American food served in a two-story wooden building built circa 1915.

Nannie Lee's Strawberry Mansion
1218 East New Haven Avenue
Melbourne
407-723-1900
American food served in a Victorian house built circa 1900.

For Information

Weona Cleveland (She conducts guided walking tours)
407-723-8725

Greater South Brevard Area Chamber of Commerce
Visitor and Convention Division
1005 East Strawbridge Avenue
Melbourne, FL 32901-4782
407-724-5400 or 800-771-9922

Other Historic Attractions

Brevard Museum of History and Natural Science 2201 Michigan Avenue
Cocoa, FL 32926
407-632-1830
Items on display chronicle the history of Brevard County. Open Tuesday through Saturday 10 A.M. to 4 P.M., Sunday 1 P.M. to 4 P.M. Adults $3, children $1.50.

Grant Historical House
5795 U.S. Highway 1
Grant, FL 32949
407-723-8543
Built in 1916 as a wood-frame Cracker house by Atley Bensen for his wife Clara. The Bensens were pioneers in the commercial fishing industry in the area.
Open Tuesday through Friday 10 A.M. to 4 P.M. Donation requested.

The Henegar Center
625 East New Haven Avenue
Melbourne, FL 32901
407-723-8698
A mini-sized cultural center housed inside the seventy-year-old Ruth Henegar School, the oldest public building in Brevard County.
Call for more information.

VERO BEACH — *Indian River County*

Suggested Dining and Lodging

The Patio Restaurant
1102 Miracle Mile
Vero Beach, FL
561-567-7215
Located in an old building that was once an ice cream parlor. Antique items on display include a fireplace from Venice.

Waldo's Restaurant at the Driftwood Inn
3150 Ocean Drive
Vero Beach, FL
561-231-7091

The Captain's Quarters at Capt. Hiram's
1606 Indian River Drive
Sebastian, FL 32958
561-589-4345
Located on the Indian River, this motel was built to resemble an old Key West–style ship captain's house, right down to the yellow paint, the green shutters, and the tin roof.

Driftwood Resort
3150 Ocean Drive
Vero Beach, FL 32963
561-231-0550

For Information

Indian River County Tourist Council/Vero Beach-Indian River County Chamber of Commerce
1216 Twenty-First Street
P.O. Box 2947
Vero Beach, FL 32961
561-567-3491

Indian River Historical Society
P.O. Box 6535
Vero Beach, FL 32961
561-778-3438
The Society conducts walking tours of Vero Beach.

Other Historic Attractions

Indian River Citrus Museum
2140 Fourteenth Avenue
Vero Beach, FL 32960
561-770-2263
Millie Bunnell conducts walking tours of Vero Beach and can be reached at the Museum.

McLarty Treasure Museum
Two miles south of Sebastian Inlet on State Road A1A
Sebastian, FL 32958
561-589-2147
Recounts, in dioramas, paintings, and recovered artifacts, the 1715 shipwreck of a Spanish treasure fleet off the Inlet. Open daily 10 A.M. to 4:30 P.M. $1 admission.

Mel Fisher's Treasure Museum
1322 U.S. 1
Sebastian, FL 32958
561-589-9875
Exhibits archaeological and religious artifacts and treasures recovered from shipwrecks.
Open Monday through Saturday 10 A.M. to 5 p.m., Sunday noon to 5 P.M. Adults $5, senior citizens $4, children six to twelve $1.50.

CENTRAL WEST

Central West

TAMPA
(YBOR CITY)
Hillsborough County

Location
Ybor City is located on Tampa Bay in Tampa on the west coast of Florida. Tampa is Florida's third most populous city. It is in Hillsborough County, Florida's fifth most populous county.

History
In 1539, while searching for gold, Hernando de Soto sailed into Tampa Bay. The Indian tribes living there called their village "Tanpa," which means "sticks of fire." Early explorers misspelled the name when they drew up maps, and the area became known as Tampa.

In 1772, a Dutch mapmaker gave the name of Hillsborough to the area's river, in honor of Lord Hillsborough, the British secretary of state for the American colonies. In 1855, the settlement known as Ft. Brooke became known as the town of Tampa.

In the late 1800s, railroad baron Henry B. Plant built an elegant hotel, the Tampa Bay Hotel, in the heart of Tampa. It cost $3 million and is still easily identifiable by its Moorish domes.

Teddy Roosevelt was a visitor to the hotel during the Spanish American War, since American troops embarked for Cuba from the Port of Tampa. The hotel is now part of the University of Tampa. The Henry Plant Museum, filled with antique treasures, is inside the former hotel.

In 1885, a cigar maker and Cuban exile named Don Vicente Martinez Ybor moved his cigar business from Key West to an area east of Tampa. In 1886, Ybor built a cigar factory, the American Cigar Manufacturing Company, in the area now known as Ybor City.

The building of Henry Plant's railroad facilitated the transport of cigars, and before long there were two hundred manufacturing operations supporting the cigar industry in Ybor City. The Ybor City cigar industry thrived because Jews, Italians, Germans, Spaniards and Afro-Cuban immigrants supported each other in a multicultural and multiracial community that enabled them to live and work harmoniously. With its shops and restaurants, Seventh Avenue became the commercial core of Ybor City. Social clubs and organizations providing economic aid sprang up. Cigar workers lived in small "shotgun" houses, with rooms lined up one behind the other.

In 1905, Casimiro Hernandez left Cuba and arrived in Ybor City with his wife and two children. He bought a small corner bar that was located across from his apartment building, and converted it into a cafe. He called it "Columbia" as a tribute to Christopher Columbus. The Columbia became a popular spot to enjoy a glass of sangria or a cup of Cuban coffee and some neighborhood gossip. In 1920, to accommodate patrons, he expanded the cafe, which today is considered to be the oldest continuously-operating restaurant in North America.

In the early 1900s, the flourishing cigar industry gave Ybor City its reputation as the "Cigar Capital of the World," but by the 1930s, the introduction of cigar-making machines and the growing popularity of cigarettes contributed to the decline of Ybor's cigar factories.

Today, Ybor City is one of only three National Historic Districts in the state of Florida. There is one in Pensacola and one in St. Augustine. The Ybor City State Museum celebrates Ybor's Latin history and culture by conducting a walking tour, which is also sponsored by the Ybor City Chamber of Commerce.

The old-fashioned street lamps, wrought iron balconies, and ornate grillwork, the stomping heels and clicking castanets of the flamenco dancers at the Columbia Restaurant, and the pervasive aroma of Cuban coffee and Cuban bread, bring Ybor City's historic heritage to life. The Tampo Rico Cigar Company continues to hand roll its cigars.

Walking Tour

Rubber-tire trolleys provide shuttle service between downtown Tampa and Ybor City. The numbered avenues run east and west. The numbered streets run north and south.

Begin the tour at the corner of Eighth Avenue and Thirteenth Street at **Ybor Square**. To get there, take I-4 to the Ybor City exit. Head south on Twenty-first Street. Turn right on Palm Avenue (Tenth Avenue) and go west. Turn left on Thirteenth Street to Eighth Avenue and Ybor Square. There is a municipal lot, and street parking throughout Ybor City. The tour is approximately one mile and takes about one hour.

Here in Ybor Square was Ybor Cigar Factory, the largest such factory in Ybor City. The three red-brick buildings now are occupied by antiques, crafts, clothing, gift shops, and restaurants. The Tampa Rico Cigar Company is housed here in the stemmery. You can watch the worker sitting in his chair as he meticulously hand rolls each cigar. The buildings comprise the factory, the warehouse, and the stemmery where cigar workers stripped the stems from the tobacco leaves. Tobacco grown in Cuba was shipped to Tampa, unloaded at the dock, and stored in the warehouse until needed.

On the first floor of the factory were the employees called "strippers" and "selectors." They'd send the tobacco up to the second floor to the employees called "rollers." The rollers rolled the cigars and sent them up to the third floor to the "boxers." The boxers packed the cigars in wooden boxes which slowed the release of moisture from the cigars.

Although basements or cellars were unusual for Florida, all cigar factories had them. Their purpose was to keep tobacco leaves damp and moist so they wouldn't dry out. The windows were always of a north and south exposure so the selectors would have good lighting to do their jobs and so that they would have a breeze blowing from the bay. This is indicative of the good working conditions that prevailed in the cigar factory.

The "lector" would sit in a lector's chair on the second floor of the factory, in the middle of the room. There, as the workers did their jobs, he would read from daily newspapers and from books. The lector was not an employee of the factory, but was paid by the workers. Beside him he kept a jar in which he collected coins placed there by the grateful workers. The lector held an important position because his loud, clear reading of the material enabled workers to keep abreast of current events and literary culture — as well as providing some sense of relief from the tedium of cigar-rolling.

Exit to Ybor Square at the door that faces east, so that you can see the iron steps where Jose Martí, the liberator of Cuba, stood to give a speech. You'll also see **El Parque de Amigos de Jose Martí**. In the mid 1950s, residents built this park and dedicated it to Martí, who championed the separation of Cuba from Spain.

Walk up to Ninth Avenue. Head east. At Fourteenth Street (Republica de Cuba) and Ninth Avenue, you'll come to **El Bien Publico**. This building was constructed in 1895 and was occupied by the Ybor Land and Improvement Company. It later became a health care facility. At Fourteenth and Ninth, you can also see the Cherokee Club, a private men's club established in 1888. It's located upstairs in the **El Pasaje Hotel**. The stained glass is original to the building.

Walk north, on the east side of Fourteenth Street, to the **Cuban Club**. This building, constructed in 1918, was a mutual aid society.

Continue north to Palm Avenue, which is also Tenth Avenue. Turn right (east). You'll pass the **Hillsborough Community College Ybor**

The Cuban Club

Campus on the north side of the street. Turn right (south) onto Fifteenth Street. Cross Ninth Avenue and Eighth Avenue.

At the southwest corner of Eighth and Fifteenth, you'll come to **El Encanto Cleaners**. This was originally a wholesale grain and grocery store. At one time, there was a gambling casino in the basement of this red-brick building. El Encanto Cleaners has continued here for three generations.

Continue south to Seventh Avenue (Broadway). At Seventh Avenue and Fifteenth Street, you'll come to **Tracks**, a popular night club on the west side of Fifteenth. It is in a blonde brick building that was built in 1917. On the east side of the street is the **Ritz Theater**, which was built in 1917 and now features rock bands.

Walk east on Seventh Avenue to approach **Centro Espanol**, where the Spanish Club formerly existed. The Spanish Club was founded in 1892 as an ethnic club designed to assist members in need of financial and moral support. El Centro Espanol is a National Historic Landmark. In the courtyard of the El Centro Espanol, called El Paseo de Ybor, there is a statue to motherhood where flowers are placed on Mother's Day. The statue, erected in May of 1948, is dedicated to the spirit of Tampa's Latin heritage, and honors mothers of the world.

Former Centro Espanol Casino and Culture Club

In 1895, the corner of Seventh Avenue and Seventeenth Street served as a meeting place and public speaking platform for Cuban exiles. Here, a young Italian revolutionary named Orestes Ferrara rallied the exiles into fighting against Spanish oppression. A street plaque in front of the presentday **Barnett Bank** explains that Ferrara joined a Tampa expedition to Cuba and became a celebrated guerilla under General Maximo Gomez. Ferrara became president of the Cuban senate, and Cuban ambassador to the United States.

The Italian Club, or L'Unione Italiana, on the corner of Seventh Avenue and Eighteenth Street, was organized in 1894 and was Tampa's first Italian-American Society. Built in 1914, the club assisted members through cultural enrichment.

As you continue walking, you'll pass a variety of shops and eateries and the famed **Columbia Restaurant/Corner Cafe**, established in 1905, which takes up an entire city block. The tile was made in Spain. The restaurant has a striking Mediterranean decor and a wonderful menu selection. The highlight of dinner at the Columbia is the flamenco floor show.

A street plaque at the intersection of Seventh Avenue and Twenty-Second Street explains that this was the site of a water trough where Teddy Roosevelt and his Rough Riders watered their horses in 1898 during training sessions during the Spanish American War.

Restored cigar worker's homes

Interior of cigar worker's restored home

From Seventh Avenue, walk to Nineteenth Street and turn left (north). Walk to Ninth Avenue to get to the **Ybor City State Museum**, located in a building that is nearly one hundred years old. The building was once occupied by the Ferlita Bakery, from which the community obtained its bread. The museum complex is comprised of the bakery, where you can see the original ovens, and three cigar workers' shotgun houses.

One house has been used as the headquarters of the Ybor City Chamber of Commerce, and another house, La Casita, is a museum. These homes were built south of the railroad tracks in 1895, and were moved to this location and restored. La Casita is furnished as a cigar worker's home would have been furnished in the early 1900s.

Through wall murals, photographs, documents, and exhibits, the Ybor City State Museum explores what life was like in Ybor City during its heyday, and how the residents, from diverse backgrounds, lived and worked cooperatively. Notice the nail on the wall outside La Casita, to the right of the front door. Fresh-baked bread was delivered and slapped onto the nail. The museum complex's surrounding brick-paved patio and gardens includes a statue of Ybor.

From the museum, walk west on Ninth Avenue to Thirteenth Street. Turn left (south) onto Thirteenth and walk to Eighth Avenue to return to Ybor Square, the starting point of the tour. An expanded version of this walking tour is sponsored by Ybor City State Museum, and Ybor City Chamber of Commerce.

PALMETTO

Manatee County

Location

Palmetto is located just north of the Manatee River in Manatee County on the central west coast of Florida.

History

The city of Palmetto was christened by Samuel Sparks Lamb after he arrived in the area in 1868 from his home state of South Carolina, which is nicknamed the "Palmetto State." For Lamb and other early settlers, the Manatee River and the waterfront were essential components of pioneer life. Everyone in the community depended on the river for delivery of mail and supplies, transportation, and citrus shipping.

In 1843, Simon Turman, an Ohio native, arrived in the Manatee area. He received a land grant of 160 acres, and he constructed a crude crib of cabbage palmetto logs which became known as Turman's Landing. Everything that was unloaded had to be rafted to shore because there was no dock connecting the crib with the mainland. Two years later, Turman moved to Tampa.

Joel Hendrix came to Palmetto in 1871. His wife Martha Ann paid Samuel Sparks Lamb $100 for six acres of land on which Hendrix built a house and a general store. He also built a dock so that supplies would no longer have to be ferried from the landing to the shore.

In 1889, the Palmetto Baptist Church was organized. That same year, the City of Palmetto was incorporated, with Peter S. Harllee elected as the first mayor. In 1895, the Palmetto Terminal Railroad was built, which enabled produce from farms north of town to be transported to Hendrix Dock. Four years later, the first bank in Manatee County, the Manatee County State Bank, opened in Palmetto's first brick building. Today, Palmetto is the center of Manatee County's agricultural industry. The Manatee Convention Center is located in Palmetto.

Walking Tour

This walking tour is approximately one mile long and takes about ninety minutes. To get to the **Regatta Pointe Marina at 985 Riverside Drive**, take S.R. 64 west to Ninth Street West in Bradenton. Take the Green Bridge over the Manatee River. On the other side of the bridge, turn left on Riverside Drive. There is parking at the marina.

Walk west from the marina to **Regatta Pointe Condominium at 1050 Riverside Drive**. This was the site of the Madame Joe Atzeroth home, later the Samuel Sparks Lamb home. Julie Atzeroth, wife of Joseph Atzeroth, was referred to as "Madame Joe." Madame Joe was known as a tough, no-nonsense woman, a feminist long before the word was coined. In 1850, Madame Joe paid $230 to purchase forty-six acres of riverfront property here. Four years later she paid $3 per acre for an additional thirty-eight acres, which she purchased from Simon Turman.

Madame Joe and her husband lived in a log cabin they built on the site. In 1886 they sold the property to Joel Hendrix's sister Sarah Campbell, of Clarke County, Mississippi. Two years later, Sarah Campbell sold the property to Samuel Sparks Lamb. The Lambs moved into the log cabin that Madame Joe had built.

Lamb operated a store from the log cabin. When he built a new house for his family, he moved the cabin farther west along the river, and used the cabin as a school. He hired a private teacher to teach his thirteen children and some neighbors' children.

In 1893, Lamb served as one of Palmetto's first aldermen. He died in 1910. His widow Sarah remained here until her death twelve years later. Regatta Pointe Condominimums were built on the site of the Lamb home.

Cross Eleventh Avenue West and continue walking west on **Riverside Drive** to **1102**, which was the home of Julius Lamb. Julius was nine years old when his family moved to the Palmetto area. His house was built in 1913 on the site to which the Lamb School log cabin had been moved. The house was ordered from a Sears and Roebuck catalog and arrived complete and ready to put together. The porches have been enclosed. The house is now **Five Oaks Inn**, a bed-and-breakfast inn.

Julius owned Guarantee Abstract Company and Lamb & Willis Real Estate and was vice president of Manatee County State Bank, which his father, S. S. Lamb, helped establish in 1899.

Continue walking to the wood frame house at **1112 Riverside Drive**. It was built circa 1900 and was owned by a farmer, J. Pope Harllee, son of Peter and Alice Harllee, who were among Palmetto's first settlers. In 1928, Harllee became mayor of Palmetto.

Along with his sons, Peter and J. P. Jr., Harllee formed Harllee Farms in 1935, which remains one of the largest operations of its kind in

Manatee County. Harllee was a member of the Manatee County Board of County Commissioners for twenty-five years. The house has been restored by its present owners, a heart specialist and his pediatrician wife.

The area between Twelfth and Thirteenth Avenues along the river was the site of a dock and boardwalk that were built in 1903 by the Howze family. Palmetto's first jail was located near here. The jail was actually a wooden building that was set out in the water. One of its prisoners escaped by setting fire to his mattress and using it to burn a hole in the prison wall. The area is now a seawall.

Turn right (north) on Twelfth Avenue (Cedar Street). The Howze Homestead, just north of **101 Twelfth Avenue West**, dates to 1885, when James A. Howze came to Manatee County from Alabama. A former captain in the Confederate Army's thirty-second Regiment, Howze opened a store west of S. S. Lamb's on the river.

During the late summer of 1888, a salesman arrived by steamer and called upon James Howze. That afternoon, the salesman caught the steamer back to Tampa. Shortly afterward, word drifted back to Howze that the salesman had died from yellow fever. Within days, Howze's wife and children came down with the disease. The children survived, but Mrs. Howze died, becoming Palmetto's first fatality from a yellow fever epidemic.

A year later, Howze remarried. His second wife was Frankie McKay, who had come to Palmetto to teach at the newly-constructed frame schoolhouse. Howze died in 1897 from a heart attack.

Walk to **325 Twelfth Avenue West**. This is where James Howze's son Stuart built a home in 1929. Stuart was a farmer and bookkeeper, and owner of Howze Grocery Store.

Walk to the white house at **330 Twelfth Avenue West**. This frame vernacular house was built circa 1900 by Macajah (Mack) O. Harrison, the son of Wade Hampton Harrison, who came to Palmetto from Alachua County in 1891. The elder Harrison was a cattle owner who lived north of Palmetto.

Mack Harrison built this house shortly before his 1903 marriage. He was a fruit packer and shipper and later served in the Florida Senate. Mack's brother William lived for a while with Mack and Mack's wife Evelyn. William, an attorney, was a judge in the circuit court from 1923 to 1959.

Next door, at **329 Twelfth Avenue West**, is the former site of the Frankie Howze house, circa 1900. When Captain James Howze died in 1897, Frankie left the Howze homestead and moved with the younger children to a home that was on this site. She continued as a schoolteacher and later became principal of the primary school. She retired in 1940. Although Frankie's house was eventually torn down and replaced by the present house at this site, some of the remaining trees on the property were planted by her.

Continue to **344 Twelfth Avenue West**. This house was built in 1887 and later occupied by Durwood B. and Minnie L. Whittle. Whittle left Georgia in 1911 and settled in Palmetto, where he opened up a plumbing company. The Whittles' son Belmont was the proprietor of Whittle's Furniture Store on Eighth Avenue.

By 1921, Assistant Postmaster W. E. Burch was living in the house. In 1929, the house was purchased by Police Chief Wade L. Oxford. Ten years later, Julian D. Howze purchased the home. Julian was the son of James and Frankie Howze. Frankie lived here with Julian and Julian's wife Kay, who was a librarian.

Turn left (west) where Twelfth Avenue dead-ends into Fourth Street West. The yellow frame vernacular house with tin roof and three-window dormer at **1209 Fourth Street West** was built in 1918. At that time, its occupants were Hattie Robertson, a saleslady, and Lela Robertson, a student. It is probable that the two women were related.

In 1921, James A. and Louise Howze lived in the house. James Howze was a real estate abstractor and a civil engineer. He was also Manatee County's tax assessor from 1924 to 1953. Upon his retirement, his son, James A. Howze Jr., succeeded him.

Turn around and walk east on **Fourth Street West** to **1118**. James K. Parrish's son Walter and his wife Nellie, daughter of S. S. Lamb, occupied this residence. They were married in 1894 and moved into the house upon its completion about six years later. Walter and Nellie had three children, Ernest, Ester and Walter Eugene. The elder Walter died after having lived in the house for only about a year. Walter Jr. and his wife Violet later lived in the house.

The white house with black trim at **1117 Fourth Street West** was built circa 1910 and was the home of Mary Emma Lamb Richards, the widow of Daniel Uriah Richards, a Civil War veteran who moved, with his brother Tuck, to Manatee County.

Daniel's first wife, Nancy Elmira Gillett, died during childbirth in 1877, leaving him with three children and a new infant daughter. A few months afterward, Daniel married S. S. Lamb's daughter Mary, with whom he had six children. When he died in 1893, he was buried next to his first wife in Gillett Cemetery.

In the 1895 census, Mary was listed as head of household with nine children aged two to twenty-four years living at home with her.

The yellow house with brown trim at **1111 Fourth Street West** was built circa 1917. In 1912, the property had been deeded by Mary Richards to a farmer named James T. DeSear, who was married to Mary's daughter Fannie Bertha.

Grocery store owner Robert Thomas, his wife Mary, and their son Elmore lived in a house built in 1913 at **1110 Fourth Street West**. Several owners later, in 1929, the house was purchased by William H. Gillett, manager of Gillett Drug Company. He was married to James DeSear's sister Velma.

Cross Eleventh Avenue West and walk to the **Palmetto First United Methodist Church at 1035 Fourth Street West**, which was built for $30,000 in 1924 on a lot donated by Mrs. S. S. Lamb.

Turn left (north), and go north on Eleventh Avenue to the **Palmetto First Baptist Church at 438 Eleventh Avenue West**. A wooden church building was built on this site in 1892 but replaced in 1926 with a new brick church. That building was torn down to make way for the present church building.

Dr. Micajah Berry Harrison, the first doctor on the north side of the Manatee River, bought the house at **427 Eleventh Avenue West** in 1890. He lived in it until his death after a horse-and-buggy accident in 1912.

Turn right (east) on Fifth Street West and head for the Oaks Hotel site at **1010 Fifth Street West**. The hotel was built here in 1905. It was an L-shaped wooden building that was torn down around 1971 to make room for the **Oaks Apartments**.

Turn left (north) on Tenth Avenue West, which is Main Street. With the arrival of the railroad in Palmetto in 1902, many businesses relocated from the waterfront area to Main Street (Tenth Street), and new buildings, made from bricks transported by railroad, sprang up along Main Street.

The beige brick **Carnegie Library at 525 Tenth Avenue West** was built in 1915. Much of the furniture was made of native cypress, and books were purchased with the help of a $1,000 donation from S. S. Lamb. The building is a museum and community hall.

Cross over to the east side of Tenth Avenue. Smith's Livery was located at **923 Sixth Street West** between 1900 and 1920. It was from the livery stables that fruit and vegetable brokers rented horses and buggies in order to inspect produce in the fields before buying it. The **Palmetto Public Library** presently occupies the site.

The Palmetto Bakery formerly operated at **512 Tenth Avenue** after being established in 1894 by Mrs. Elizabeth Toft, a native of England who

Crusader Building

had moved to Palmetto from Maine. Mrs. Toft's bread was said to be baked from a secret recipe containing leavening made from peach tree leaves.

Cross Fifth Street West on the east side of Tenth Avenue. Walk to **449 Tenth Avenue West**, the location of the former Palmetto State Bank, which was incorporated in 1912 and is now used as offices. Notice the bank's name spelled out in the black-and-white floor tiles inside the front of the building.

The gray stucco building at **435 Tenth Avenue West** was built in 1918 as the S. B. Black Grocery. At one time, a barbershop rented space on the first floor, and the upstairs was used as apartments.

The brick building with green awnings at **431–433 Tenth Avenue West** was built in 1918 to house the Palmetto Fire Insurance Company and other businesses.

The white brick **Palmetto Masonic Lodge building at 404 Tenth Avenue West** was built in 1923, and originally served as an open-air post office.

Cross Fourth Street West and walk to the former Higgins Garage at **337 Tenth Avenue West**, a white building that flourished in 1918 as an auto repair garage. It now contains apartments.

The three-story stucco building painted seafoam green at **323 Tenth Avenue West** was built in 1921 as an apartment building. It has been renovated to serve as an office complex. In honor of sailors who lived here while training for the America's Cup aboard their boat *The Crusader*, the building's name was changed to the Crusader Building.

Walk south, back to Regatta Pointe, which completes the walking tour.

BRADENTON

Location

Bradenton is located in Manatee County, on Florida's central west coast, north of Sarasota and south of Tampa, with the Gulf of Mexico to the west and Tampa Bay to the north.

History

Timucuan and Calusa Indian tribes were the first known inhabitants of Manatee County. In 1539, explorer Hernando DeSoto led the first European expedition into the area. During the latter half of the eighteenth century, members of the Seminole tribe relocated here from northern Florida.

In 1843, Josiah Gates and other early settlers founded the Village of Manatee which is now East Bradenton. That same year, Joseph Addison Braden arrived here to establish a sugar plantation and mill. Braden built Fort Braden to protect his business.

Manatee County separated from Hillsborough County in 1855. In 1857, Braden's sugar plantation closed down. Another sugar plantation, owned by Maj. Robert Gamble in nearby Ellenton, also ceased production. With the demise of the sugar producing business in the county, farmers began growing fruits and vegetables. Today, tomatoes are the county's biggest crop.

In 1878, in recognition of Joseph Braden, the town was officially named Bradentown, although documents sent to Washington, D.C., incorrectly spelled it as "Braidentown."

Braidentown was incorporated in 1903. In 1927, it officially became Bradenton. In the 1880s, a fishing village was established in Bradenton. It was called Cortez Village, and has remained a fishing community, dotted with old bungalows and craftsman-style homes.

Manatee County includes five incorporated cities: Bradenton, Palmetto, Anna Maria, Holmes Beach, Bradenton Beach, and the township of Longboat Key, part of which is in Sarasota County and part of which is in Manatee County. (Until 1921, Sarasota was part of Manatee County as well.)

Walking Tour

This tour is approximately one mile and takes about forty-five minutes. To get to the **Manatee County Historical Records Library at 1405 Fourth Avenue West**, take I-75 to S.R. 64 west to Fourteenth Street West. Turn right and go to Fourth Avenue West. There is metered parking across the street to the east of the library.

Construction of this library, a neoclassical building that has a Doric portico with columns at the elevated entrance, began in 1918 with a $10,000 grant from the Carnegie Corporation to the City of Bradenton. The property and the funds to cover the operating expense for continued operation were provided by the city of Bradenton. The building was used as a city library and then as a county library. All of the historical public records at the county courthouse were moved here in 1977 after being transferred onto microfilm, thus making this the first archival library in Florida under the auspices of a Clerk of Circuit Court.

From the Records Library, walk east on Fourth Avenue West, across Fourteenth Street West, to the corner of Thirteenth Street West. The pale blue brick building at **406 Thirteenth Street West** is Bradenton's **City Hall**, built circa 1914. At one time, the building was occupied by a fire station. In fact, the brickwork above the first floor windows to the left of the entrance distinguishes the location of the door to the garage where the fire engine was stored.

City Hall

This was also the site of the Braden stockade, which housed the employees and slaves of Joseph and Hector Braden, who came to Manatee County in 1843. Under the Armed Occupation Act, they claimed 160 acres of land, part of which was used to build their sugar plantation.

Continue walking on Fourth Avenue West to Twelfth Street West or Old Main Street. Cross Twelfth Street and turn left, toward the Manatee River. Walk south on the east side of Twelfth Street West.

The Bakery Building at **320 Twelfth Street West** was built in 1910 in early twentieth century commercial architectural style. It was once home to the Bradenton Board of Trade and also once served as a bakery. It later became the Union Bus Station.

The large white stucco building with a long green awning is the **Coe Block Building at 302–318 Twelfth Street West**. It was built between 1897 and 1912 as three separate structures. They were joined together in 1914. One end was once used as servants' quarters for the St. James Hotel, which was on the second floor of the building along Main Street. A post office and a movie theater were two of the building's earliest tenants.

Cross Third Avenue. Walk north to the historical marker in the city parking lot across from **The Courtyard at 222 Twelfth Street West**. The City Auditorium and the Manatee Players buildings are here. In 1878, Bradenton's first post office was established on this site, inside the general store owned by the city's first postmaster, Maj. William Turner. Turner had fought in the Second Seminole War and in the Civil War. A citrus and vegetable grower, Turner built a store, warehouse, and wharf here as well as a small hotel.

Historical buildings that are visible from this site are the **Manatee River Hotel at 309 Tenth Street West** and the **Cox Building at 1111 Third Avenue West**. The pink Manatee River Hotel was built in 1925 at a cost of $850,000. Each of the 285 rooms had its own bathroom. It is now a retirement residence. The Cox Building was built in 1926 as a Chevrolet dealership.

Turn around and walk south on the east side of Twelfth Street West. Cross Fourth Avenue West and continue on the east side of Twelfth to the **Tri-City Trust Building at 402–406 Twelfth Street West**. This Mediterranean revival–style building, finished with liberal use of decorative ceramic and Spanish tile, was constructed in 1925 and was first occupied by a restaurant and various businesses.

The **Wyman and Green Building at 414 Twelfth Street West** was built in 1923 and was the location of Crews Department Store and the W. S. Babcock Corporation Furniture Store. Notice the original hound's tooth course along the parapet. The blue-gray brick, three-story **Harvey Building at 420 Twelfth Street West** was built in 1910. A dry goods store operated here until 1920. The Cecil Hotel was on the second and third floors.

The **Jennings Arcade at 417 Twelfth Street West** was built in 1926. Skylights, open air vents, and wrought iron grillwork are architectural elements of this gray stucco, Mediterranean-style building which contained upper level stores and offices.

The **Juplinor Hotel addition at 435 Twelfth Street West** was built

Jennings Arcade

in 1912 by Mrs. S. A. Reasoner. It flourished until the mid-1920s, and was named for the first syllable of her children's names: Julia, Pliney, and Norman.

The **Bradenton Publishing Company Building at 436–440 Twelfth Street West** was used in 1910 as a commercial printing shop and then a Western Union office. It has recently been the location of a restaurant.

An eclectic Renaissance revival style describes the **Fuller Block and Clifton addition at 442–456 Twelfth Avenue West and 1206 Manatee Avenue West**. The travertine mosaic tile was added in the 1940s. Built in 1905 and 1906 of yellow rock from Mr. Fuller's quarry up the Manatee River, the building was occupied by a drug store, an attorney's office, and a bank.

Cross Manatee Avenue and turn left (east) to the front of the blond brick **Manatee County Courthouse at 1115 Manatee Avenue West**, which was built in 1912. The county jail operated on the fourth floor of the courthouse. There was a dome on the roof of the building, but it was deemed a fire hazard and was removed in 1925.

Walk east on Manatee Avenue to **1023 Manatee Avenue West**, the location of the **Bradenton Bank and Trust Company Building**. This neoclassical revival–style, blond brick building was constructed in 1926. There were ninety tenants on the floors above the main level bank, but by 1929, the Great Depression decreased that number to twenty. In 1933, the bank was liquidated. In later years the building became known as the Professional Building, because doctors, lawyers and other professionals rented space there.

Continue walking east on Manatee Avenue to Tenth Street West. Turn right (south) on the west side of Tenth Street. Cross Sixth Avenue West and turn right (west) to the corner of Eleventh Street West.

The **First Methodist Church at 603 Eleventh Street West** was built in 1922 in the neoclassical revival style. The church boasts beautiful stained and leaded glass windows. The building was expanded in 1956.

Cross Eleventh Street West and continue walking west on the south side of Sixth Avenue, to the **Washington Square Building at 1115 Sixth Avenue West**. This white building, containing several stores, got its name because when it was built in 1925, it fronted on Washington Avenue, now called Sixth Avenue. The wooden awning suspended from the parapet is supported by iron tie-rods.

Cross Sixth Avenue and walk north on the east side of Twelfth Street West to **Curry's Garage and Machine Shop at 544–546 Twelfth Street West**. A travel agency currently operates out of the green and brown building. The building opened in 1913 as the city's first automobile garage. It was owned by Whitney Curry. His one-cylinder Cadillac was the first car to be owned by anyone living in Manatee County.

The gray building at **528–532 Twelfth Street West** is the Iron Block building. You can, in fact, see the words "iron block" on what is considered to be one of the best-preserved pressed metal facades in Florida. It was built in 1896.

The blond brick building at **526 Twelfth Street West** is the **United Abstract Building**, constructed in 1925. It was built in a beaux arts, neo-classical revival style, with touches of Georgian limestone. United Abstract still occupies the building.

Turn left (west) and cross Twelfth Street West. Walk west on the south side of Manatee Avenue. Cross Thirteenth Street West. **The First Baptist Church at 1306 Manatee Avenue West** was built in 1912. This magnificent brick structure was designed in an eclectic Romanesque revival style.

Walk north on Thirteenth Street West to Fourth Avenue Drive West, which is between the Baptist Church and the former City Hall. Walk west on Fourth Avenue Drive West, and go through the city parking lot to return to the Historical Records Library at 1405 Fourth Avenue West.

BRADENTON
(FOGARTYVILLE)

Manatee County

Location

Fogartyville, a residential section of Bradenton, is located on the Manatee River in Manatee County on the central west coast of Florida. Bradenton is just south of Tampa Bay.

History

The area called Fogartyville was settled in 1868 by brothers John, Bartholomew, and William Fogarty, who had come from Key West to establish a trading post and schooner base. In 1865, Capt. John Fogarty's fishing boat was caught in a storm. Seeking protection, John Fogarty sailed into the mouth of the Manatee River and waited out the storm so that he could investigate this unfamiliar area.

Fogarty was so impressed with the abundant wildlife and fish and the oak and cedar woods, that he, his brothers Bartholomew (Tole) and William, and their families relocated from Key West in order to homestead 135 acres in government land grants. The area became known as Fogartyville.

The Fogartys set up their shipbuilding business and trading post here. Seven members of the Fogarty family became ship captains. Tole Fogarty's son Bartholomew, or Captain Bat as he was called, followed in his father's profession. Bat Fogarty had two large buildings behind his house, one for shipbuilding and one that he used as a machine shop.

When Captain Bat died in 1944, so did the family's shipbuilding business, a business that had constructed hundreds of sailing vessels. In 1993, Captain Bat's grandson Charles died. His family donated the boatyard to the South Florida Museum to be preserved. Fogartyville was incorporated into the city of Bradentown (its original spelling) in 1903.

Walking Tour

This walking tour is approximately one mile and takes about forty-five minutes. To get to **Lewis Park/Manatee River Garden Club at 3120 First Avenue**, take I-75 to S.R. 64 west to Thirty-second Street. Turn right.

Go to First Avenue West. There is street parking.

In 1868, the land that Lewis Park sits on was part of the seventy-three acres owned by Bartholomew Fogarty. Because of Fogarty's failure to pay taxes during the Depression, the area encompassing what is now Lewis Park and the Garden Club was claimed by the city of Bradenton. H. O. Lewis was the city's mayor at the time.

From the park, walk east on First Avenue West for two blocks to Thirtieth Street Northwest. Turn left (north) and walk toward the Manatee River. The site of the Madame Joe Atzeroth home is at **209 Twenty-ninth Street Northwest**.

In 1870, Joseph Atzeroth and his wife Julie, who was politely referred to as "Madame Joe," were living north of Palmetto when their daughter Eliza married William Fogarty. By 1873, Madame Joe had been widowed for two years, so Eliza persuaded her mother to move to Fogartyville.

Madame Joe paid thirty dollars to buy three-and-a-half acres from William's brother John. Two years later, she was living in a house built on the property. In 1878, after John Fogarty returned from a trip to Mexico, he gave coffee seeds to Madame Joe. According to Atzeroth family records, the first pound of coffee produced in the United States was grown in Madame Joe's garden.

In 1879, Madame Joe wrote to the Commissioner of Agriculture in Washington, D.C., to describe her coffee bushes. A year later, she sent a pound of coffee to the commissioner and received in return a $10 gold piece. After sending more coffee, she received a thank-you note from President Rutherford B. Hayes. When Madame Joe died in 1902, her daughter Eliza sold the property to a clergyman for $400.

Cross the street to **208 Twenty-ninth Street Northwest**. The white house with green trim was built in 1890 as Robert Fogarty's wedding gift to his bride Martha (Mattie) Tillis. Robert Fogarty was the adopted son of John and Mary Fogarty. His natural mother was Madame Joe's niece who, along with her husband and three other children, died from yellow fever when Robert was two years old. Robert became a ship captain. He lived in this house with Mattie and their eleven children.

Walk north on Twenty-ninth Street Northwest, heading to Riverview Boulevard. On Riverview Boulevard turn right (east) and walk to **2835 Riverview Boulevard** Northwest. This white frame house belonged to Henry Fogarty. He was born to Robert and Mattie Fogarty on May 2, 1893. Henry lived here with his wife, Ruby Mitchell. He and his brothers operated a motor van business called Fogarty Brothers Transfer Company, which began in 1912.

William and Eliza Atzeroth Fogarty house

Walk to the John and Mary Fogarty house at **2813 Riverview Boulevard** Northwest. John died in 1916. Mary continued to live here until 1925. Continue walking until you reach a nearby empty lot on the Manatee River. The site next to where a two-story white house now stands was once the location of the Fogarty store and docks.

Inside the store, which began operating around 1875, there was a post office. The store itself sold a variety of foods and clothing. There were two docks: one for small boats and unloading seafood and one for bigger boats. In 1914, Mrs. Herrick Ward's pottery shop was here. She sold pottery that she made from clay obtained from the river bottom. Ward Pottery has become very collectible.

From the empty lot, turn back and head west on Riverview Boulevard to Twenty-ninth Street Northwest. Turn right (north) on Twenty-ninth Street Northwest and go to **320 Twenty-ninth Street Northwest**. The big gray, two-story house with four white columns was built circa 1872 by William H. Fogarty and his wife Eliza Atzeroth Fogarty. It is the third oldest house in Fogartyville. It followed the John Fogarty house, built in 1866, and the Capt. Bartholomew Tole house, built in

Capt. Bartholomew Tole Fogarty house

1871. William died in 1901. Eliza moved to St. Petersburg and rented out this house. It is now used as a private residence.

Walk south and return to Riverview Boulevard on Twenty-ninth Street Northwest. Turn right (west) on Riverview Boulevard, and walk to **3101 Riverview Boulevard Northwest**, to the Capt. Bartholomew Tole Fogarty House. This green frame house, on which construction began in 1871, orginally faced east, but in 1941 it was turned to face the river. The Toles used the house as a hotel. The family included Tole, his wife Mary Ellen, and their children John Joseph, Bartholomew William (Bat), Kate, Elizabeth, and Letitia. Alterations have been made to the house. The porch is gone and colonial columns have been added to the front of the house.

Walk west on Riverview Boulevard to Thirty-first Street Northwest. Turn right (north) on Thirty-first Street Northwest. Walk to **408 Thirty-first Street Northwest**. This house was built circa 1890 by shipbuilder Bartholomew (Captain Bat) Fogarty. Bat married Mamie Duckwell in 1890. When she died, Bat was left to raise their seven-year-old son named Charles. Bat later married Mary Mahoney, and they lived in this house.

Walk south on Thirty-first Street Northwest. Turn right onto Riverview Boulevard. Walk west to Thirty-second Street Northwest. Walk south on Thirty-second Street Northwest back to Lewis Park.

BRADENTON
(OLD MANATEE)

Manatee County

Location

Old Manatee, in eastern Bradenton, is located in Manatee County, north of Sarasota and south of Tampa on Florida's central west coast. The Gulf of Mexico is to the west and Tampa Bay to the north.

History

Old Manatee was settled in 1842 by Josiah Gates who was given 160 acres of land under the Armed Occupation Act. The land grant was contingent upon a settler clearing five acres, building a house, living there for five years, and agreeing to serve in the militia if needed.

Gates had been an innkeeper at Fort Brooke which later became part of Tampa. He heard about the Manatee River area from a captain who frequently sailed between Cedar Key and Key West. Gates built his homestead at what is now Fifteenth Street East and the Manatee River.

In 1843, several families settled in Manatee, including Dr. Joseph Braden who built a log house, and Ezekiel and Abigale Glazier who had come from Massachusetts. In 1845, Edmund Lee, a Presbyterian minister, and his wife Electa came to Manatee from Vermont. They opened a day school called the "Dame School for Boys."

In 1850, residents built a one-room meeting house which, during the week, served as a school similar to the Dame School. Electa Lee was the schoolmistress.

The Village of Manatee was part of Hillsborough County from 1842 to 1855. In 1855, Manatee County was created. A county seat was to be established and called Palos, but local residents successfully petitioned the legislature to designate Manatee as the county seat.

A courthouse was built in 1860. It was used for only five years, because in 1865 the county seat was moved to Pine Level. The Union Congregation bought the building and used it as their church until 1887. It now sits with other historic buildings in Manatee Village Historical Park.

In 1868, James Warner, the inventor of the Springfield rifle, arrived here with his family. In 1888, the Village of Manatee was incorporated as a city. In 1944, to avoid declaring bankruptcy, the village merged with Bradenton. Many people refer to Old Manatee as East Bradenton.

Walking Tour

This tour is approximately one mile and takes about forty-five minutes. To get to the starting point, the **Manatee Methodist Church at 315 Fifteenth Street East**, take I-75 to S.R. 64 West to Fifteenth Street East. Turn right. There is street parking.

In 1887, construction began on the Manatee United Methodist Church on the corners of Church Street (Fourth Avenue) and Main Street (Fifteenth Street). Within its two-year construction period, many members of the congregation, along with the minister, J. R. Crowder, died from yellow fever. The church continued to serve its congregation for nearly one hundred years until 1974. That year, the church was relocated to the Manatee Village Historical Park in Bradenton. A new church on the original site was completed that year.

Walk south on Fifteenth Street East for one block, to Fourth Avenue East. Turn right (west) and walk to Fourteenth Street East, where you'll come upon the Whitaker/Casper house at **322 Fourteenth Street East**.

This house was first owned by Dr. Franklin Branch, who operated an apothecary and a sugarcane press. When Dr. Branch's wife Matilda Vashti Branch died in 1859, Dr. Branch abandoned his plan to open a sanitarium on his land, which included a fresh water spring. He had intended to use the mineral water to heal the sick.

Dr. Branch sold his house and the land to Capt. John Curry. In 1864, Union soldiers destroyed the Curry family gristmill and captured John Curry's schooner, Ariel. Curry had hidden a small boat from the Union soldiers. He used this boat to transport Confederate Secretary of State Judah P. Benjamin to safety at the Gamble Mansion in nearby Ellenton.

In 1880, the spring property was deeded to George Casper for $200. Dr. Casper ran a small drugstore and soda fountain called Spring Pharmacy. In 1882, he sold the property to William H. Whitaker for $1800. Six years later, William and his wife Mary Jane sold the property to their daughter-in-law Nellie Whitaker for $5.

In 1896, Samuel Gates, a descendant of Manatee's original settlers, bought the property as a wedding gift to his bride, Lula Curry. Two years later, he built a front and back porch onto the house as his anniversary present to Lula. In 1948, Dr. Fred Williams and his wife Leah bought the property. They remodeled the house and filled in the underground pantry.

The house was subsequently owned by a pastor and his wife, who sold it to its present owner, Trudy Williams. The house has been used as an apothecary, doctors' offices, a boarding house, and finally a single-family home. The house was built without indoor plumbing, but became the first residence in the community to install indoor plumbing.

Walk north on Fourteenth Street East for one block to Indian Spring Park. The former mineral spring and Indian encampment on this site both explain the name of the park. This land, including the mineral spring, was occupied and later abandoned by Indians. It was the land Dr. Franklin Branch purchased in 1849 and which he sold ten years later to the Curry family.

Continue north on Fourteenth Street East past Second Avenue East until it ends at the Manatee River. This is the approximate location of Henry S. and Ellen Clark's home and store. The Clarks were friends of the Gateses, who first settled the area. The Clarks soon followed their friends to Manatee, where they homesteaded the land that included the spring where Dr. Branch later hoped to build his sanitarium.

Turn right at the end of Fourteenth Street East, and walk along the unmarked road to **102 Fifteenth Street East**. It was on this street that John A. Graham built his home in 1903. He ran a streetcar line from his house all the way down to Fogartyville, to steamships that moored at a dock he owned. In 1910, Graham sold his house to Christopher H. Davis, who built a toll bridge across the Manatee River. The town of Wimauma surrounded Davis's sawmill, and derived its name from Davis's daughters Wilma, Maude and Mary.

Head south on Fifteenth Street East to a historical marker at **105 Fifteenth Street East**. It was on this site near the riverbank in 1842 that Josiah Gates built his first home. Despite the high pine-log wall that Gates constructed around his family home to keep out Indians and wild animals, a panther found its way onto the property and wandered into the detached kitchen where Mary Gates was cooking. Her screams summoned her brother, who shot the panther. The Gates family welcomed passing visitors, and soon the house became known as the Gates Hotel.

Walk south on Fifteenth Street East to Second Avenue East. Turn left (east) on Second Avenue. Walk two blocks on Second Avenue East to **1603 Second Avenue East**, the Arthur H. Brown house. Arthur and Mary Brown moved to Manatee County from Ocala, Florida, in search of a warmer climate. In 1898, Arthur managed a citrus grove. When he built his house in 1903, local newspapers touted it as the finest house in Manatee.

Walk right (south) on **Sixteenth Street East** to **205**. This was the

Arthur H. Brown House

Foster house, built in 1899 by R. B. Foster and his wife. The Fosters transported their belongings from Illinois to Manatee aboard a covered wagon. Foster worked in the citrus industry.

Keep walking south on **Sixteenth Street East** to the **corner of Fourth Avenue**. In 1844, Rev. Edmund Lee, his wife Electa, and their daughter Sarah built a home a block east of this spot. The minister had moved here to a warmer climate in hopes of curing his consumption. The Lees used their upstairs room as a schoolroom, where Electa became the county's first schoolteacher. She charged $5 tuition for each school term. The house no longer exists. After Electa died, Lee remarried twice. Ironically, Lee, who had arrived in Manatee in near-death condition, thrived in the Florida climate, and outlived three wives.

From Sixteenth Street East, turn west on Fourth Avenue and go to **1527 Fourth Avenue** to the location of the Josiah Gates Jr. house, which was built in 1881. In 1873, Josiah Gates Jr. married Christine Pelot, the sister of Dr. Pelot, who was welcomed into the community when he replaced Dr. Franklin Branch, who had moved to Tampa. Josiah Jr. and Christine ran the Gates Hotel for many years. After it was sold, they built the house at 1527, in order to be closer to Christine's family. Josiah Jr. became mayor of Manatee.

Walk west on Fourth Avenue to the corner of Fifteenth Street East which brings you back to the Methodist Church.

SARASOTA
(LAUREL PARK)
Sarasota County

Location

Sarasota is located on Florida's central west coast, about one hour from Tampa and two and a half hours from Orlando.

History

Native Americans were the primary inhabitants of what is now Sarasota until the Seminole Indian Wars forced them out. In 1842, at the end of the Second Seminole War, settlers began to homestead along the Manatee River, where they founded Manatee, which is now Bradenton.

In December of 1842, a young man named William H. Whitaker sailed from Tallahassee in search of greener pastures. He established a homestead south of Bradenton along the Gulf Coast, in an area known as Whitaker Bayou, which is part of present-day Sarasota. In 1851, Whitaker married Mary Jane Wyatt, who was a native of Tallahassee and the daughter of Col. William Wyatt. William and Mary Jane had eleven children.

In January of 1855, Manatee County was formed from Hillsborough County. Sarasota was part of Manatee, and remained so until 1921. By 1868, the communities of Bee Ridge, Fruitville, and Osprey had been founded, spawning cattle ranches and citrus groves. Within two years, a sprinkling of homesteads was developed in a village known as "Sara Sota." In 1878, the first post office opened for business, enabling area residents to receive their mail at a specific location.

In 1885 one hundred upper-middle-class Scottish colonists came to Sara Sota to join in a thriving community they heard existed there. They were heartbroken to find out how primitive the place actually was. They attempted to establish a community in this Gulf coast wilderness but failed partly due to a long, harsh first winter. The next year J. Hamilton Gillespie arrived from Glasgow and revived the struggling colony. He later became mayor of Sarasota.

In 1910, Bertha Palmer visited the town to inspect land she had seen advertised in the Chicago newspapers. She was so impressed, she quickly purchased property. The Palmer House in Chicago was named for her banker husband, Potter Palmer. By the 1920s, socialites were spending their winters in Sarasota, which had become a fashionable resort.

Oilman William Selby and his wife Marie soon followed. The Selbys later donated to Sarasota the land on which Selby Gardens is located. Owen Burns was another important figure who moved to Sarasota around 1910. He bought up large parcels of land and became Sarasota's first major developer. Burns built many private residences and commercial structures, including the El Vernona Hotel, which opened in September of 1925. He named the Spanish Colonial hotel after his wife Vernona Freeman. Today, the hotel is John Ringling Towers. Burns also improved upon the Gillespie Golf Course, which had been laid out by J. H. Gillespie and is believed to be the first golf course in America.

Oilman Calvin Payne also bought property in Sarasota. He donated Payne Park to the city. Sarasota's posh hotels, its gay night life, and the land boom of the 1920s drew celebrated visitors and residents including Thomas Edison, Henry Ford, and New York Mayor Jimmy Walker.

Despite the land boom bust in 1926, John Ringling made Sarasota the winter quarters of his Barnum & Bailey Circus. He and his wife Mable lived in their opulent residence, Cà d'Zan, which means "House of John." The mansion reflects a combination of Venetian gothic, Florentine and Spanish Renaissance architecture and is a popular sightseeing attraction.

The house is part of a complex that includes Ringling Circus Galleries, which exhibits Ringling Brothers and Barnum & Bailey circus memorabilia, and the John and Mable Ringling Museum of Art. On March 30, 1930, when Ringling opened the gallery and museum to the public, fifteen thousand people came to see it. The museum contains one of the world's most important collections of seventeenth-century baroque paintings. Ringling's development of the area resulted in the formation of such communities as Longboat Key, St. Armand's Key, Bird Key, and Lido Key, accessible via the Ringling Causeway.

The Asolo Theater opened in January of 1953. The theater, which had been built in Scotland in 1798, was relocated from Venice, where it had been in storage. The Asolo is now part of a theater complex called the FSU Center and is one of four state theaters in Florida.

Walking Tour

This walking tour of the Laurel Park neighborhood is approximately three-quarters of a mile long and takes about thirty minutes. To get to the **Sarasota Trust Center building**, which faces Washington Boulevard and Oak Street, take I-75 to Exit 38 (Bee Ridge) west to U.S. 41. Head north on U.S. 41 to U.S. 301 (which is Washington Boulevard).

The road splits here, so bear right onto Washington Boulevard, and continue approximately two blocks to Oak Street. Turn left. The Sarasota Trust Center now houses antique shops. There is a parking lot at the Center, and there is ample street parking.

Walk west on Oak to **1922 Oak Street**. This house was built around 1925. It is a simple, cream-colored, craftsman-style bungalow that is recognizable by its aqua-colored front door. The front of the house was once an open porch that is now enclosed. The original casement windows have been replaced by smaller windows. In the mid-1930s, the house was moved from Main Street to Oak Street by its owner Pat Valdo, a former clown with Ringling Brothers Barnum & Bailey Circus. Valdo later became a general manager for the circus. His wife was a trapeze artist. In 1952, Valdo served as a technical consultant during the filming of *The Greatest Show On Earth*.

Continue west. The house at **1876 Oak** is a Mediterranean revival style, with decorative tiles from Seville and three scuppers that drain water from the upper deck. It was built in 1925 by Owen Burns, a former Midwestern banker who came to Sarasota around 1910. He was greatly responsible for developing the area.

The house was formerly occupied by a general practitioner, Dr. Walter Kennedy, a robust, portly man. According to local lore, an overweight woman who had never met Dr. Kennedy came to his office to seek dietary advice. When she laid eyes on him, she supposedly uttered, "This will never do," and promptly left his office.

The **Gesneriad Research Foundation** is at **1873 Oak**. The Foundation is a private, non-profit, scientific institution dedicated to the preservation of the Gesneriaceae, a large tropical plant family, including African violets and lipstick vines, that thrives in tropical rain forests and faces extinction.

The verdant beauty behind the Foundation house is unexpected and fascinating. The grounds boast a live collection of five hundred species of rare or extinct gesneriads and 300 species of tropical forest plants that are grown in on-site greenhouses or in the simulated rain forest, complete with bubbling spring, fog and raindrops. Tours of the rain forest and greenhouses are available by appointment.

The house itself was built in 1925 by Owen Burns, and designed by Thomas Reed Martin, a well-known Chicago and Sarasota architect.

The Thomas Reed Martin home is at **1855 Oak Street**. Built in 1925 by Owen Burns, the house is a Mediterranean revival style, with antique tile roof and terra-cotta-toned stucco walls. Behind the wrought iron gates, you can see the cypress board-and-batten door with its porthole-like window and hammered door pull. Bougainvillea and confederate jasmine add lush color to the landscaping.

At the **corner of Oak Street and Madison Court**, turn right onto Madison. The corner house is occupied by the Honorable John Early. Early is a former judge, state representative, and Sarasota mayor who moved to the area during the land boom of the 1920s. Early is considered the oldest surviving Eagle Scout in America. His wood-frame house was built circa 1925 in a Dutch colonial revival style. Notice the oolitic limestone on the sun porch and the chimney, and the huge Florida slash pine tree by the screened porch.

Walking along Madison, you'll see the **Madison Court Bungalows**. These quaint homes were built in 1925 as duplexes. If you peer up at the aqua terra-cotta element on the side of **517**, you'll notice that it represents a lighthouse and a wave.

At the corner of Madison Court and Laurel Street, turn left onto Laurel. The **Robar Apartments** are at **1836 Laurel Street**. They were built in 1924, during the land boom, by real estate developers and speculators Roades and Barr.

At the corner of Laurel Street and Osprey Avenue, turn right onto Osprey. The **Seminole Apartments at 404 Osprey Avenue** were built in 1925 by Rhodes & Hale Contracting. The peach stucco structure was built in a Mediterranean revival style.

Seminole Apartment

Across the street and down a ways is the **Valencia**, a large pale blue building dating to 1925, when it was known as the Silva Apartments. Three Craftsman-style bungalows stand alongside to the north of the building. One of them was occupied by Silva, who was a local druggist.

Go back a half-block to the corner of Osprey Avenue and Morrill Street, turn left onto Morrill. The **Young Apartments at 1759 Morrill**, consisting of four apartments, were built in 1924 by Rhodes & Hale Contractors, and sold to the Youngs in 1925. The Youngs paid $15,000 for the white Mediterranean revival building. About a year later, they sold it for $30,000. Note the arched parapet with a sunburst medallion.

At the corner of Morrill Street and Ohio Place, turn left onto Ohio. The **El Dorado Apartments at 325 Ohio Street**, were built in 1925 by Rhodes & Hale Contractors, and were originally known as the San Juan.

Rhodes and Hale lived in the Spanish bungalow homes at 320 and 326. Among the interesting architectural features of the house at **326 Ohio** are its two recessed arches in the tall piers on either side of the front door.

At the corner of Ohio Place and Laurel Street, turn right onto Laurel. Just past Laurel Park, with its graceful gazebo and wrought iron and brick fence, is the **Seventh Day Adventist/Grace Fellowship Church at 1702**, with its red doors and window frames. It was built in a mission style in 1926 by original congregation volunteers. It is said that the applied arches on the front of the building were put there by a blind member of the congregation.

The tin-roofed, gray Queen Anne folk-Victorian bungalow at **1677 Laurel** was built circa 1890. The house was originally owned by a tombstone carver. A subsequent owner found discarded tombstones under the house.

Unusual for the neighborhood is the red brick foundation beneath the gray Craftsman-style bungalow at **1667 Laurel**. The house was supposedly built from a Sears and Roebuck kit in 1925. Notable features are the box columns, triangular knee brackets, wide overhang, and the starburst pattern above the gable.

The pink, green-trimmed Spanish colonial home at **1646 Laurel** was built in 1925 by T. M. Byron, an architect from Tennessee. A colorful broken-tile walkway leads to the house. Byron also designed the Valencia Apartments.

Continue on Laurel to a little alleyway on the left, which is Rawls Avenue. Turn left into the alleyway, which leads to a row of twenty-four **Khatadin Court Apartments**. This stucco, Spanish-style building with green trim was built in 1925 by Logan and Currin Contractors. After serving in World War I, Frank Logan experimented with a mask that could protect soldiers from mustard gas. The gas mask that looks like an elephant trunk, became known as the Logan mask.

The apartments he and Currin built were occupied by employees of the Sarasota *Herald* which had not yet bought the *Tribune*. The Sarasota *Herald* building sat across from the apartments. The building is now the Woman's Exchange. The Khatadin Court Apartments have become so popular that prospective tenants must put their names on a waiting list.

Continue to the corner of Rawls Avenue and Oak Street. Turn left on Oak to return to your point of origin.

CENTRAL WEST FLORIDA
HISTORICAL ATTRACTIONS, DINING, AND LODGING

TAMPA — *Hillsborough County*

Suggested Dining and Lodging

Bern's Steak House
1208 South Howard Avenue
Tampa, FL
813-251-2421
Filled with antiques, gilded columns, Tiffany lamps, and murals of French vineyards, to create an Old World atmosphere.

Cafe Creole
1330 East Ninth Avenue
Ybor City
813-247-6283
Located in the Cherokee Club building.

Columbia Restaurant
2117 East Seventh Avenue
Ybor City
813-248-3000

Bayboro House
1719 Beach Drive SE
St. Petersburg, FL 33701
813-823-4955
Located on Tampa Bay. A 1907 Queen Anne bed-and-breakfast inn furnished with antiques.

Ruskin House
120 Dickman Drive SW
Ruskin, FL 33570
813-645-3842
Two-story antiques-filled bed-and-breakfast inn built in 1910.

For Information

Tampa/Hillsborough Convention and Visitors Association
111 Madison Street
Suite 1010
Tampa, FL 33602-4706
813-223-1111

Ybor City Chamber of Commerce
1800 East Ninth Avenue
Tampa, FL 33605
813-248-3712

Ybor City State Museum
1818 Ninth Avenue
Tampa, FL 33605
813-247-6323

Ybor Square
P.O. Box 384
Tampa, FL 33601
813-247-4497

Other Historic Attractions

Henry B. Plant Museum
401 West Kennedy Boulevard
Tampa, FL 33606
813-254-1891
Located in the former Tampa Bay Hotel, which was built by railroad magnate Henry Plant. Exhibits include furnishings and antiques collected by Plant and used in his hotel. Open Tuesday through Saturday 10 A.M. to 4 P.M., Sunday 1 P.M. to 4 P.M. Donation $3.

Tampa Bay History Center
601 South Harbor Island
Boulevard
Tampa, FL 33602
813-228-0097
Changing exhibitions reflecting Tampa
Bay history.
Open Monday through Saturday 10
A.M. to 9 P.M., Sunday noon to 5 P.M.
Free admission.

Tampa Rico Cigar Company
1901 North Thirteenth Street
Tampa, FL 33605
813-247-6738 or 800-892-3760
Open Monday through Saturday 10
A.M. to 6 P.M., Sunday noon to 5:30 P.M.
Call for cigar-rolling demonstration
times. Free admission.

Tampa Theatre
711 Franklin Street Mall
Tampa,FL 33602
813-223-8981
A restored 1926 movie palace featuring
a Mighty Wurlitzer organ and replicas
of Greek and Roman sculptures. The
movie house was designed to resemble a Moorish courtyard.
Call for event schedule and
admission fees.

Ybor City Brewing Company
2205 North Twentieth Street
Tampa, FL 33605
813-242-9222
Located in a renovated one-hundred-
year-old cigar factory. Open Monday
through Saturday 7 A.M. to 6 P.M.
Admission: $2.

**BRADENTON, FOGARTYVILLE,
PALMETTO** — *Manatee County*

Suggested Dining and Lodging

The Pier Restaurant
1200 First Avenue West
941-748-8087
Located on the pier, which was built
in the 1920s.

Duncan House Bed and Breakfast
1703 Gulf Drive
Bradenton Beach, FL 34217
941-778-6858
Victorian home built in 1910 and
moved by barge in 1946 from downtown Bradenton.

Five Oaks Inn Bed and Breakfast
1102 Riverside Drive
Palmetto, FL 34221
941-723-1236
An original Sears and Roebuck home
occupied by early Palmetto settlers.

Harrington House Bed & Breakfast
5626 Gulf Drive
Holmes Beach, FL 34217
941-778-5444
Restored 1925 house filled with
antique furnishings.

For Information

*Manatee County Convention &
Visitors Bureau/Bradenton Area
Convention & Visitors Bureau*
P.O. Box 1000
Bradenton, FL 34206
941-729-9177

Cathy Slusser
*c/o Manatee County Historical Records
Library*
1405 Fourth Avenue West
Bradenton, FL 34205
941-741-4070

Other Historic Attractions

Cortez (Fishing) Fleet
12507 Cortez Road (S.R. 684)
Cortez, FL 34215
941-794-1223
Provides beachcombing and sightseeing trip to Fort Dade, accessible only by boat. Call for more information.

De Soto National Memorial
Seventy-fifth Street NW
Bradenton, FL 34209
941-792-0458
An exhibit commemorating the exploits of conquistador Hernando De Soto, who began his exploration of the southeastern United States in 1539. Open daily 9 A.M. to 5 P.M. Free admission.

Florida Gulf Coast Railroad Museum
P.O. Box 355
Parrish, FL 34219
941-776-3266
Dedicated to the preservation of classic examples of American railroad rolling stock. Includes locomotives, coaches, cabooses, and lounge cars. Call for schedule.

Gamble Plantation
3708 Patten Avenue
Ellenton, FL 34222
941-723-4536
The only antebellum plantation house remaining in south Florida.
Open Thursday through Monday 8 A.M. to 5. P.M. Guided tours. Adults $3, children $1.50.

Manatee Village Historical Park
Manatee Avenue and Fifteenth Street East
Bradenton, FL 34208
941-749-7165

Nineteenth- and early twentieth-century buildings have been relocated here to preserve local heritage and history.
Open Monday through Friday 9 A.M. to 4:30 P.M., Sunday 1 P.M. to 4 P.M. Donation requested.

SARASOTA — *Sarasota County*

Suggested Dining and Lodging

Bijou Cafe
1287 First Street
941-366-8111
A former gas station built in the 1920s and renovated.

Carmichael's Restaurant
1213 North Palm Avenue
941-951-1771
Located in a 1920s Spanish-style house filled with antiques.

Crescent House Bed and Breakfast
459 Beach Road
Sarasota, FL 34242
941-346-0857
Located on Siesta Key.

Duncan House Bed and Breakfast
1703 Gulf Drive
Bradenton Beach, FL 34217
941-778-6858

Five Oaks Bed and Breakfast Inn
1102 Riverside Drive
Palmetto, FL 34221
941-723-1236

Harrington House Bed and Breakfast Inn
5626 Gulf Drive
Holmes Beach, FL 34217
941-778-5444

For Information

Sarasota Chamber of Commerce
1551 Second Street
Sarasota, FL 34236
941-955-8187

Sarasota Convention & Visitors Bureau
655 North Tamiami Trail
Sarasota, FL 34236
941-957-1877 or 800-522-9799

Whit Rylee
Mango Tours
1345 Second Street
Sarasota, FL 34236

Other Historic Attractions

Asolo Center For the Performing Arts
5555 North Tamiami Trail
(U.S. 41)
Sarasota, FL 34243
941-351-8000
Eighteenth-century Scottish opera house inside a State Theater.

Bellm's Cars & Music of Yesterday
5500 North Tamiami Trail
(U.S. 41)
Sarasota, FL 34236
941-355-6228
A collection of antique cars, music boxes, and games. Open daily 9:30 A.M. to 5:30 P.M. Admission: $7.50.

Gesneriad Research Foundation
1873 Oak Street
Sarasota, FL 34236
941-365-2378
Tours available without an appointment Saturdays between 2 and 3 P.M. Call for information on scheduling tours for larger groups.

Historic Spanish Point
500 North Tamiami Trail (U.S. 41)
Osprey, FL 34229
941-966 5214
Indian shell middens and a pioneer Victorian homestead. Open daily 9 A.M. to 5 P.M. Admission: $5.

John and Mable Ringling Museum of Art/Cà d'Zan/Circus Galleries
5401 Bay Shore Road
Sarasota, FL 34243
941-355-5101
The estate home and museum complex of John and Mable Ringling, built in the 1920s, and exhibiting ornate furnishings, circus memorabilia, and Renaissance art. Open daily 10 A.M. to 5:30 P.M. Admission: $8.50, $7.50 for seniors. Children and Florida students are admitted for free.

Sarasota Opera House
61 North Pineapple Avenue
Sarasota, FL 34236
941-366-8450
A Mediterranean revival building built in 1926.

Selby Botanical Gardens
811 Palm Avenue South
Sarasota, FL 34236
941-366-5730
Indoor and outdoor museum of tropical plants. Open daily 10 A.M. to 5 P.M. Admission: $7 for adults, $3 for children 6–11, children 5 and younger admitted free.

South

SOUTH

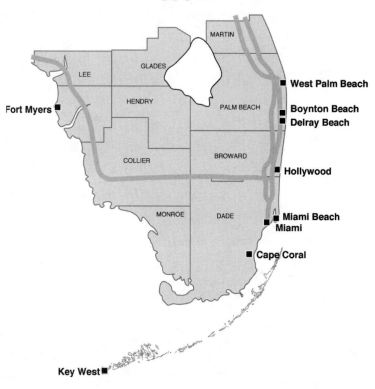

MARTIN

GLADES

LEE

HENDRY

PALM BEACH

Fort Myers ■

COLLIER

BROWARD

MONROE

DADE

West Palm Beach ■

Boynton Beach ■
Delray Beach ■

Hollywood ■

Miami Beach ■
Miami ■

Cape Coral ■

Key West ■

WEST PALM BEACH

Palm Beach County

Location
Palm Beach County is on the southeast coast of Florida, approximately sixty miles north of Miami. It is the largest of Florida's sixty-seven counties.

History
In the 1870s, a small settlement existed on an island we now know as Palm Beach. In 1878, a two-masted ship sailing from Trinidad to Cadiz washed ashore on the island, spilling its cargo of coconuts and spurring a subsequent growth of coconut palm trees. When the island's post office was built, it needed a name, and "Palm Beach" seemed a fitting name for the island settlement.

The area west of Palm Beach was largely uninhabited until 1875, when homesteader Benjamin Lanehart built a palmetto cabin near Barcelona Road. Lanehart became a pineapple planter. By 1883, a cook named Elizabeth Wilder Moore was homesteading land she had bought south of Lanehart's.

In the early 1890s the island of Palm Beach was visited by Henry Flagler, who had founded the Standard Oil Company and who had built the Florida East Coast Railway. Flagler, noting the lack of hotel facilities, decided to build the Royal Poinciana Hotel there. He extended his railroad as far south as Lake Worth to provide transportation to the hotel. Condos and shops have replaced the Royal Poinciana.

Flagler also purchased 140 acres of oceanfront property in Palm Beach and converted an existing wooden house on the property into the Palm Beach Inn, which opened in 1896. In 1901 he renamed it The Breakers. The hotel burned down in 1903 and was replaced with a new building that burned down in 1925. It was reported that when the 1925 fire started, Marjorie Merriwether Post, actress Billie Burke (the good witch Glinda in *The Wizard of* Oz), and The Unsinkable Molly Brown of Denver, were in the hotel. In 1926, Flagler's heirs rebuilt The Breakers, which still stands.

Flagler had investigated the western mainland, across Lake Worth, and decided that it was a convenient place for his construction workers to live. He established a commercial center there. By 1895 the town of West Palm Beach had been incorporated.

By 1900, pineapple growing was a major commercial operation in the West Palm Beach area, but a pineapple disease and competition from Cuban pineapple growers doomed the local industry. As of 1910, much of the Lanehart and Moore homesteads had been bought up by arriving pioneers and divided into nearly two dozen residential parcels.

In the sixteen years since its incorporation, the population of West Palm Beach had quadrupled. With the coming of the land boom in the 1920s, Palm Beach materialized into a fashionable resort and a winter residence for the rich and famous. Visiting celebrities shopped at the boutiques of tony Worth Avenue and checked into The Breakers.

In the early 1920s, the old pineapple fields were bought by Jay Phipps of Pittsburgh, whose father, Henry, was Andrew Carnegie's partner in U.S. Steel Corporation. Phipps developed them into a subdivision which he named "El Cid," after the Spanish hero Rodrigo Diaz de Vivar, whom the Moors called "Cid" (Lord).

During the land boom of the 1920s, elegant and expensive Spanish colonial–, Mediterranean-, and mission-style houses, designed by cream-of-the-crop architects, sprang up in West Palm Beach neighborhoods such as El Cid and Old Northwood. These houses were bought by prominent businessmen and officials.

During the 1970s and 1980s, many of the houses suffered from neglect and disrepair. The neighborhoods experienced a revitalization as the homes came under new ownership and were restored or remodeled. The El Cid Historic Neighborhood Association oversees its well-maintained historic district.

Walking Tour

To get to the Ann Norton Gardens, take I-95 to Exit 52. Head east on Okeechobee Boulevard to Flagler Drive. Turn right (south) on Flagler and proceed for approximately one mile. There is street parking. The walking tour is approximately half a mile and takes about thirty minutes.

Begin at **the Ann Norton Sculpture Gardens at 253 Barcelona Road**, across from the Intracoastal Waterway. This white, two-story Spanish-style house, listed on the National Register of Historic Places, was built in 1924.

Ralph Norton, founder of the Norton Gallery and School of Art, married Ann Weaver in 1948. She had taught at his school for six years, but marriage enabled her to work on her monolothic sculptures which sit in the Nortons' garden amidst exotic palm trees. She died in 1982.

If you face the house, the Intracoastal Waterway beyond the sea wall of South Flagler Drive will be on your right. Walk east, to the corner. Turn right (south) on Flagler.

The Marshall Rinker House at **2111 South Flagler** was built in 1938 and designed by noted architect Maurice Fatio. Rinker was the founder of a rock and sand hauling company. In the 1930s, he began producing concrete blocks. By the 1980s, Rinker Materials was one of the largest concrete manufacturers in the country. The School of Business at Palm Beach Atlantic College in West Palm Beach is named after Rinker. He died in early 1996.

Continue south on Flagler for two blocks until you get to Granada. Turn right (west) on Granada. The front of the beige Mediterranean-revival Moorish-style house at **257 Granada** faces sideways. The house was built circa 1925. It was the residence of Charles C. Chillingworth, who came to West Palm Beach in 1894 to become the first Town Attorney. He was also Lantana Florida's first Town Attorney. Chillingworth helped develop Palm City in Martin County, and was the local Rotary Club's first president. Chillingworth's son, Circuit Court Judge Curtis E. Chillingworth, lived on Dyer Road and was murdered in 1955. You'll learn more about the murder when you get to Dyer Road.

Charles Chillingworth house

The Charles Watkins house at **285 Granada** was built in 1924 in a Mediterranean revival style. In the late 1920s, the house was singled out by *Home Building* magazine for its architectural excellence. Watkins was mayor of the District of West Palm Beach from 1933 to 1934. Around 1921, he founded the Deep Rock Mineral Water Company, which today operates in West Palm Beach under the name of Deer Park Spring Water, Inc.

Walk back to Flagler and turn right. Walk one block to Valencia and turn right. The pale peach-colored Mediterranean-revival home at **245 Valencia** was built in 1925 and was owned by Jerome Wideman. Wideman was a graduate of Stetson Law School who began his West Palm Beach law career in 1914. He was also a county prosecuting attorney and a judge. In 1989, an episode of Burt Reynolds's TV series *B. L. Stryker* was filmed here.

The house at **196 Valencia**, on the corner of Medina Way and Valencia, is architecturally notable for its huge windows, its atrium with fountain, its third-story tower room, and its wrought iron widow's walk.

Cross Medina Way. The George Mann house at **204 Valencia** was built in 1936 and designed by Maurice Fatio.

The mission-style Joseph Earman house at **217 Valencia** was built in 1923. Earman was the publisher of the *Palm Beach Post*, and later a Municipal Court judge and a city commissioner. He was also instrumental in bringing to West Palm Beach the first diagnostic laboratory in south Florida.

Walk to the next corner, which is Aravale Road, and turn left at the stop sign. A large, majestic tree and a lamppost flank the front yard of **2416 Aravale**. The house on this property was built in 1925 for E. B. Walton, a native of Nebraska who moved to West Palm Beach in 1917. Walton was a civil engineer who built fourteen homes in the El Cid Historic District.

Aravale Road is a short street that leads out to Sunset Road. The low door on the house to your left will indicate that you're at the Hon. Rufus Robbins house at **223 Sunset Road**, at the corner of Aravale and Sunset. Robbins was born in Titusville, Florida and graduated from Stetson Law School in DeLand, Florida. He was a Palm Beach County judge from 1917 to 1920. His Mediterranean-style house of pale pink stucco with rust-red trim was built in 1925.

Turn left onto Sunset. The little pink house at **190 Sunset** was designed in the 1930s by Belford Shoumate, a well-known Palm Beach architect who died in 1991 at the age of eighty eight.

Walk to the corner of Sunset and Flagler, where on your left you'll

Casa Blanca de Lago

see, at **2433 South Flagler**, a white stucco Spanish-style house with a third-floor tower. This house, owned by the Parker family, was built in 1925. The Karl Kallman house next door to it, at **2421 South Flagler**, was built in 1936 and designed by Maurice Fatio.

Turn right on Flagler, heading south. Architect W. B. Eckler designed the 1926 Mediterranean-revival style house at **2527 South Flagler**. Stone lions sit on the walls facing the water. The white house with green shutters features a third-story tower. The house is called Casa Blanca de Lago.

Turn right onto Pershing Way. The Christian Kirk house at **200 Pershing Way** is a gray, three-story, shingled house that is one of the oldest residences in El Cid. The house was built circa 1914. Kirk was a Finnish carpenter who worked on titan Henry Morrison Flagler's hotel and railroad, and on Flagler's massive home in Palm Beach. Kirk's great-grandson now lives in the house.

Turn back (east) on Pershing and return to Flagler. Turn right on Flagler to the Ralph Wagner house at **2631 South Flagler Drive**, which is considered one of the best examples of art moderne in Palm Beach County. The five-bedroom house was designed by Belford Shoumate, and built in 1937. Notice the two typical components of the art moderne–style: "porthole" windows and the vertical lines flanking the front door. Ralph Wagner and his wife Edna moved to the art deco home in El

Art Moderne house designed by Belford Shoumate

Cid from a more modest home elsewhere in West Palm Beach. Wagner was president of the Palm Beach Gas Company which is now part of the Florida Public Utilities Company in West Palm Beach. In April of 1996 the house's last owner, attorney Ward Wagner — no relation to Ralph Wagner — sold the house to attorney Homer Marshman Jr. for $775,000.

Continue on South Flagler. Cross Belmont Road and Almeria Road. At the next corner, Dyer Road, turn right. The beige Mediterranean-style house on the right, at **211 Dyer Road**, was built in 1924 and was the home of Curtis Chillingworth. In 1917, Curtis joined his father Charles's law firm in West Palm Beach. Five years later Curtis became the youngest circuit judge in Florida. He was only twenty-six.

Joseph Peel, a local municipal court judge, was afraid Curtis would have him disbarred for unethical legal practices. In 1961, Peel was sentenced to life in prison for his 1955 hiring of two men to kill Curtis and Marjorie Chillingworth. The killers abducted the couple, bound them, and placed a lead-weighted belt on Marjorie. Later testimony revealed that Curtis told his wife, "Remember, honey, I love you," and that Marjorie replied, "I love you, too," just before the killers pushed her into the ocean. They tied a twenty-five-pound anchor around Curtis's neck and dumped him overboard. One killer has been paroled. The second killer will be eligible for parole in 2013.

El Cid Apartments, built in 1926

Peel was paroled in 1979 and again imprisoned following a convic-
tion for mail fraud. He was released in 1982 because he was dying of cancer. He died nine days later.

Cross South Olive Avenue and continue up Dyer Road to **315 Dyer
Road**. This white house with red trim was built in 1924 and occupied by
Emile Anthony. In 1896, he and his brothers established a men's clothing store, Anthony Brothers. The small chain of Anthony's stores specializes in women's fashions.

The beige mission-style house at **328 Dyer Road** was built in 1925
and is known as the Dr. William Van Landingham House. The doctor was
a superintendent of Good Samaritan Hospital and served as the county
public health officer.

Continue up Dyer to Dixie Highway. Turn right. Walk to Almeria and
turn right. The yellow-awninged **El Cid Apartments at 315 Almeria** were
built in 1926 in the Mediterranean revival style and are now occupied by
senior citizens.

Continue east on Almeria, to Olive Avenue. Turn left and walk up to
Barcelona Road. Turn right and continue back to the Ann Norton House.

BOYNTON BEACH

Palm Beach County

Location

Boynton Beach is located in southeast Palm Beach County. It is south of West Palm Beach and north of Delray Beach.

History

In 1895, retired Civil War Major Nathan Boynton vacationed in Palm Beach. Looking for a suitable site to build a hotel, this insurance and real estate salesman and former mayor of Port Huron, Michigan, took a boat ride down the East Coast Canal (now the Intracoastal Waterway). Boynton purchased five hundred acres of land down by the beach north of Linton, which is now Delray Beach. He built a fifty-room hotel, completed in 1897, one year after Henry Morrison Flagler's Florida East Coast Railroad came through Boynton Beach.

One of the carpenters who worked on the hotel was Horace Murray, who had come from the Midwest with his family. By 1896, two black families, the Kings and the Cades, were living on land they had bought from Maj. Boynton. Their small farms were located on what is now U.S. 1.

S. B. Cade and L. A. King showed Horace Murray and other settlers how to grow pineapples, which, along with tomatoes, were primary crops. The building of Flagler's railroad made it easy to transport this produce.

Around 1900, another black settler arrived. W. C. Girtman bought two acres north of the Boynton Canal, where he raised pheasants and grew oranges and avocados. In 1905, he built his house where he raised his nine children. Settlement continued. In 1907, Marcus Weaver came to Boynton Beach, where he grew pineapples and later founded Weaver Dairies.

In 1911, Maj. Boynton died. In addition to founding Boynton Beach, the major is remembered for inventing the Boynton fire truck and the Boynton hook and ladder truck.

Boynton Beach was incorporated in 1920. The Boynton Beach Hotel was torn down five years later. During the 1940s, in addition to tomatoes, pineapples, and avocados, Boynton Beach's farms were producing corn, beans, cabbage, okra, eggplant, and cucumbers. Today, residential developments sit upon much of that farmland.

Walking Tour

The walking tour is short in terms of historic sites, but it gives you an idea of the history of the area. It centers around Ocean Avenue, which runs east and west, and it begins at the 1913 schoolhouse. The tour is approximately three-quarters of a mile if you include the Woman's Club. It takes about forty-five minutes.

To get to the **1913 schoolhouse**, take I-95 to the Boynton Beach Boulevard exit. Head east to Seacrest Boulevard. Turn right on Seacrest and go two blocks to Ocean Avenue. Turn left. There is street parking, or you can park by the old schoolhouse or at the Civic Center across the street.

The last graduating class of the 1913 cement block schoolhouse was the class of 1947. The high school next door was built in 1927 and was used as a hurricane shelter the following year. The elementary school is listed on the National Register of Historic Places. A campaign is underway to convert the school into a cultural center, part of a renovation project for the downtown area.

With your back to the elementary school, turn left and walk southward on East Ocean Avenue to Southeast Third Street. Turn right and walk to **217 Southeast Third**, to the white, two-story frame house on the west corner of the street. The house is easily recognizable by the large yellow flower in the stained-glass panel in the front door. This is the Horace Murray house, which was built in 1909 by Murray, who had come from Michigan to do carpentry work at the Boynton Beach Hotel.

In 1909, a Norwegian barkentine, the *Coquimbo*, ran aground near the Boynton Beach Inlet and broke apart, sending its shipwrecked cypress floating to the shore. Some Boynton Beach residents salvaged the cypress and used it to build their homes. The Murray house has cypress shingles that came from the *Coquimbo*. The house has been restored and is now owned by Micheline Many, a real estate broker who lives upstairs and rents out the downstairs apartment.

On March 5, 1996, Horace Murray's daughter Rose died at the age of eighty-six. She was believed to have been the oldest living native of Boynton Beach. She delighted in telling the story of how she helped the 1913 elementary school to be built: In 1912, residents were told that there were not enough children to justify the construction of a school. To increase the enrollment figures, Rose was enrolled at age four.

Turn around and head back toward East Ocean Avenue. The first cross street you'll come to is Southeast First Avenue. The white house on the **southeast corner of Southeast First Avenue** is in disrepair, but it sits on nearly an acre of desirable property. This two-story, six-bedroom New England clapboard-style house was built around 1909 from the salvaged wood of the *Coquimbo*.

In 1926, Katie Andrews became the new owner of the house. Katie was the wife of Charles Lee Andrews, a former Civil War officer who had moved to Florida because of his poor health. Katie and Charles Lee had two sons, Charles and George.

During World War II, George, a lieutenant colonel in the 9th Air Force, was stationed in England where he met and married his wife Edith, who, accustomed to the cold climate of northern England near Scotland, was reluctant to move to Florida. He preferred Florida's semi-tropical climate and was unable to adapt to England. Edith and George "compromised." The young war bride moved to Miami with her husband.

As a source of income, Katie Andrews had turned her upstairs bedrooms into a rooming house by renting them to young gentlemen. Especially during spring break, the overflow of young boarders would string up hammocks in the backyard for a place to sleep.

In 1977, Edith and George became owners of the old white house. George died in 1993. At the time of his death, he and Edith had been wed for nearly fifty years.

Andrews House, built circa 1909

Tom Walsh House, built circa 1910

Continue north on Southeast Third, back to East Ocean Avenue. As you come to the corner at East Ocean, Scully's Market will be directly to your left. Across the street, directly opposite Scully's, at **211 East Ocean**, you'll see a vintage white house partially hidden by the front yard tree.

This two-story, tin-roofed house, circa 1910, was partially built from the cargo of the *Coquimbo*. The house features ten-foot ceilings, Dade County pine floors, and a large porch. Tom Walsh, a local real estate agent, has renovated the house. One remaining original feature of the house is the walk-through closet on the second floor, which is accessible from two bedrooms.

In its earlier years, the house was occupied by Eunice Magnuson and her husband Oscar, who was a fern farmer. Their daughter, Harriet Magnuson, grew up in the house. Harriet's daughter, Barbara Scott, remembers frequent visits to her grandparents' home. In particular, Barbara remembers "porch time," in which the family members sat together on the porch as they watched passersby along East Ocean Avenue.

With your back to the Walsh house, turn left and walk east on Ocean Avenue to U.S. 1 (Federal Highway). At U.S. 1, turn right and cross over to the east side of the street. Walk for approximately six blocks until you come to a residential area with an entrance sign that says "Boynton Isles." You will be on the corner of Isles Road and Greenbriar Drive. Bear to your right so that you are not heading into Boynton Isles, but rather you are walking south on the narrow street that is Greenbriar Drive.

The first structure you'll see on the west side of the street is a white office building in an art deco style that was designed by Conrad Pickel as a monument to art. It is now occupied by attorneys' offices.

Just south of this building is the **Boynton Beach Woman's Club, at 1010 South Federal Highway**. It is on the National Register of Historic Places. You'll be walking along the side of the building. Turn right to approach the entrance to the building. The cargo from the shipwrecked *Coquimbo* was used to build the original Woman's Club on East Ocean Avenue, which was sold when this new building was constructed.

The present Club was designed and built by Addison Mizner in 1926 as a gift to the city. The impressive peach stucco building with dark green trim was built in a Mediterranean revival style. The Woman's Club building is rented out for special events. In its earliest years it was a hub for social and cultural events and was at one time used as a library. There is a ballroom on the second floor.

On the first floor there is a large Bernard Thomas mural which depicts the early history of Florida. The mural shows the different flags of Florida, the famous barefoot mailman, early crops such as tomatoes and pineapples, the old Boynton Beach Hotel, a portrait of Maj. Nathan Boynton, and the club women of the 1920s as they rode their bicycles and presided over meetings.

When you come out of the Woman's Club, walk back to the Boynton Isles entrance and cross over to the west side of U.S. 1. Walk back to East Ocean Avenue. Turn left. Just past the railroad tracks, on the south side of East Ocean, you'll see the **500 Block**. This old building dates to the earlier part of the century and was once a hotel. It is now occupied by storefronts on the street level and apartments upstairs.

At the corner you'll notice an old, weathered, two-story building. This is the **Beane Building**, which in 1910 was the original home of the Boynton Woman's Club. The *Coquimbo* cypress from which it is constructed has been allowed to weather. The building's original porch and balcony are gone. The Boynton Woman's Club, which paid $10,000 for this building in 1910, sold it for the same amount to the Masons, who used it until 1954. The present owner, Bob Beane, rents it to an antique store.

Cross the railroad tracks and walk back to the 1913 elementary school.

DELRAY BEACH

Palm Beach County

Location
Delray Beach is called the Ocean City because of its close proximity to the Atlantic. It lies between Boca Raton to the south and Boynton Beach to the north. It is in southeastern Palm Beach County.

History
In 1894, in response to an advertisement for undeveloped land for sale in what we know as Delray, thirty-eight-year-old William S. Linton convinced his friend, bookstore owner David Swinton, to travel with him to Florida from their homes in Saginaw, Michigan, where Linton was postmaster.

What Linton found was a jungle of pine and palmetto trees and a plethora of alligators, snakes, and mosquitoes. None of this daunted him. He invested in 160 acres at $25 per acre, and he established the town of Linton. David Swinton backed Linton's investments.

Linton returned to Saginaw where he convinced a group of men to buy five-acre tracts. These investors followed him back to Delray. One of the settlers from Michigan was Nathan Boynton, who purchased a tract of land around 1895 and later established Boynton Beach to the near north.

In 1894, black pioneers settled on land west of the Linton Tract. Led by Fagan and Jane Monroe, they came from the Panhandle, from Alabama, from the Carolinas, the West Indies, and South Dade. At that time, Delray was part of Dade County. They immediately petitioned the Dade County School Board to establish a colored school. By 1897, they had established a school, churches, and a neighborhood of modest homes where they raised their families. Delray Beach owes much to these black pioneers who helped to drain land, dig canals, lay roads, and cultivate the pineapple fields.

Good soil and climate attracted pioneers from other parts of the country and from Europe. In 1895, German immigrants Adolph and Anna

Hofman arrived in Delray Beach on the recommendation of someone aboard the ship the Hofmans took to the United States. They were advised that they could grow crops year-round in Delray. This information made an impression upon Hofman, because he had studied agriculture and planned to become a farmer. The large Hofman farm produced tomatoes, beans, eggplants, and pineapples.

By 1900, the town of Linton had a population of 150. The town was eventually renamed Delray, after a suburb of Detroit where several residents had previously lived. Agriculture became the primary industry. A group of Japanese farmers, led by George Morikami, created the Yamato Colony, which grew vegetables and pineapples. The coming of Henry Flagler's Florida East Coast Railroad brought winter tourists and made it easier to market Delray's agricultural crops.

During the 1920s, Delray land values became inflated, a result of the land boom. The towns of Delray and Delray Beach became incorporated as the city of Delray Beach. By 1935, Delray was recovering from the Depression because new residents were enticed by the affordable housing, the warm weather, and the beaches. In 1942, a military base and training school opened in nearby Boca Raton, which couldn't keep up with the housing needs of the growing population. A building boom began again in Delray.

Walking Tour

This walking tour is simple if you remember that West Atlantic Avenue and East Atlantic Avenue run east and west, and South Swinton runs north and south. When you cross Atlantic Avenue while heading north, South Swinton Avenue becomes North Swinton Avenue.

The walking tour is approximately two miles long and takes about ninety minutes. To get to the Sundy house, take I-95 to Atlantic Avenue east to Swinton Avenue. Turn right (south) on Swinton and continue a few blocks to the Sundy House. It has a small parking lot, and there is street parking.

The Sundy house at **102 South Swinton Avenue** was built for John and Elizabeth Sundy and their eight children in 1902. The two-story, wood frame Sundy house was constructed in a Queen Anne style, with five gingerbread gables, multiplaned roof lines, and a wraparound porch. Henry T. Grant, who was one of Henry Flagler's carpenters as well as a supervisor on Flagler's railroad, used South Carolina and Dade County pines to build the house.

The Sundy house is on the National Register of Historic Places. It remained in the Sundy family for about seventy years, until it was sold,

Sundy house

renovated, and turned into a tea room and antiques shop. The royal poinciana tree in the backyard is one of the oldest such trees in Palm Beach County. The gardens include lime, lemon, orange, and avocado trees.

During the Great Depression, Elizabeth Sundy was a Latin teacher. She and John Sundy saw all eight of their children graduate from college, a rare accomplishment in the 1920s. In 1911 the town of Delray was incorporated, and John Sundy became the first mayor. He served eight mayoral terms. He was also a judge, and a cobuilder of the Alterep Hotel on East Atlantic Avenue, which is now the Colony Hotel. Sundy owned the Sundy Feed and Fertilizer Company. The company building is now preserved as a museum on the grounds of the Morikami Park in Delray Beach.

From the Sundy House, walk north on South Swinton Avenue until you come to a low stone wall, behind which sits the Cathcart house at **38 South Swinton**. This beautiful white house with kelly green trim is surrounded by gardens and fruit trees. This house's past and present histories are equally interesting.

The house was built in 1902 from black ironwood which was shipped from the Bahamas to Delray and then carried by mule to the property site. The wood is so strong that the house survived the 1926 and 1928 hurricanes that destroyed many other buildings. The house has two

Cathcart-Snyder house

wraparound porches with a two-tier ornamental balustrade. It also has a double-hipped and broken-sloped roof.

The artesian well and the windmill are no longer part of the property, but the cistern is still in place, as are the sapodilla tree that was planted in 1911 and the original etched glass panes in the front doors of the house. The house is touted as the oldest inhabited house in Delray Beach. It is Delray's only remaining example of Bahamian-style architecture.

The first owner of the house was a minister named John Leatherman. Eight years later it came under the ownership of a Delray businessman named W. J. Cathcart, who purchased it as a wedding gift for his bride. According to a romantic story, Cathcart carried his bride over the threshold past the two front doors, which he had decorated with big red ribbons. He then presented her with the deed to the house. She lived in the house for the next fifty years.

In 1971, the house was purchased by Virginia and Ross Snyder who still reside there happily. Virginia is a spry, warm, grandmotherly private investigator in partnership with her husband Ross and her nephew Wayne Campbell, all of whom work out of an office the Snyders added to the back of the house.

An episode of Burt Reynolds's former TV series, B. L.Stryker, was shot on the grounds of the Cathcart (Snyder) home. According to Virginia, guest star Maureen Stapleton was so taken with the beautiful trees in the yard that, during the filming of one scene, she ad-libbed a line about them.

Two doors northward from the Cathcart (Snyder) House, on the corner of South Swinton and East Atlantic Avenue, is the **Methodist Church Rectory at 14 South Swinton Avenue**. During a 1926 hurricane the church next door blew away but the rectory remained intact. Until recently, the Sundy house was believed to be the oldest house in Delray. When Jane Baxter bought the rectory to use as a studio and offices for her design work, Ross and Virginia Snyder helped her to search through historic records. They learned that the rectory was built in 1900, making it the oldest house in Delray Beach.

Cross Atlantic Avenue to continue north on Swinton. At the corner of Atlantic and North Swinton, you can see Doc's All American, a fast-food type commercial structure with a green awning and a neon sign reminiscent of fast-food signs of the 1950s.

Next door to it, at **20 North Swinton**, is a yellow and white, wood frame building, with green trim and green door. This Monterey-style house, dating from 1939, was converted into office space. The house was carried by barge from its former West Palm Beach neighborhood to its present location. It had stood abandoned from 1987, after the Palm Beach International Airport noise abatement buyout, until 1994 when it was acquired by Delray Beach's Historic Palm Beach County Preservation Board.

The beige stucco and wood building next door to it, at **24 North Swinton**, is a bungalow-style house built in 1925 that has been converted to office use. Its most notable features are its stone piers and stone chimney. It was acquired at the same time as the house at 20 North Swinton, and was also carried by barge from its former West Palm Beach location. It is the headquarters of the Community Redevelopment Agency.

Damiano's Restaurant, at **52 North Swinton**, advertises itself as specializing in transcontinental cuisine. The owners of Damiano's are Anthony and Lisa Damiano, former chefs at the Russian Tea Room in New York. They opened their restaurant inside Tarrimore, a yellow stucco bungalow-style house surrounded by a white picket fence. Russian carpets, hand-painted chandeliers and sconces, and hand-carved Japanese dividers decorate the restaurant.

The two-story, 2,686-square foot house is believed to have been built in 1926 by John Cason, Jr., Delray Beach's first permanent doctor. It sits on what is known as the "Four Corners" of Swinton Avenue and Northeast First Street, across from several historic buildings. In the late 1980s, two local women bought it and named it Tarrimore with the intention of turning it into a bed-and-breakfast inn, using three of the five bedrooms for that purpose, but the house fell into foreclosure.

The simple wood frame vernacular house with blue-green trim and screened porch at **102 North Swinton** is the Clark House. It stands on the northwest corner of Swinton. It was built circa 1898 and is now occupied by law offices.

If you look across Swinton, you can see Cason Cottage on the northeast corner and Old School Square at **51 North Swinton** on the southeast corner. **Old School Square** is actually three school buildings that have been restored and converted to an archive, museum, and cultural center. The barrel tile roof reflects its Spanish-style look. Old School Square is on the National Trust for Historic Preservation and the National Register of Historic Places.

The 1913 former elementary school is now the **Visual Arts Center** which includes the Cornell Museum, named after a Delray couple. The museum features four galleries, a formal tea room, and a gift shop as well as a collection of thousands of military miniatures displayed in three-dimensional panoramas. There is no admission fee to the museum, and tours are available.

Old School Square

The Performing Arts Building, once the original Delray High School, is now the **Crest Theatre**, a 320-seat facility that presents cultural programs and lecture series. The gymnasium is rented out as a reception hall.

Although **Cason Cottage** and its parking lot are visible from North Swinton Avenue, the house, with its 1930s arts and crafts–style entrance door, faces Northeast First Avenue.

The white five-room house was built circa 1915 in a Florida wood-frame vernacular style for Dr. J. R. Cason Sr. The windows are detailed with crown moldings, the floors and siding are built with Dade County pine, and the ceilings are nine feet high.

Dr. Cason was a retired minister who later became a Delray municipal judge and minister of the First Methodist Church in Delray, which was renamed Cason United Methodist Church in 1924. Cason also founded the first orphanage in Florida between 1925 and 1930. The Methodist Children's Home was located in Enterprise, Florida.

Cason's children were as community-minded as he was. One son became Dade County Attorney in 1931, a daughter became a dairy-woman and ran Ives Certified Dairy, and another daughter became the first principal of Citrus Grove Junior High School in Miami. Dr. J. R. Cason Jr. was Delray's first physician.

In anticipation of Dr. and Mrs. Cason Sr.'s fiftieth wedding anniversary, the Cason Cottage was renovated and expanded to include a porte cochere and a roof line that encompassed three styles — gambrel, flat, and gable. Cason Cottage is now a museum that exhibits furnishings, photographs, and other memorabilia showcasing Delray's past. It is open to visitors Tuesdays through Sundays from 10 AM. to 3 PM.

The yellow, four-square house at **124 North Swinton**, a few doors away from the Clark house, has four rooms upstairs and four rooms downstairs. It has been converted to an arts and crafts shop called Nanny's Attic. The house was built in 1910.

At the corner of North Swinton and Northeast Second Street, turn right. Walk one block to Northeast First Avenue, and turn left. Welcome to **Banker's Row**, a picturesque little street with imposing Mediterranean revival homes on the left and pleasant little bungalows on the right. In the 1920s, the grand homes on this street and the little bungalows facing them were occupied by businessmen and artists.

There are two theories as to why the neighborhood is called Banker's Row: because of the bankers who lived there, or because the banks took ownership of so many of the homes.

During the 1980s, many of the houses fell into disrepair and were inhabited by vagrants and drug dealers. Slowly, Banker's Row was transformed by new residents who made repairs and restorations from a disintegrating neighborhood to a pristine one. Although some of the houses are still boarded up or neglected, the continuing facelift has added charm and character to the street.

At the far corner of the street, Villa Abrigo, at **248 Banker's Row**, is a 1925 Mediterranean-revival house built by real estate developer Matt Gracey and designed by Samuel Ogren, with decorative details by Addison Mizner. In 1992, it underwent a major restoration at the hands of Frank McKinney and his wife Nilsa, an interior designer, who lived in the house briefly.

Frank refers to himself as a Delray Beach redeveloper who buys and restores old buildings to their original beauty. It was his intention to buy Villa Abrigo as an investment, restore it, and sell it. Instead, Frank and Nilsa fell so in love with the house, the beautiful old floors, the pecky cypress beams, and the layout of the rooms, that they decided to move into it.

Nilsa researched records to find out exactly how the house looked inside during its heyday. She replicated the curtains, the Victorian furniture, and other details. Frank worked double-time to restore its grandeur. For the McKinneys, completing the house quickly was imperative, because the couple had decided to hold their wedding reception there, and move into it on their wedding night. They sold the house in 1993 after deciding that they wanted to live nearer to the beach.

In 1926, A. G. Evans, vice president of the Delray Bank and Trust Company, built the house at **238 Northeast First Avenue**, next door to Villa Abrigo. Subsequent owners Elizabeth and William Gearhart ran a private day school in the main house during the 1940s. Kindergarten classes were held in the two-story garage.

J. C. Keen, who was proprietor of the East Coast Produce Company, vice president of a lumber company, and director of a Delray bank, owned lots along Banker's Row, most of which he sold to several wealthy businessmen. In 1924, Leslie H. Walker bought one of the lots. He was a prominent builder and contractor. Walker's house was at **234** and Keen's house was at **226**.

The **little houses on the east side of Banker's Row** were built in the late 1930s by the sons of Frank E. Mackle. The Mackle name later became synonymous with General Development Corporation. These five-room bungalows are referred to as "traditional minimal" in style. They were advertised at a selling price of $3,000. The first of a group of twenty homes was sold in January 1939. It took only one month for the remaining homes to sell out.

Banker's Row bungalows

During the winter months, many of the houses were rented out to tourists. Two of those tourists were purported to be Chic Raymond, the Blondie cartoonist, and Wood Cowan, who drew the Major Hoople comic strip.

From Banker's Row, head south on Northeast First Avenue. Cross Northeast First Street and walk one block farther to Atlantic Avenue. Turn left (east) on Atlantic. You'll pass Worthing Park on the corner of Atlantic and Southeast Second Avenue. Walk on the south side of Atlantic, which is on the park side.

The Cathcart Building at **135 East Atlantic Avenue**, on the north side of Atlantic, was built in 1912. It was a general store constructed of rusticated cement blocks. The masonry vernacular-style beige building with blue-striped awnings maintains all of its original features except for the windows. Sal's, a sports shop, is located there.

Cross the railroad tracks. The Flamingo Service Station at **301 East Atlantic Avenue** was built in 1941 and has been cleverly converted into a restaurant, Ellwood's Dixie Bar-B-Que. The old oil rack in this stream-line moderne-style building serves as a bar countertop. The list of drinks on the menu can be found under "lubricants."

Cross Southeast Third Avenue and walk to the corner of Southeast Fourth Avenue. The Green Owl Cafe at **30 Southeast Fourth Avenue** was built in 1928. The blonde brick masonry vernacular-style building with green awning was originally an office building.

Cross Fourth Avenue to the Arcade Tap Room **at 411 East Atlantic Avenue**. The pink Mediterranean revival–style building was built in 1923. Architectural features include matching barrel-tiled octagonal towers and a fifteen-foot center entrance portal breezeway which once led to a courtyard of shops and offices.

The Arcade Tap Room was originally a sandwich shop. When Ohio native William Kraus purchased it in 1933, he transformed it into the Tap Room. Between 1933 and 1948, the Arcade Tap Room became a favorite hangout for visiting presidents, artists, writers, financiers, and polo aficionados. Cartoonists also congregated here. At one time, their autographed cartoons decorated the walls.

Cross Southeast Fifth Street, which is U.S. 1. On the left, you'll see the **Colony Hotel at 525 East Atlantic Avenue**. The concrete and stucco hotel was built in 1926 in a Spanish colonial mission revival style. Its architectural features include domed matching towers, a street-level, triple-arched entrance leading onto an open loggia with cracked Cuban tile flooring, and decorative shields and galleons. The furnishings came from John Wanamaker of Philadelphia.

The Colony was originally the Alterep, a name that was probably derived from combining letters from the name Albert T. Repp, a Delray

Colony Hotel, built in 1926

businessman who owned the Colony Hotel site. Of the nine hotels that at one time lined Atlantic Avenue, the Colony is the only one that has survived.

When the hotel opened in January of 1926, Miss Ida Greenwood's Chicago Three, a female orchestra, played at the reception. A $5 dinner marked the formal opening in March. Financing problems caused the Alterep to foreclose in December 1926. In 1935 it was bought by its present owners, the Boughton family, and continues to open on a seasonal basis. The Boughtons also own the Colony Hotel in Kennebunkport, Maine.

Turn around and head west on Atlantic. Continue walking until you come to the end of the tennis center. At the northwest corner of Atlantic and North West Third Avenue, turn right onto North West Third, to the historic black community of Delray.

The house at **30 Northwest Third Avenue** is typical of the south Florida bungalow style that could be found in Delray Beach during the 1920s and 1930s. This is where a tall, thin black woman named Susan Currie Williams lived during the last four years of her life. It is referred to as the Susan Williams house.

Susan was born in the Bahamas in 1870, where she grew up to become a midwife. Around 1898, Susan, her husband, and their daughter Agnes sailed to America. They settled in Delray where Susan continued as a midwife for both black and white families. Eventually, she went into home nursing. Susan's daughter Agnes married Grover Cleveland Munnings in 1924. In 1935, Isaiah Bruin, from the Florida Panhandle town of Quincy, built the Munnings's bungalow at **30 Northwest Third Avenue**. In 1950 Susan suffered a stroke. She moved into her daughter's house where she died four years later, at the age of eighty-four.

Vinyl siding now covers the original exterior wood facing of the Susan Williams house. Its bungalow features include multipaned casement windows, exposed rafters, a gabled roof, and a porch roof supported by piers.

Continue walking north on Northwest Third Avenue to Northwest Second Street. Turn left and walk two blocks west to Northwest Fifth Avenue. Turn left on Northwest Fifth Avenue and walk to **170 Northwest Fifth Avenue**, which is the Solomon David Spady house, built in 1926.

S. D. Spady was a black educator who was born in Virginia in 1890. At Hampton Institute (now Hampton University), Spady was a student of George Washington Carver. Spady was a cofounder of the New Farmers of America, which encouraged black people to become independent farmers. In 1923 Spady moved to Delray. He became a teacher and principal at a school designated as "Delray Colored No. 4." After his death the school was renamed in his honor.

Spady was committed to improving the educational quality of segregated schools and inspired his students by recounting personal anecdotes involving himself and Booker T. Washington and George Washington Carver. He retired to Virginia in 1956.

The Spady house was built in a simplified mission revival–style with a flat roof concealed with a parapet. The chimney has a bell tower covering, and there are drain tile scuppers set into the parapet walls. The house, of stucco-over-frame construction, was built as an eight-room, two-story house. Aluminum windows now enclose the openings of the original screened porch.

Continue walking south on Northwest Fifth Avenue. Cross Northwest First Street and walk to the **B. J. James and Frances Jane Bright Park** on the east side of Northwest Fifth. This unusual mini-park is named for two revered local teachers. It commemorates buildings established by Delray's earliest black settlers and is listed on the Florida Black Heritage Trail. It officially opened on Martin Luther King, Jr. Day in 1995. It is only twenty-two feet by sixteen feet and is enclosed by coquina walls. There is a bench inside the park where visitors can reflect upon the importance of Delray's black pioneers. The entrance panel has leaf cutwork, to signify the community's agricultural beginnings. Another panel provides information about the five sites.

In addition to Delray Colored No. 4, which was founded in 1895 and no longer exists, the black community founded Greater **Mt. Olive Missionary Baptist Church** in 1896. It is located on the corners of Northwest Fourth Avenue and Northwest First Street. **St. Paul African Methodist Episcopal Church** was founded in 1897 and is located on Northwest Fifth Avenue between Northwest First Street and Northwest Second Street.

The Free and Accepted **Masons Lodge** #275 was founded in 1899 and is located on the corners of Northwest Fifth Avenue and Northwest First Street. **St. Matthew Episcopal Church** was founded in 1911 and is located on the corners of Southwest Fourth Avenue and Southwest Third Street. In 1989, these sites were placed on the Local Register of Historic Places.

Walk south a very short distance to Atlantic Avenue. Turn left on Atlantic and walk back to Swinton. At Swinton turn right and walk back to the Sundy House.

HOLLYWOOD

Broward County

Location

Hollywood, with its six miles of beaches, is located north of Miami and south of Ft. Lauderdale on Florida's southeast coast. It is Florida's ninth most populated city.

History

Before the turn of the century, the Hollywood area and the Broward County region were part of Dade County. They were populated by runaway slaves, a smattering of white settlers, and Indians who had been driven south from Georgia and the Carolinas and who later became known as the Seminoles.

The arrival of Henry Flagler's Florida East Coast Railway was a boon to the local farming industry. Now, produce could be shipped to new markets. The railroad also carried new settlers, and it gave birth to tourism.

In 1904, Napoleon Bonaparte Broward, a former gunrunner during Cuba's fight for independence from Spain, mounted a successful gubernatorial campaign based on his promise to drain the Everglades for farming. He kept his promise. The New River was dredged, and the North New River Canal was built, making it possible to cruise from Ft. Lauderdale all the way to Ft. Myers.

Around 1920, Indianapolis real estate developer Joseph Wesley Young purchased an initial five plats of land south of Ft. Lauderdale on which he would build his dream city. He would call it Hollywood, a name he associated with the area in southern California where he had once lived.

Young's dream city had parks, a golf course, lakes, and a wide tree-lined boulevard stretching from the ocean to the Everglades. He built houses fit for people in every class of life. He hired a staff of star real estate salesmen to promote Hollywood. The people of Hollywood elected to re-name their city after Young, but he modestly refused.

Hotels and motels sprang up along Hollywood Beach, attracting vacationers to its shores. The deepest port harbor in Florida was built at Port Everglades, near Hollywood and what is now Ft. Lauderdale/ Hollywood International Airport. It became home to two dozen cruise ships. Despite the port and the proliferation of beach-front hotels, Hollywood has remained a large, nonindustrial city. It was incorporated in 1925.

Walking Tour
This walking tour is approximately one mile and takes about forty-five minutes. To get to the starting point of Dixie Highway and Hollywood Boulevard, take I-95 to the Hollywood Boulevard exit and head east to Dixie. There is plentiful street parking.

Begin at the **corner of Dixie Highway and Hollywood Boulevard**, east of the railroad tracks. Dixie is North Twenty-first Avenue. Hollywood Boulevard runs east and west. Dixie Highway runs north and south.

Walk east on the left side of Hollywood Boulevard. You'll be strolling through a pleasant shopping district lined with trees and parking meters. You'll come to the corner of Hollywood and North Twentieth Avenue and the peach stucco **Sun Bank at 2001 North Twentieth Avenue**. In 1923, the year it was built, the bank was called Hollywood State Bank. Much of its original Moorish-style architecture has been changed throughout the decades. It is one of the oldest buildings in Hollywood.

The building at **1921 Hollywood Boulevard** was the site of the area's first movie theater, aptly called the Hollywood Theater when it opened in 1925. Its name later changed to the Ritz Theater. It is now a dance center.

The **Great Southern Hotel, on the corner of North Nineteenth Avenue**, looks as though it was once a grand building along the Boulevard. For a two-year period during the 1930s, gambling was legal here, and the gambling tables of the hotel were a great enticement. Most of the hotel's upper windows are now boarded up and painted over. Its Spanish-style architecture is evident in the barrel tile roof, the arched windows, the textured stucco, and twisted columns.

Cross Young Circle to **Young Circle Park** facing you. Here you'll encounter the bronze bust of Joseph Young. Young Circle was first known as Park Circle. In 1924, Warren G. Harding made a golfing visit to the area, prompting a name change to Harding Circle. A year after Joseph Young's death, the Circle again changed names — to honor Young.

The short stroll to the end of the park leaves you facing a small shopping strip at East Young Circle, anchored by a Publix Supermarket.

Cross over U.S. 1 to the Publix and turn right. Walk through the parking lot and to the corner. Cross over to Harrison Street and turn left to Harrison Street and South Sixteenth Avenue.

On this corner you have a view of the **Art & Culture Center of Hollywood, at 1650 Harrison Street**. Cross over to the Center. It was originally the home of Jack Kagy, who was one of Joseph Young's star salesmen. The Mediterranean-style mansion, built circa 1924, was a funeral home before its present use as an art school, a gallery, and the site of discussion groups, educational programs, and traveling exhibits.

Walk past the Art & Culture Center, heading east on Harrison Street, which parallels Hollywood Boulevard.

The **Maison Harrison Bed & Breakfast is at 1504 Harrison**. This two-story Spanish colonial house was built in 1934 by a family member of Joseph Young. Some of Young's squad of real estate salesmen were purported to have lived here. The house was later purchased by Emma Ennis, an Englishwoman who turned it into a guest house. She sold it in 1991. The new owners restored the house to its 1930s look and opened it as Maison Harrison, the only bed-and-breakfast establishment in this area of Hollywood.

The refinished wood floors and French doors, the brass beds, wool throw rugs, and other furnishings accentuate the history of the house. Among the guest rooms is a honeymoon room that features a canopy bed that was once part of the Patty Duke Suite in the old Diplomat Hotel. A white picket fence surrounds the house, courtyard, and garden.

The pale blue house at **1421 Harrison** is in the art moderne style. Behind its white wrought iron gate and the royal palms that flank the front, the house has a sleek art deco look to it, especially because of its racing lines, parapet, and rounded corners.

Turn left at Fourteenth Avenue and Harrison. Walk to Hollywood Boulevard and turn left. Peer eastward, to your right. The panoramic view will give you an idea of what Joseph Young envisioned. He wanted a grand street all the way down to the beach and the Hollywood Beach Hotel, which you can see if you look far enough eastward.

Continue left (west) on Hollywood Boulevard. The house at **1506 Hollywood Boulevard** was built in 1924 in a Spanish style with baroque touches. Facing it from the north side of Hollywood Boulevard is a pink house with white awnings and a barrel tile roof.

The latter house, at **1515 Hollywood Boulevard**, was built circa 1935 in a Mediterranean revival style. The 1945 city directory indicates the house was owned by Helen Hart Brown. It was used as a small private school. The exterior of this wood frame house was designed so that

1930s *hybrid-style home*

Carlton House Apartments

the wood looks like big slabs of stucco.

At North Sixteenth Avenue and Hollywood Boulevard, cross over to the north side of the Boulevard. The corner house at **1555 Hollywood Boulevard** is a hybrid style from the 1930s. Cheerily painted in yellow, it has green and orange floral bas-relief panels on each side of the entrance doorway. The panels and the glass block on the west side of the house are elements of a 1930s art deco style that combines with 1920s Spanish elements such as the arched doorway and a cast stone decorative panel above the door.

Continue down North Sixteenth Avenue to Polk Street. Turn right (east). The Hollywood Country Club is on the north side of Polk, and it faces **1536 Polk**, the location of the peach stucco Carlton House Apartments which was designed with a double-sloped, bungalow-style roof.

The house with the flagpole on the lawn at **1520 Polk** has a Spanish style but incorporates some modern touches, including the vertical lines around the front doorway. This house, built in 1934, was designed by architect Bayard Lukens. It was the home of Clarence

Eversoll House

Hammerstein, a successful salesman who willed his house to the city of Hollywood. It is now the headquarters of the Hollywood Historical Society. Hammerstein was a World War I prisoner. He returned to Evansville, Indiana, after the war. In 1922, he married his sweetheart. Hammerstein was employed in the advertising industry when he met Joseph Young at a Kiwanis convention. Young convinced Hammerstein to come to Florida in 1925. In addition to working for Young, Hammerstein was a citrus grower, and he also grew mangoes. He developed a mango called the Ham mango — Ham being short for Hammerstein.

Walk to the corner of North Fifteenth Avenue and Polk Street. Turn right onto North Fifteenth. Walk to the next street which is Tyler Street. Turn left, and cross the street.

1455 Tyler was built circa 1940. Its turret entranceway is an interesting design detail. From 1957 to 1986, it was the home of physician Dr. Norton Eversoll and his wife. At the time of Dr. Eversoll's death in 1993, he was ninety-seven years old and he was writing a book to be called "My First Hundred Years."

At this corner, turn right and walk back to Hollywood Boulevard. Turn right, and you'll be heading back in the direction of Dixie Highway/North Twenty-first Avenue.

MIAMI BEACH
(ART DECO DISTRICT)
Dade County

Location

Miami Beach is located in Dade County, on the southeast coast of Florida. The beach stretches for ten miles along the Atlantic Ocean. The art deco district of South Beach covers more than one square mile in area.

History

Hundreds of years ago, Tequesta Indians lived in settlements in the Miami Beach area. In the early 1800s, the primary residents were white Bahamians and Spanish settlers. They were homesteaders living among mangroves and swamps. In 1892, Dade County built the first paved road on Florida's east coast. But the Miami Beach area remained sparsely settled until Henry Flagler's railroad came southward.

The Florida East Coast Railway opened the doors to civilization and development. During the latter part of the nineteenth century, Northerners paid twenty-five to thirty cents an acre as they began to invest in the land around what we know as Miami Beach.

One of those investors was John Collins, who was a Quaker from Morristown, New Jersey. He cultivated avocado and orange groves on the Florida land he bought. The long stretch of Collins Avenue in Miami Beach is named after him. Another Miami Beach developer, Carl Fisher, was a millionaire from Indiana who had accumulated his wealth from the manufacture of a component that illuminated car headlights.

Miami Beach was incorporated in 1915. During its busy real estate development period, it was a boomtown, but after the 1926 hurricane and the Depression, it slumped. From the 1930s to the 1960s, Miami Beach enjoyed renewed popularity as a tourist resort.

Some people describe the colorful Miami Beach hotel style as art deco, but technically the majority of these hotels were designed in a style that is called streamline moderne. Particular aspects of this style include slender, sleek lines, porthole designs, and rounded corners. Many hotels combined streamline moderne with Mediterranean or Spanish elements such as arches, tile roofs, and stucco.

Although Miami Beach was a popular tourist mecca during the 1930s and into the 1950s, it was well known for being "restricted." Some hotel signs were reported to blatantly read, "Gentiles only," or "No dogs. No Jews," or "Always a view. Never a Jew." The irony is that the architects of many of these hotels were Jewish.

In the 1960s, the popularity of Miami Beach declined, forcing the closing or demolition of many of its hotels. The area began to attract poorer people and retirees. In recent years, Miami Beach's art deco district has evolved into a hot spot for models and celebrities. Many of the hotels and their restaurants have been restored.

Walking Tour

This walking tour is approximately one mile and takes about forty-five minutes. Many of the buildings on this tour of the Miami Beach art deco district do not have readily visible street numbers, but they are easily identifiable because of certain colors or characteristics.

Ocean Drive runs north and south along the beach and the Atlantic Ocean. To get to the starting point, the Cardozo Hotel at Ocean Drive and Thirteenth Street, take I-95 to Exit 395E, which takes you to the beaches. At Ocean Drive, turn left. There is street parking and there is a parking lot behind the hotel.

Begin your walk by standing with your back to the beach, so that you are facing the **Cardozo Hotel**. You'll be facing west. If you stand on the beach (east) side of Ocean Drive, you'll get a wide view of the stretch of buildings flanking the Cardozo.

Cardozo Hotel

The Cardozo Hotel, which faces the Atlantic Ocean, was designed by New York architect Henry Hohauser and built in 1939. It was named after U.S. Supreme Court Justice Benjamin Cardozo. Notice the keystone (marble) trim on the facade, the porthole designs, the ship's rail, and the glass block. Step into the lobby and hallway areas of the hotel to see how vibrantly they are painted. The hotel's rooms, dominated by bright oranges, purples, greens, and aquas, have been restored. The original hardwood floors remain. A *Hole In The Head*, with Frank Sinatra and Edward G. Robinson, about a Miami hotelier faced with foreclosure, was filmed at the Cardozo. (The 1959 Oscar-winning song, "High Hopes," came from that movie.)

To the left of the Cardozo, you'll see the **Carlyle Hotel**. Typical of what we think of as art deco, the Carlyle's architectural features include eyebrows, rounded contours, terrazzo floors, and a parapet above the roof line.

Walk west on Thirteenth Street, past the Cardozo and the municipal parking garage (which is also in keeping with the overall art deco appearance) to Collins Avenue. Cross over to the west side of Collins to the **Alamac**, a Mediterranean revival building with balconies, barrel tile roof, arches, and a navy-toned awning with the name "Alamac."

Continue on Thirteenth Street to the next street, which is Washington Avenue. Cross Washington, to the northwest corner and the **U.S. Post Office**. The post office was designed in 1937 by Howard Cheney. Its stark architectural style is described as depression moderne. The post office was a public project funded by Roosevelt's New Deal. The interior's center rotunda is decorated with a massive mural, a triptych painted in 1940 by Georgia artists. The panels depict historic Florida incidents. Above the mural, a Dome of Heaven boasts forty-eight stars edged in bronze and silver. The center of the sun is a skylight.

Turn right (north) on Washington Avenue. This was a heavily Jewish-occupied section. You can still see the **Kosher Meat Market**. Walk to Fourteenth Street. Look to the southeast side of Fourteenth, and you'll see the **Club Deuce Bar**. The building dates from the 1920s.

Glance across to the east side of Washington Avenue to see **South Beach Realty**. Notice the building's cantilevered ceiling. Nothing visible is holding it up, yet it is supported by reinforced steel and concrete.

While walking along Washington Avenue, you'll pass the mission-style **Fisher-Leroy Feinberg School** on your left. It was built by Carl Fisher and sold to the public school system. It is the oldest elementary school on the Beach. Leroy Feinberg was a principal at the school during the 1960s.

Espanola Way

Continue north on Washington Avenue to the next street, which is Espanola Way. As you peer down this street to your left, you may feel as though you're in Old San Juan or Madrid. Wrought iron balconies, clay-potted plants, facade tiles, barrel tile roofs, archways, and courtyards create a picturesque scene.

Before you turn left to walk up Espanola Way, look instead to the northeast corner of Espanola Way, across Washington Avenue. You'll see the **Cameo Theatre**, built in the 1930s. Glance eastward, farther down Espanola Way, and you'll glimpse old buildings with turrets, and a nightclub that was once Hoffman's Cafeteria and later the Warsaw Ballroom. Turn left (west) on Espanola Way. On your left is the **Clay Hotel**, an American Youth Hostel with white columns, pink arches, and wrought iron gate leading to a courtyard. To the left of the courtyard is a shoe repair shop that has been in that location for sixty years.

At the next corner, Drexel Avenue, turn left. Walk to a dead end, which is the location of the **Ida Fisher Elementary School**. Built in 1936, the school exhibits Spanish-style design elements such as textured stucco and a courtyard. Notice also the white medallion designs atop the front of the building. As you stand in front of the school building, there will be a playing field to your left. Walk across the field and out to the street. You'll be on the corner of Fourteenth Street and Drexel Avenue. Continue on Drexel.

Heading south, you'll see a hodgepodge of architectural styles

The Habana and other hotels and apartments along Drexel

among the hotels and apartments, such as the **Windsor Plaza** and the **Habana**, both of which were built in the 1920s. Continue on Drexel and cross Thirteenth Street. On the right (west) side of the street, you will notice the buildings' streamline moderne style — the rounded contours, parapets, portholes, racing lines, and the yellows, blues, and aquas of the condos.

The rental apartments and condos on Drexel come with a heavy price tag, yet renovation and restoration busily moves forward here. Parking meters line up like metal soldiers along the street, yet parking is at a premium. The residences on the west side of Drexel create a pretty pastel pallette.

As you near the corner of Drexel and Twelfth Street, look up toward the top of the **old Miami Beach City Hall**, which now houses law offices and other businesses. Stone urns perched on top of the building once toppled during a hurricane, so the urns that are now there have been reinforced with steel rods. This old city hall was built in 1920 by Carl Fisher at a cost of $200,000.

Turn left on Twelfth Street. You'll be heading east, alongside City Hall. Turn right at Washington Avenue and walk into the lobby of the City Hall. Here you can see the building's original lighting and elevators. Continue south on Washington Avenue to the corner of Washington and Eleventh Street.

To your right will be **Rocky Pomerance Plaza** and the Bahaus-style

Kenmore Hotel, built in 1938

police station. Pomerance was Miami Beach's police chief from 1963 to 1977.

Cross Eleventh Street. As you stand on the southwest corner of Washington and Eleventh Street, you'll be in front of the **Kenmore Hotel**. Built in 1938, the yellow and turquoise hotel was once a Kosher hotel for the Jewish elderly.

Look across Washington to the southeast side of Eleventh Street. Notice something out of the rock 'n' roll era? It's an old-fashioned **stainless steel diner** built in 1948 and shipped from its home in Wilkes Barre, Pennsylvania.

Continue south on Washington Street. You'll pass the **Taft**, a very art deco structure partially hidden behind a long half-wall of white concrete. With a wavy top and holes like portholes, the wall resembles a ship at sea.

At Tenth Street, turn left and cross over to the east side of Washington Avenue. Here you can peek through the doors of the **Wolfsonian Foundation's International Museum and Study Center**. Once a furniture storage building, it is now dedicated to the collection, exhibition, and preservation of the decorative, design, and architectural arts. It houses some 50,000 objets d'art and rare books. The Wolfsonian is named for the Wolfson family, who built Wometco Theaters. Among the treasures in the Wolfsonian is the old facade of a Pennsylvania movie theater. There is a Spanish frieze on the building's upper facade.

If you look up the street to your left, you'll notice an unusual little structure — a **bridgetender's house** made of aluminum.

Remaining on the east side of Washington Avenue, cross to the south side of Tenth Street. You'll be able to see the side of the Wolfsonian. Let your eye wander across the pink frieze-work. That's when you'll spot Wolfson's face etched into the frieze.

Continue south to the corner of Ninth Street. From this distance, you'll see the **Blackstone** which was formerly a hotel and is now an apartment building for senior citizens. It was supposedly in the hotel's solarium that George Gershwin composed part of Porgy and Bess. In 1954, a convention of Southern Baptist black ministers could not find an accepting hotel in Miami Beach. The Blackstone welcomed the conventioners. The Blackstone was the first resort north of Fifth Street to accept Jewish guests.

Turn left on Ninth Street, heading toward Collins Avenue. You'll pass an office building with yellow awnings. This building was erected in 1918 by Avery Smith. It was built with oolitic limestone.

Continue east on Ninth, back to Ocean Avenue, which was your starting point. Cross Ocean and head toward the beach. With your back to the ocean, glimpse up and down the west side of Ocean Drive.

You'll see the **Waldorf** with its lookout tower; and the **Locust**, an old pink apartment building with a Venetian design, although some people describe the style as Moorish. Also notice the yellow and blue **Breakwater Hotel**, with its tall parapet and large lobby area, its neon illumination and etched glass. The Venetian-style peach and white **Edison Hotel**, next to the Breakwater, was designed by Henry Hohauser.

Walk up to the Tenth Street Beach where Pavarotti once performed a free concert. Look toward the ocean. Rising from the sand is an art deco pink and yellow lifeguard station. The beach's patrol headquarters building was designed in 1939 by architect Robert Taylor in a moderne style. Among the notable design features of the yellow and aqua building are the ship railing, portholes, and industrial pipe.

From the beach side of Ocean Drive, head north, back toward Thirteenth Street and the Cardozo Hotel. You'll see the **Adrian Hotel**, designed in a pink art nouveau style. Notice the turquoise "waves" at the top of the building. Next, you'll see the impressive **Casa Cuarina** which

Gianni Versace residence

was built in 1930 and was once an apartment complex. The 18,000-square-foot estate was purchased in early 1993 by Italian fashion designer Gianni Versace. It contains sixteen bedroom suites, a two-story library, and a copper-domed observatory. Versace is said to have paid $2.95 million for his showplace, which features keystone around the door, wrought iron balconies, a barrel tile roof, and gardens.

Continue on to the Cardozo to complete your tour.

CORAL GABLES

Dade County

Location

Coral Gables is located in southwestern Dade County approximately seven miles south of Miami International Airport.

History

In 1898, a Congregational minister named Solomon Merrick arrived in South Florida from Massachusetts with his wife and children. He bought 160 acres of undeveloped land southwest of Miami and cultivated thriving citrus and avocado groves.

Reverend Merrick's son George had a vision of developing the area into a picturesque, affluent suburb — a desirable residential community with manicured lawns, gateways and fountains, and a decidedly Mediterranean theme.

Merrick's vision, which he called Coral Gables after the house in which he had grown up, became a successful reality during the land boom years of the 1920s. Through the efforts of Merrick's team of prominent architects and contractors, hundreds of homes sprang up, including an affluent country club section complete with a golf course.

In 1924, Merrick joined forces with Biltmore Hotel magnate John Bowman to build the 275-room hotel and resort now known as "The Biltmore Hotel, Coral Gables, Westin Hotels and Resorts." It attracted dignitaries, celebrities, and the notorious. Al Capone once stayed in the Everglades Suite.

During World War II, the Biltmore served the wounded as the Army Air Forces Regional Hospital. Windows were sealed with concrete, and marble floors were covered with government-issue linoleum. The hotel has been restored to its original opulence.

The Biltmore's Mediterranean revival style includes a 315-foot, copper-clad tower that was inspired by the Giralda bell tower in Seville. Hand-painted cathedral ceilings, a brick and stone courtyard, and a 22,000 square foot swimming pool — the largest of any hotel pool in the continental United States — reflect George Merrick's dream of a grand and elegant hotel.

In 1924, the Venetian Pool on DeSoto Boulevard was created from a limestone rock quarry. Phineas Paist designed this public swimming pool with towers, loggias, porticoes, and coral rock caves. The pool is listed on the National Register of Historic Places. The city's Alhambra water tower, conceived by artistic advisor Denman Fink, was designed to resemble a lighthouse. It was built in 1924.

In the early 1920s, the University of Miami was established in Coral Gables. The hurricane of 1926 did such severe damage to campus buildings that the school was given the nickname "The Cardboard College."

Coral Gables' fountains, elaborate entrances, and commercial and residential buildings characteristic of the architecture of Spain and Italy, created an Old World ambiance that made the city a fashionable address. The stores along Coral Way (now known as Miracle Mile) attract shoppers from near and far.

After the land bust in the late 1920s, Merrick lost nearly everything. He operated a fishing camp in the Florida Keys, and he later became the Miami postmaster. He died in 1942.

Walking Tour

This is a walking tour of residences that surround the Granada Golf Course within Coral Gables' largest historic district, **The Country Club of Coral Gables**. The tour is approximately one and a half miles and takes about one hour.

To get to The Country Club, take U.S. 1 to LeJeune Road north to Coral Way. Go west on Coral Way to the two stone piers and the sign that marks the entrance to the Country Club of Coral Gables. There is parking on the swales along North and South Greenway Drives inside the entrance to the Country Club.

Many of the homes are significant either because of the people who lived in them or because of the architects who designed the homes. North and South Greenway Drives surround the Granada Golf Course, which was the first golf course in the City of Coral Gables. It opened on New Year's Day in 1923 and was designed by the Chicago-based architectural firm of Langford and Moreau, who were considered the leading golf course architects in the United States.

The first house you'll see is **611 North Greenway Drive**. As are nearly all the houses in the district, this 1939 house was built in a Mediterranean revival style. Its first owner was Frank Holley, who operated a chain of five and dime stores. He was president of the Coral Gables Chamber of Commerce and a director of the Coral Gables First National Bank.

The architect of **641 North Greenway** is unknown, but the house was built in 1924 and was at one time owned by Dr. William McKibben, who was chief of pediatric staff at Miami City Hospital and founder of the Dade County Tuberculosis Association. He was also a vice president of the Coral Gables Chamber of Commerce. The stucco house is recognizable by the two spiraling palms in the front yard.

A ring of flowers surrounds the two trees that are on either side of the walkway leading to **647 North Greenway**. A canopy shades the single-door entry to this house, which was built in 1937 by the architectural firm of Kiehnel and Elliott. This Pennsylvania architectural firm opened a Florida office in 1922. Kiehnel and Elliott specialized in Spanish colonial architecture. They also designed the Coral Gables Congregational Church and the Coral Gables Elementary School. Among their many residential designs are the homes at 647, 701 and 1133 North Greenway Drive.

Cross Casilla and walk to **701 North Greenway**, the house on the corner of Casilla and North Greenway. Built in 1935, this was another Kiehnel and Elliott design. The oval window above the balcony and the decorative use of wrought iron are distinguishing features of this house.

Royal palms line up at the entrance to the house at **717 North Greenway**. Built in 1929, the house was first owned by Achille Renuart, president of Renuart Realty Company, one of the primary real estate companies in Coral Gables.

John and Coulton Skinner designed the house at **725 North Greenway**, which was built in 1929. Four years earlier, the brothers, orig-

1935 Kiehnel and Elliott design

Edwin Belcher house

inally from Ohio, had established their architectural firm in the Miami and Coral Gables area. They designed such notable buildings as the French Normandy Village on LeJeune Road and had a substantial number of other large residential commissions.

Three unusually-shaped vertical hedges add interesting landscape detail to the peach stucco house at **737 North Greenway**. The hedges are cylindrical. Note the stonework around the arched entry and the bell tower above the barrel tile roof. The house was built in 1929. One of its earlier owners was Edwin Belcher, president of the Belcher Oil Company.

The architect of the beige stucco house at **751 North Greenway** is unknown. The house was built in 1924 and occupied, in 1926, by an architect named C. L. Lewis Jr. The scuppers above the left window awning are a common detail of the home's mission style of architecture.

Cross Cortez. Continue on North Greenway to the corner of Granada, where the Country Club is located. Cross Granada. The white two-story house at **1021 North Greenway** was built in 1936. It stands out among the neighboring homes because it is designed in an art deco style with the typical porthole, racing lines, and curved corners.

The white, two-story house with barrel tile roof at **1101 North Greenway** was built in 1937. It is rather plain in style, with little ornamentation. The architects were Paist and Steward. Phineas Paist was Supervising Architect of Coral Gables. He was one of the architects of Vizcaya, the James Deering estate in Miami. In 1926, Paist formed a partnership with Harold Steward. In addition to residential design, they worked on the Colonnade Building and Coral Gables City Hall.

Kiehnel and Elliott were the architects of the beige stucco house at **1133 North Greenway**, which was built in 1923. The scrollwork columns between the arched windows add a decorative touch to the otherwise plain mission style.

As you walk along North Greenway, you'll notice, by peering ahead, that you are walking toward the **Alhambra water tower** that looms above the rooftops at the intersection of Alhambra Circle and Ferdinand Street. It was built in 1924 under the guidance of architect Denman Fink. The water tower resembles a lighthouse.

Cross Columbus. On the corner of Columbus and North Greenway, you'll come to a peach stucco house at **1203 North Greenway**. It was built in 1923. In 1926 it became the residence of William S. Maxwell, director of the Coral Gables Chamber of Commerce. The house was designed by H. George Fink, who was George Merrick's cousin. In 1921, at the age of thirty-one, he became the youngest architect to be admitted to the American Institute of Architects.

Coral Gables water tower

Fink designed many Mediterranean revival houses and commercial buildings in Coral Gables. In 1924, he was honored by King Alphonso XIII of Spain for his creativity and imagination in reproducing the Spanish arts in America.

Cross Madrid. Continue on North Greenway and cross Greenway Court. The Alhambra water tower will now appear high on your right. The next street is South Greenway. Turn left here. Continue walking. You will cross both Madrid and Columbus.

A white stone wall with wrought iron gates surrounds the house at **1100 South Greenway**. This house, at the corner of Cordova and South Greenway, was built in 1923 and was owned by Jan Garber, a bandleader who often performed in Coral Gables with his orchestra.

Cross Cordova. Paist and Steward designed the house at **1036 South Greenway**. This yellow house with white shutters and wrought iron fence and gate was built in 1935. Cross Toledo. George Merrick's former residence is **at 832 South Greenway**. Built in 1922, it was designed by H. George Fink.

Walk to the **corner of Castile and South Greenway**. This is the site of the packinghouse of the Coral Gables plantation established by George Merrick's father, Reverend Solomon Greasley Merrick. The post in the fig tree is the only remaining evidence of the packinghouse.

Turn right on Castile. Walk to the corner of Castile and Toledo. Turn left on Toledo. There is a driveway on your right that leads to the Coral Gables Merrick House. This is actually a back entrance to the house and is the visitors' parking lot. Walk through the rear entrance, up the path to the front of the house, which sits at **907 Coral Way**.

The Merrick house, built circa 1899, was constructed of coral rock and Dade County pine, and gave George Merrick the idea to call his development Coral Gables. This was the boyhood home of George Merrick and the plantation home of his parents, Solomon and Althea Merrick, who designed the house in a New England colonial style.

The property includes a one-and-a-half-acre garden filled with citrus trees, vegetable beds, and a variety of other trees and plantings. The grounds are maintained organically. Visitors can take a self-guided tour of the gardens, where some of the plantings from 1908 remain.

Return to the parking lot at the back of the house. Walk back out onto Toledo and walk briefly in the direction of the golf course. This puts you onto South Greenway. Turn right on South Greenway and continue to circle the golf course until you return to your origination point.

KEY WEST

Monroe County

Location

The southernmost city in the continental United States, Key West is about ninety miles from Cuba. Key West is four miles long and two miles wide. Located 150 miles from downtown Miami, Key West is reached by the Overseas Highway, which includes 43 island-hopping bridges.

History

Key West was first inhabited by Calusa Indians. According to legend, Spanish explorers who found the island strewn with the bones of Indians named it Cayo Hueso — Island of Bones — which was turned into English as "Key West." In 1823, the island was so inundated with privateers that the U.S. Navy dispatched Commodor David Porter and his squadron to successfully end the pirates' power.

Around 1830, wrecker and harbor pilot Capt. John H. Geiger built a three-story house in Key West that was large enough for his wife and twelve children. In 1832, the Geigers hosted John James Audubon, who captured many of the island's birds in his engravings.

Key West became populated by wreckers, men who salvaged goods from ships that had gone down on nearby reefs. The booty from that lucrative industry made Key West the wealthiest city in the United States. During the 1830s, the harbor was filled with ship chandleries and auction houses. This area was named Mallory Square, after Stephen R. Mallory, the U.S. senator from Florida and Confederate secretary of the navy. Sponge fishermen here found a good market for sponges harvested in the waters.

In the late nineteenth century, the cigar industry flourished in Key West. Cuban-born Benito Alfonso's cigar factory, with fifty employees, competed with Francisco Marrero's larger factory of six hundred employees. Yet so profitable was the cigar-making business that, in 1891, Alfonso was able to pay $2,000 to buy a house. By the 1920s, hundreds of people were employed at the Key West Box Company, where they made containers for the cigars.

From the 1870s to the 1890s, the United States and Spain were at conflict over Spain's policies toward Cuban patriots who wanted independence from Spanish rule. United States sympathy ran high for the Cuban freedom fighters. On January 25, 1898, the U.S.S. Maine was dispatched from Key West to Havana to protect American interests and property in Cuba. On February 15, 1898, the battleship blew up and sank in Havana Harbor, resulting in a loss of 260 men. Although a subsequent U.S. naval inquiry could not place the blame on anyone, "Remember the Maine" became a rallying cry among outraged Americans. Many of the men killed aboard the Maine were buried in Key West Cemetery. The sinking of the Maine was the catalyst that led to the Spanish-American War.

In 1912, the Overseas Railroad gave tourists easy access to Key West. The Florida Keys Overseas Highway was built in the 1920s through the 1940s.

From the late 1920s until the early 1940s, Ernest Hemingway was probably the most famous resident of Key West. In 1946, and for the remainder of his presidency, Harry S. Truman vacationed in Key West in officers' quarters located on the U.S. naval station. It came to be called The Little White House.

Walking Tour

The walking tour described here is approximately one mile and takes about one hour. To get to the **Donkey Milk House/Peter A. Williams House at 613 Eaton Street**, take U.S. 1 south into Key West. Turn right on North Roosevelt Boulevard, which becomes Truman Avenue. Continue on Truman to Simonton Street. Turn right on Simonton. Travel to Eaton Street and turn right. There is street parking.

The Donkey Milk House is a white Greek revival–style house that was built circa 1866 and was owned by Fire Marshall Peter Williams. Members of the Williams family continued to live in the house for 120 years. It is called the Donkey Milk House because mule carts once delivered milk to houses along the alley behind the Williams house. The house is now owned by Denison Tempel, who restored it to its original beauty a few years ago, and who conducts tours of his home.

The house is 3,500 square feet and contains ten rooms, which no doubt were needed to accommodate Williams's eight children, including two sets of twins. There is a porch or verandah off every room. Tempel furnished the house with an eclectic mix of furniture styles representing periods from 1830 to 1930.

Donkey Milk House, built circa 1866

The restoration work revealed that the ceilings were painted around 1890 in a blue and beige flower and leaf design by an Italian artist. The floor is covered with a nineteenth-century Barcelona tile in a geometrical pattern. The staircase in the Donkey Milk House is of note because it was made from black walnut rather than the mahogany that was commonly used during that era. The staircase was built with dust corners which are dust-catching triangles of brass on each step.

Across the street from the Donkey Milk House is the George H. Curry House at **620 Eaton**. This white Greek-revival residence was built circa 1885 for Curry, who was president of the Key West Light and Power Company.

With your back to the Donkey Milk House, walk to your left (east) along Eaton Street until you come to **709 Eaton Street**. This is a Bahamian white house with a picket fence and a two-story verandah. It was built circa 1853 by William Uriah Saunders and his wife Eliza.

Calvin Klein was a former owner of the octagon-shaped, aqua-shuttered house at **712 Eaton Street**, which was built between 1892 and 1899 by grocery store owner Richard Peacon. The house was restored by the late designer Angelo Donghia. The house with white columns at **713 Eaton** was once used as a hospital and was later decorated by Angelo Donghia.

A mix of Bahamian and Victorian architecture defines the black-shuttered, white house at **724 Eaton**. This is the Filer house, built in 1885. Turn right on William Street.

The Gideon Lowe House/Whispers at **409 William Street** was built in the Classical revival style. The first section of the house was constructed in the 1840s, and the second section was constructed around thirty years later.

The three-story Island City House at **411 Eaton** was built in the early twentieth century and served as a hotel for many years.

Cross Fleming Street. The Charles Roberts House, painted pink, is at **512 William Street** and is described as an eyebrow house because the roof overhangs the second-story windows to provide shade. Roberts's brother John owned the house at **516 William Street**, which was built in the Classical revival style, but with Victorian influence. Both houses were built in the 1890s.

Turn right on Southard Street. The William Albury house sits at **730 Southard**, on the corner of Southard and William. This white house with green shutters is one of Key West's oldest. It features double porches and a widow's walk.

Cross Elizabeth Street. John Lowe Jr. owned a sponging fleet. His pink house with gray shutters at **620 Southard** has an eyebrow overhang on the third floor. The house was built in the mid–nineteenth century. Note the widow's walk and wide porches surrounding the house which, behind its white fence, sits on the largest plot in Old Town, which is a historic eight-street area west of White Street.

The white, dormered Benjamin Curry house at **610 Southard** is set back onto its property. The Currys bought the property from Pardon Greene in 1856. Members of the Curry family have lived in the house for the past six generations.

The beige William C. Lowe house at **603 Southard** was built after 1865 and has a distinctive roof because of its deep pitch.

When you come to Simonton Street, turn right. The James Haskins Building/Marquesa Hotel is at **600 Fleming Street**, at the corner of Fleming and Simonton. A few years after it was built in 1884 as a single family home, the first floor was converted to commercial space. The upper floors were eventually used as a boarding house known as the "Q-Rooms" because of the quiet accommodations. It functioned as such for nearly a hundred years.

In 1988, the building reopened as the Marquesa Hotel. Adjacent buildings were acquired in 1995, and the hotel became a twenty-seven-room compound with two swimming pools and a waterfall. The main building is Greek revival style and is listed on the National Register of

Historic Places. The poolside buildings are West Indies–style frame vernacular. The hotel rooms feature four-hundred-pound Indonesian sleigh beds and antique English armoires. A focal point of the grounds is a wall covered with orchids from around the world. The Cafe Marquesa inside the hotel is decorated with canterra stone floors and a trompe l'oeil wall with a kitchen scene. In the middle of the scene there is a spot where diners can see the chefs at work.

The Pilot House at **414 Simonton**, behind a wrought iron gate, is a gray building with lots of decorative Victorian details. The house has been restored and converted into a guest house. The house next door, at **410 Simonton**, was built in 1876 by architect William Kerr in a carpenter gothic style.

The **Methodist Church on the corner of Eaton and Simonton**, at 600 Eaton, was built around the original wood church that stood in this spot. The stone walls of the church are two feet thick. The church was built out of stone in 1877 and is the oldest religious building in Key West.

Turn left onto Eaton and walk to **529 Eaton**, the Otto House/Artist House. This gray turreted house with lavender trim was built in 1898 in a mix of Queen Anne and West Indian styles. It was owned by druggist Thomas Otto, Jr. After his death it was cared for by a relative, Gene Otto, an artist, which may explain why it was called the Artist House. It is now a guest house.

The tallest above-ground cistern on the island is located on the premises of **511 Eaton Street**. This 1886 Conch house was the home and office of Dr. Richard Warren, who was one of Key West's physicians. The house has a beautiful garden and a Spanish lime tree that grows through the roof.

St. Paul's Episcopal Church at 401 Duval, on the corner of Duval and Eaton, boasts stained glass that was recycled from three previous churches on the site. The first service at this location took place in 1832, making the church the oldest Episcopal church in the diocese of south Florida.

Turn right on Duval Street and walk to **336 Duval**. Mr. and Mrs. William Pickney owned this house. Mrs. Pickney's sister conducted private education classes here in 1842.

The **Wreckers Museum at 322 Duval Street** is touted as the oldest house in Key West. In 1832, three years after it was built, this white house with green shutters was moved from its original location several blocks away to its present location. Originally the home of merchant seaman and wrecker Capt. Francis B. Watlington, this Conch house has a ship's hatch in the roof. Inside the house/museum, ship models, artifacts, and paintings document the history of the wrecking industry in the Keys.

The red brick house located at **319 Duval Street** was built in 1892 as the home of Capt. Martin Hellings. It has been the headquarters of the Key West Woman's Club for more than fifty years.

Turn left on Caroline Street. The French mansard–style house at **429 Caroline Street** is the J. Y. Porter house, which has remained in the family for seven generations. It was built in 1838. Nine years later, Dr. J. Y. Porter II was born in the house. Thanks to his research into yellow fever, the doctor was appointed Florida's first public health officer.

Judge W. Hunt Harris owned the house at **425 Caroline Street**, which was built circa 1898. Harris was a former lieutenant governor of Florida.

Jessie Porter's Heritage House and Robert Frost Cottage, at **410 Caroline Street**, was built in 1834 by a sea captain, George Carey. It was later owned by Jessie Porter Newton and now operates as a museum that exhibits furnishings, artifacts, and antiques. Notice the cranberry glass panels above the front door. Behind this Caribbean colonial house, there is a cottage surrounded by a pretty flowering garden. The cottage is where Robert Frost lived and worked when he visited Key West.

Jessie Porter's Heritage/Robert Frost Cottage

Presidential Gates outside Truman Little White House

The house at the corner of Caroline and Whitehead Streets, at **301 Whitehead**, is now home to Kelly's Caribbean Bar, Grill, & Brewery. It is owned by actress Kelly McGillis and her husband. The restaurant has an art gallery, a local writers library and a display of Pan American Airways memorabilia. Historians argue about whether the building was once the office for Pan Am. The memorabilia celebrates Key West aviation and Pan American's first international flight — to Havana.

Across the street are the Presidential Gates, which were built in 1908, and which lead to the **Harry S. Truman Little White House**, which was President Truman's vacation house. Truman first visited Key West in 1946 and became so enamored with Key West that he visited the island usually twice a year during his presidency. It is now a museum that is open to the public.

Turn right on Whitehead. Walk to Greene Street. The Audubon House/Geiger Home is on the corner of Whitehead and Greene at **205 Whitehead Street**. Capt. Geiger was a harbor pilot who owned this American vernacular home in the early 1800s. As a guest of Geiger's, John James Audubon stayed here during his visit to Key West in 1832.

Each morning, sometimes as early as 3 A.M., Audubon would explore the mangroves in search of native birds to draw. He spent a great deal of time sketching plants and birds. Many of his famous Birds of America engravings are on display in the house. The house is filled with

237

Key West Cigar Factory

period furnishings, and is surrounded by beautiful tropical gardens.

Whitehead curves into Front Street. As you walk along Front Street, you'll pass a red brick building on your left, which is the old **Customs House**, built in a Romanesque style in 1891. This building has served as a U.S. Post Office and as a courthouse as well as the Customs House. The Key West Art and Historical Society is revamping the building into a historical museum.

Continue on Front Street. You'll see the **Key West Cigar Factory**, which has been owned for more than twenty -five years by Eleanor Walsh. She surprised her competitors, and Key Westers in general, by building up and continuing to run what may be the most successful cigarmaking business on the island. Visitors can stand outside the factory window to watch her cigars being hand rolled.

Walk back to Front Street to **423 Front Street**, the site of the first Bank of Key West, which was destroyed by a fire in 1886. Harbor House, the present red brick building, was built in a New Orleans style. You can see the words "Bank of Key West" embedded into the top of the building.

Continue on Front Street to Duval Street and turn right. Walk to Greene Street and turn left. Walk to Ann Street and turn right. Walk to the Curry mansion at **511 Caroline Street** on the corner of Ann and Caroline Streets. The original Curry house was part of the 1855 homestead of William Curry, a lumber and salvage millionaire. Curry's son Milton demolished the house and built a new house in 1905.

Milton Curry and his wife Euphemia patterned their stately, Victorian mansion after a twenty-two room Newport, Rhode Island "cottage" they had admired. In 1919, banker George Allen bought the house. In 1965, it passed to his daughter, Mrs. Sam Goldsmith. After Mrs. Goldsmith's death in 1969, the house had two more owners.

In 1973, it was purchased by Edith and Al Amsterdam, who had retired to Florida from their apple orchard business in upstate New York. They painstakingly restored the mansion to its present splendor. The Amsterdams converted the mansion into an award-winning bed-and-breakfast inn. Four rooms in the main house are used as guest rooms. More accommodations are available in an addition that the couple built.

The mansion is on the National Register of Historic Places. Every room in the house is brimming with fascinating antiques and furnishings that date from the eighteenth century to the 1930s. It is an astounding collection that includes an 1853 Chickering grand piano that belonged to Henry James, Dresden and Meissen figurines, original Audubon prints, a French inlaid table made in 1798, and Ernest Hemingway's big game gun. Curry Mansion is open for tours.

Turn left on Caroline Street and walk to Simonton. The corner house at **532 Caroline Street** is the Delaney House, built circa 1899. This white, three-story house with wraparound verandah was owned by clothing merchant John J. Delaney.

Cypress House, 1887

The Cypress House sits across the street, at **601 Caroline**. This weathered brown wood, three-story house was built in 1887 in a Bahamian style. It was owned by William Kemp, who pioneered the sponge industry in Key West.

Turn right on Simonton. Walk to Rose Lane. Cross Rose Lane. In the 1920s, the Ford Motor Agency was located next door to the Trevor-Morris Apartments at **314 Simonton**. In 1928, young novelist Ernest Hemingway and his wife Pauline ordered a new Model A Ford, but it was late in arriving. While awaiting delivery of the car, the Hemingways lived for seven weeks on the second floor of the apartment building. It is there that Hemingway drafted his novel, A *Farewell to Arms*. Today, the Pelican Poop Shoppe occupies the first floor of the brown-trimmed, white concrete building.

Walk to Eaton Street and turn left to walk back to the Donkey Milk House.

Location
Fort Myers is located in central Lee County on southwest Florida's gulf coast between Naples and Sarasota. It is the county seat.

History
Lee County was named in honor of Gen. Robert E. Lee. It was founded in 1887 with 1,414 residents. The first visitor to the Lee Island coast was Ponce de León, who deposited a stone marker on Pine Island in 1513.

In 1841, a U.S. Army outpost was given the name Fort Harvie, after First Lt. John Harvie, but it was later renamed Fort Myers, after Col. Abraham C. Myers. The southernmost land battle of the Civil War was fought in Fort Myers on February 20, 1865. Runaway black slaves formed part of the Second U.S. Union Federalists Color Troops stationed here after the Confederates abandoned the fort.

In 1866, the first pioneer families arrived at the fort outpost, which had been abandoned by the Union Army at the end of the Civil War. One of the settlers was a Spanish sailor from Key West, Capt. Manuel A. Gonzalez. In 1872, Gonzalez moved his family a mile south to homestead a large tract of riverfront land. There was a creek running through his property. He named it Gonzalez's Creek. Today, it is known as Manuel's Branch and forms the southern boundary of the Fort Myers subdivision known as Edison Park. Gonzalez's wife Evelina opened a school in the Gonzalez home, where she taught four children. Gonzalez is considered to be Fort Myers's first permanent settler.

In 1878, a North Carolina schoolteacher named Howell A. Parker became Ft. Myers's first school principal. Nearly all present-day Edison Park consists of the tract of land that Parker purchased for eighty cents an acre in 1879.

In 1885 the cow town and cattle-shipping center of Fort Myers on the Caloosahatchee River was incorporated. It had approximately 350 residents. A year later, Thomas Edison established his winter home in Fort Myers. Edison would later be responsible for Fort Myers's nickname,

The City of Palms, because he planted two hundred of the statuesque royal palm trees which line fifteen miles of McGregor Boulevard.

In 1901, wealthy cattleman John Murphy built a Georgian revival–style home on 450 feet of river frontage that cost him $3,500. Murphy died in 1914. In 1919 the property was purchased by entrepreneur Nelson Thomas Burroughs. In 1916, automobile pioneer Henry Ford made Fort Myers his winter home by moving next door to his close friend Thomas Edison.

In 1925, during the land boom, the New Homes Development Company, with James D. Newton as its president, developed a subdivision, Edison Park, named in honor of Thomas Edison. Newton, a twenty-year-old Philadelphian, marketed Edison Park as an exclusive neighborhood complete with city water and sewers, gas, electricity, and other amenities.

Walking Tour

To get to the **Edison and Ford Homes at 2350 McGregor Boulevard**, take I-75 to Exit 22 (Colonial Boulevard). Head west to the end of Colonial Boulevard. Turn right onto McGregor Boulevard. Head north for approximately two and a half miles to the white picket fence that surrounds the ticket office to the Edison and Ford Homes. Turn right (east) into the parking lot. The ticket office is on the same side of McGregor Boulevard as the parking lot. The Edison and Ford Homes are directly across the street, on the west side of McGregor Boulevard, and also are surrounded by a white picket fence. From the ticket office, you can walk across the Boulevard to tour the two historic homes.

The walking tour can take up to three hours, depending on how much of the museum, houses, and gardens you want to view. Add a half hour if you take a walking tour of the Edison Park neighborhood next door to the ticket office. There is a $10 admission fee to the Edison and Ford Homes whether you take one of the continuous tours led by docents or explore on your own. If you take a self-guided tour, begin by walking around the grounds.

The fourteen-acre Edison estate is largely landscaped with an experimental garden of tropical and subtropical specimens that Edison lovingly tended between 1886 and 1930. He was quite interested in horticulture and botany. Many of the plantings are identified by small explanatory signs. One of the most intriguing trees is the Moreton Bay Fig or *Ficus macrophylia*, which is Australia's national tree. The tree has 200-foot-long roots that coil out from the trunk.

The banyan tree outside Edison's laboratory is the largest banyan

The Edison Winter Home

in Florida. It was given to Edison by Harvey Firestone in 1925 and has an aerial root circumference of 390 feet. Other specimens you'll see are giant bamboos, an Australian seagrape, an African sausage tree with its heavy, inedible, sausage-shaped fruit, and the goldenrod which Edison experimented with as a source of rubber.

The gardens include exotic fruit trees, flowering trees, pincushion trees, palm trees, chenille plants, lipstick bushes, bougainvillea, magnolia trees, and queen's wreath vines.

An office and small laboratory detached from the main house were built in 1929 as a gift from Mina Edison to her husband. The wood desk is the focal point of the office, which is surrounded by a garden that blooms with flowering plants. The laboratory is neatly filled with an assemblage of racks, test tubes, and various apparatus that Edison used in his experiments. Edison was mostly deaf, which he looked upon as an advantage. He felt it enabled him to concentrate on his work.

The nine-foot-deep swimming pool, built in 1910, was one of the first in Florida. It was made from cement that came from Edison Portland Cement Company. Edison's children spent many hours splashing about in the pool, but today it is occupied by a variety of tropical fish.

From the garden, signs will lead you to the Edison Museum. Here, you'll see Edison's Model T Ford, circa 1915, and the 1908 Cadillac that was custom made for him. A tour of the Edison museum on the estate

243

Phonographs exhibited in the Edison Museum

grounds gives testimony to Edison's genius. "I find out what the world needs, then I go ahead and try to invent it," Edison once said, and his more than 1,000 patents are proof.

On exhibit are his inventions — hundreds of phonographs, stock-tickers, embossing telegraphs, talking dolls whose sounds came from a hand-wound mechanism, incandescent lamps, movie cameras, and storage batteries. There is a towering bronze bust of Edison in the center of the museum.

The Edison home and connected guest house were built in 1886 from pre-cut spruce lumber transported from Maine to Fort Myers. Wide porches are integral parts of the houses. The living room contains an unpretentious assortment of wicker and wood furniture, brass chandeliers lighted by carbon filament bulbs that were turned on and off via a hanging switch, and a brick fireplace above which hangs a portrait of Edison's second wife, Mina.

The dining room is furnished in a yellow-accented early American style. The hand-painted china sits on a lace cloth-covered dining room table. The china turkey platter was made by Haviland in 1879. The same platters are on display in the White House and in the Smithsonian Institute.

Thomas and Mina's bedroom is cheerful and feminine, with pink

The Henry Ford Winter Home

and white accents, wicker furniture, a vinepatterned wallpaper, and a red brick fireplace. All of the rooms were heated by fireplaces. He was an avid reader.

From the Edison Home, walk next door to the Ford Home. In 1916, Edison's good friend Henry Ford paid $20,000 for three-and-a-half acres of property and an existing fourteen-room home on the property. This became the winter estate of Henry and his wife Clara. It was named "The Mangoes."

The "friendship" gate between the Edison and Ford homes was always open when the two famous men wintered in Fort Myers, so that they could freely visit each other. The wide front veranda of the Ford house was a relaxing spot for Edison and Ford to share conversation as they sat on the wicker furniture.

The Fords' living room has a cozy, almost rustic look. An area rug partially covers the wood floor. A hurricane lamp, wicker and wood furniture, beamed ceiling, and red brick fireplace complete the room. It was here that Henry and Clara would square dance to the sounds coming from the Edison phonograph. The home's Queen Anne–accented dining room is dominated by a dining room table covered with a lace tablecloth and topped with Wedgewood china.

It is not commonly known that the Fords were avid music-lovers and dance enthusiasts. Henry Ford played the fiddle and formed the Henry Ford Orchestra. Clara enjoyed sewing, a pastime she pursued in the quiet of the upstairs master bedroom. A sleeping porch adjoins the bedroom. Henry spent many tranquil moments here as he gazed out at his gardens, his dock, and the Caloosahatchee River.

The upstairs hallway is decorated with a carpet-runner on top of the wood floor, a bookcase, and simply-framed prints reflecting nature. There is a room upstairs that served as a trunk room for storage of the trunks the Fords filled with clothing when they traveled to Fort Myers in their private railway car. The Fords' son Edsel often slept in the guest room.

When you come out of the Edison Home and Ford Home onto McGregor Boulevard, cross over to the east side of the Boulevard. The Edison Park subdivision is located next door to, and just south of, the ticket office. This subdivision, which was begun in the early 1920s, became Fort Myers's first local historic district in the fall of 1995.

The entrance to Edison Park is flanked by arched walkways. Henry Ford is said to have frequently rested on the shortened wall at one of the archways after he strolled around the neighborhood. Here, he could watch with amusement as curious passersby peered over his picket fence across the Boulevard.

The Edison Park walkway arches are made of cement block with a stucco veneer. They have an obelisk on the top, and contain a crest of the city of Ft. Myers. At the center of the entrance, there is a cement statue of a Greek maiden, believed to be Aphrodite, that was dedicated in 1926 and that is part of a large fountain behind which are the words "Edison Park." Mina Edison was dismayed that the statue was indiscreetly nude and requested that it be clothed in some way. To appease her, and several other ladies who had complained, Edison Park developer James Newton had a marble epoxy veil applied to Aphrodite. The substance was the precursor of cultured marble.

When you enter Edison Park, you'll be walking on Llewellyn Drive. During your walk, you'll see one of the sixteen remaining cast iron Arcadian-style steet lamps that were installed in 1926. The homes described are representative of the upscale Edison Park neighborhood.

To your left, at **1601 Llewellyn**, you'll see a Spanish colonial–style house that was built in 1937 by a local builder named Howard Wheeler. He occupied the house for many years. The house is built out of red clay, hollow tile blocks with a stucco veneer. Wheeler popularized the use of hollow tile and after making design changes to it he named it "speedy tile." It was a precursor to cement block.

On your right, at **1622 Llewellyn Drive**, there is a Spanish-style ranch house. If you peer into the garden, which is visible from the street, you can see part of an elaborate two-story Mediterranean-style house behind the ranch. (It can be seen in full view if you later walk to 2413 McGregor Boulevard.) The two-story house was built in 1928 out of hollow tile and was designed by local architect Nat Walker. Through the 1940s it was owned by Edward Smith, district manager of Florida Power and Light Company. Since the 1960s it has been owned by the same family that owns the ranch at 1622 Llewellyn. The ranch was built in 1948. The family remodeled it to match the Mediterranean style of the two-story house. They added an exotic garden and use both houses as a family compound.

Straight ahead of you at **1619 Llewellyn**, you'll see the Mediterranean-style **Thomas A. Edison Congregational Church** which was built out of hollow tile in 1931 on land donated by Edison. The church was known simply as the Congregational Church until its name was changed in 1964. Mina Edison taught Bible classes here.

The road will fork at Llewellyn Drive and Houston Road. Hug the church side of the road by bearing to your left, which is a continuation of Llewellyn. Walk one short block to the house at the **corner of Llewellyn Drive and Marlyn Road**. This beige stucco two-story mission-style house at **1666 Llewellyn** was built in 1926 and designed by Nat Walker. It was owned by Thomas Edison's local physician, Dr. Robley Newton, the father of James Newton, who developed Edison Park. During the Depression, the house was owned by a local Coca-Cola distributor. A balcony on the front of the house has been removed. The house is now owned by a banker.

Turn left on **Marlyn** and walk to **1662**. This white wood-frame ranch-style house with green awnings was built in 1940 and was occupied by a prominent physician, Dr. Grace. The previous owners enclosed the garage to turn it into a guest room. The house was rcently purchased by a physician.

The peach stucco Mediterranean-style house with blue trim at **1750 Marlyn** was built in 1926 by Nat Walker. Notable original architectural features of the facade are the spiral columns and the lion-head medallions between the three arches. The house was constructed of wood lath and a stucco veneer. It has been occupied by Lee County's head engineer, by a realtor, and by a California physician who compared it to his vacation home in Barcelona. The current owner, an interior designer, recently expanded the second floor.

The yellow two-story Spanish colonial–style house with art deco

1750 Marlyn, built circa 1926

details at **1766 Marlyn** was built in 1939 out of hollow tile. There are three Spanish-tiled steps leading to the front door. There is a guest house in the rear yard. The swimming pool, with its detailed tile work, is original to the house and was the first swimming pool in Edison Park. A local jeweler once owned the house. It was later purchased by a judge, the first black circuit court judge in Ft. Myers.

Edison Park is designed with many curved streets. At this point, you'll be facing a triangular intersection, a sort of island where Marlyn Road, Monte Vista Avenue, and a one-block-long street called Harvard Street all connect. In the center of this small intersection, there is a triangular area that residents sodded and decorated with a canary date palm tree and a park bench. The area is called **Edison Park Triangle**. James Newton's girlfriend, Ruth Malcolmson, was Miss America in 1925. She bought a homesite near the Triangle but never built a house on the site. A subsequent owner has built a house on the lot.

At the triangle, cross over to Harvard Street from Marlyn. At the corner of Monte Vista and Harvard, you'll see a Georgian-style house at **1806 Monte Vista**. It was built in 1940 of hollow tile by Howard Wheeler for Frank Prather Sr., whose familty occupied it for thirty years. Prather operated a dry-cleaning business, which still exists. The garage with its "mother-in-law quarters" was originally detached from the house, but in 1943 a family room was added in the rear of the house to connect the two

1807 Monte Vista Avenue, built in 1926

buildings. A graphic designer and her husband, a physician, currently own the house.

Cross to the opposite side of **Monte Vista Avenue** to the green and white house at **1807**. Residents of Edison Park describe the house as a Mediterranean-style chalet. It was built in 1926 and was the first model home in Edison Park to show hollow tile construction. It has two symmetrical upper porches which were originally above two open areas which have since been enclosed to add a family room to the house. The house was formerly owned by Thomas Smoot Sr., a businessman who lived in three other nearby Edison Park homes during a sixty-year period.

The front of the house faces Monte Vista, but the side of the house faces Marlyn Road and an opening between the houses on the street. There a yellow sign indicates that the opening is a back entrance to the Edison Home parking lot. You can cross Marlyn and return to the ticket office by walking through the parking lot.

Another option is to take a short scenic route that leads you back to McGregor Boulevard and the fountain entrance to Edison Park. If you choose this route, head back (south) on Marlyn for a very short distance to the corner of Marlyn and Menlo Road. Turn right on Menlo, which was named for Menlo Park, New Jersey, Thomas Edison's northern home. Walk for one short block to the intersection where Menlo curves into

Llewellyn. You'll see the back of the fountain entrance and McGregor Boulevard. Continue on Llewellyn for a short block, which leads you out to McGregor Boulevard. Turn right and walk next door to the Edison Home ticket office.

The advantage to taking this route rather than walking through the Edison parking lot is that Menlo Road is lined with beautiful oak trees that form a canopy over the street. You'll also be able to see the house at **1668 Menlo Road**. It was built in 1927. For more than forty years the family of Ft. Myers's first pediatrician, Dr. Louis Girardin, has lived in the house.

SOUTH FLORIDA
HISTORICAL ATTRACTIONS, DINING, AND LODGING

WEST PALM BEACH — *Palm Beach County*

Suggested Dining and Lodging

Amici Ristorante
2885 South County Road
Palm Beach, FL
561-832-0201
Italian restaurant in a 1926 Mizner-designed Mediterranean-style stucco building. Features a wood-burning oven.

Centennial
45 Cocoanut Row
Palm Beach, FL
561-659-8460
Victorian-themed restaurant located in an 1897 golf clubhouse located on the grounds of The Breakers Resort.

Florentine Dining Room at The Breakers Resort
1 South County Road
Palm Beach
561-655-6611
Painted ceilings, tapestries, antiques, and furnishings reflect the Italian Renaissance.

Renato's
87 Via Mizner
Palm Beach
561-655-9752
Located along a route or via of courtyards and shops, and the five-story towers in which architect Addison Mizner lived. The Via was designed by Mizner in 1924. Mizner's pet monkey, Johnny Brown, was buried in 1927 in a marked grave in one of the courtyards.

391st Bomb Group Restaurant and Cabaret
3989 Southern Boulevard
West Palm Beach
561-683-3919
Housed in a replica of a World War II-era English farmhouse, and filled with artifacts from that era.

Brazilian Court Hotel
301 Australian Avenue
Palm Beach, FL 33480
561-655-7740 or 800-552-0335
Built in 1926, this two-story, 130-room, Spanish style hotel was an apartment house for ladies. It was built in a figure eight to overlook two massive gardens with fountains.

The Breakers
One South County Road
Palm Beach, FL 33480
561-655-6611
Famous 586-room hotel rebuilt in 1926 in Italian Renaissance style.

Hibiscus House Bed and Breakfast
501 Thirtieth Street
West Palm Beach, FL 33407
561-863-5633
Built in 1922 by Mayor David Dunkle, and restored and decorated with eclectic European antiques and furniture. A lovely tropical garden surrounds the pool.

Palm Beach Historic Inn
365 South County Road
Palm Beach, FL 33480
561-832-4009

Built in a Mediterranean-revival style in 1923 and designed by Harvey and Clarke Architects, who built the Town Hall. It was originally occupied by shops and upstairs apartments.

Plaza Inn
215 Brazilian Avenue
Palm Beach, FL 33480
561-832-8666 or 800-233-2632
European style, fifty-room boutique hotel with art deco exterior. Built in the 1930s.

West Palm Beach Bed and Breakfast
419 Thirty-Second Street
West Palm Beach, FL 33407
561-848-4064 or 800-736-4064
A charming 1937 Cottage-style home with Caribbean flair. It resembles a Key West guesthouse and includes a carriage house.

For Information

El Cid Historic Neighborhood Association
561-833-2708

Palm Beach County Convention and Visitors Bureau
1555 Palm Beach Lakes Boulevard, Suite 204
West Palm Beach, FL 33401
561-471-3995

Other Historic Attractions

Florida History Center and Museum
805 North U.S. 1
Jupiter, FL 33477
561-747-6639
Three museums dedicated to South Florida history. The Historical Museum houses exhibits depicting the area's development from the time of the earliest pioneers. The DuBois Pioneer

Home is an interpretive exhibit of two rooms of an 1898 pioneer home. The Jupiter Lighthouse Museum is located in the oil house of the lighthouse, which is the oldest still-existing structure in Palm Beach County. Open Tuesday through Friday 10 A.M. to 5 P.M., Saturday and Sunday 1 P.M. to 5 P.M. Adults $4, senior citizens $3, children six and older $2.

Ann Norton Sculpture Gardens
253 Barcelona Road
West Palm Beach, FL 33401
561-832-5328
Open Tuesday through Saturday 10 A.M. to 4 P.M.

Whitehall (Henry Flagler Museum)
1 Whitehall Way, Cocoanut Row
Palm Beach, FL 33480
561-655-2833
The opulent fifty-five-room mansion built in 1901 by the Florida East Coast Railroad tycoon as a wedding present to his last wife.
Open Tuesday through Saturday 10 A.M. to 5 P.M., Sunday noon to 5 P.M. Adults $7, children six to twelve $3.

BOYNTON BEACH — Palm Beach County

For Information

Boynton Beach Chamber of Commerce
639 East Ocean Avenue
Boynton Beach, FL 33435
561-732-9501

Boynton Cultural Centre/1913 Schoolhouse
141 East Ocean Avenue
Boynton Beach, FL 33435
561-375-6397

Boynton Beach Historical Society
P.O. Box 12
Boynton Beach, FL 33425
561-375-6380

Boynton Woman's Club
1010 South Federal Highway
Boynton Beach, FL 33435
561-369-2300

DELRAY BEACH — *Palm Beach County*

Suggested Dining and Lodging

Addison's
2 East Camino Real
Boca Raton
561-391-9800
Set in a huge Spanish-style building said to resemble El Greco's home in Toledo, Spain. It was built in the 1920s as administrative offices for Addison Mizner, the famed architect of The Cloisters, now the Boca Raton Resort and Club. A glass roof encloses the courtyard.

Bennardo Ristorante
116 North East Sixth Avenue (U.S. 1)
Delray Beach, FL
561-274-0051
Cozy upscale Italian restaurant in a 1925 Mediterranean revival-style house.

Ellie's '50s Diner
2410 North Federal Highway
Delray Beach, FL
561-276-1570
Music and mementos from the 1950s.

Elwood's Dixie Bar-B-Que
301 East Atlantic Avenue
Delray Beach, FL
561-272-RIBS
An old gas station, transformed into a restaurant.

La Veille Maison
770 Palmetto Park Road
Boca Raton, Fl
561-391-6701
Located in 1932 Mediterranean-style house furnished to reflect the Riviera and designed by one of Addison Mizner's architects.

Boca Raton Resort and Club
501 East Camino Real
Boca Raton, FL 33431
561-395-3000
The original section, The Cloisters, was designed by architect Addison Mizner in 1926. Guided tours of the hotel are offered.

Colony Hotel
525 East Atlantic Avenue
P.O. Box 970
Delray Beach, FL 33447
561-276-4123 or 800-552-2363

For Information

Delray Beach Chamber of Commerce/Downtown Development Authority/Community Redevelopment Agency
64 Southeast Fifth Avenue
Delray Beach, FL 33483
561-279-1384

Delray Beach Historical Society at Cason Cottage
5 Northeast First Street
Delray Beach, FL 33444
561-243-0223

Palm Beach County Historical Society
400 North Dixie Highway
West Palm Beach, FL 33407
561-832-4164

Other Historic Attractions

Morikami Museum and Japanese
Gardens
4000 Morikami Park Road
Delray Beach, FL 33446
561-495-0233
Presents exhibits and festivals to
honor the living culture of Japan and
to pay tribute to George Morikami who
founded the Yamato Colony, a
Japanese farming settlement in Delray
Beach in the early 1900s.
Open daily except Monday, 10 A.M. to 5
P.M. Adults $4.25, seniors $3.75, ages 6
to 18 $2. Admission is free on Sundays
between 10 A.M. and noon.

HOLLYWOOD — Broward County

Suggested Dining and Lodging

Hemingways Restaurant
219 North Twenty-first Avenue
954-926-5644
Located in a Mediterranean revival-
style building built in the 1920s. The
City Hall was once located here, as
was the Hollywood Publishing
Company. The restaurant has a "Gay
Nineties" atmosphere.

Hollywood Beach Club Resort and
Hotel
101 North Ocean Drive
Hollywood, FL 33021
954-921-0990
The pink Mediterranean revival hotel
was built by Young in 1926.

Maison Harrison Guest House
1504 Harrison Street
Hollywood, FL 33022
954-922-7319

Riverside Hotel
620 East Las Olas Boulevard
Ft. Lauderdale, FL 33301
954-467-0671
Built in 1936, this is the oldest
hotel in Ft. Lauderdale.

For Information

Dr. Paul George
c/o The Historical Museum of Southern
Florida Metro-Dade Cultural Center
101 West Flagler Street
Miami, FL 33130
305-375-1625

Hollywood Chamber of Commerce
4000 Hollywood Boulevard,
Suite 265S
Hollywood, FL 33021
800-231-5562

Hollywood Historical Society
P.O. Box 222755
Hollywood, Fl 33022-2755

Other Historic Attractions

Art & Culture Center of Hollywood
1650 Harrison Street
Hollywood, FL 33032
954-921-3274
Open Tuesday through Saturday 10
A.M. to 4 P.M., Thursday 7 P.M. to 9 P.M.,
Sunday 1 P.M. to 4 P.M. Admission:
Wednesday through Saturday $3,
Sunday $5 (including concert),
Tuesday donation.

Bonnet House
900 North Birch Road
Ft. Lauderdale, FL 33311
954-563-5393
The waterfront winter estate of artists Frederic and Evelyn Bartlett. It includes a plantation-style house, a shell museum, and eight outbuildings, all reflecting the history of south Florida. Guided tours Wednesday through Friday 10 a.m. and 1 p.m., weekends 1 p.m. and 2 p.m. Adults $7, seniors $6, students $5.

Ft. Lauderdale Historical Museum
219 Southwest Second Avenue
Ft. Lauderdale, FL 33301
954-463-4431
Collections and exhibits that reflect the growth and development of Ft. Lauderdale.
Open Tuesday through Saturday 10 A.M. to 4 P.M., Sunday 1 P.M. to 4 P.M. Admission: donation.

Old Dillard High School Cultural Arts Museum
1001 North West Fourth Street
Ft. Lauderdale, FL 33311
954-765-6952
A former "colored" school, now a living chronicle to Ft. Lauderdale's black history. Call for information.

Stranahan House
335 South East Sixth Avenue
Ft. Lauderdale, FL 33311
954-524-4736
Ferryman Frank Stranahan's 1913 home, the oldest surviving structure in Broward County. The house has served as a post office, town hall, general store, and currently is a museum of south Florida pioneer life.
Open Wednesday through Saturday 10 a.m. to 4 p.m., Sunday 1 P.M. to 4 P.M. Adults $5, children $2.

MIAMI BEACH — *Dade County*

Suggested Dining and Lodging

Allioli South Beach Cafe
1300 Ocean Drive
305-538-0553
Located in the Cardozo Hotel.

Colony Bistro
Colony Hotel
736 Ocean Drive
305-673-6776
Located in a historic art deco hotel.

Eleventh Street Diner
1065 Washington Avenue
305-534-6373

I Paparazzi Ristorante
Breakwater Hotel
940 Ocean Drive
305-531-3500
Located in a historic art deco hotel.

Raleigh Restaurant and Bar
Raleigh Hotel
1775 Collins Avenue
305-534-1775
Located in a historic art deco hotel.

Avalon Hotel
700 Ocean Drive
Miami Beach, FL 33139
305-538-0133 or 800-933-3306

Cardozo Hotel
1300 Ocean Drive
Miami Beach, FL 33139
305-535-6500 or 800 782-6500

The Delano Hotel
1685 Collins Avenue
Miami Beach, FL 33139
305-538-7881

Marlin Hotel
1200 Collins Avenue
Miami Beach, FL 33139
305-673-8770

Waldorf Towers Hotel
860 Ocean Drive
Miami Beach, FL 33139
305-531-7684 or 800-933-BEACH.

For Information

Dr. Paul George
c/o The Historical Museum of Southern
Florida Metro-Dade Cultural Center
101 West Flagler Street
Miami, FL 33130
305-375-1625

Greater Miami & the Beaches Hotel
Association
407 Lincoln Road, Suite 10G
Miami Beach, FL 33139

Greater Miami Convention & Visitors
Bureau
701 Brickell Avenue, Suite 2700
Miami, FL 33131
305-539-3094

Other Historic Attractions

Sanford L. Ziff Jewish Museum of
Florida
301 Washington Avenue
Miami Beach, FL 33139
305-672-5044
Built in 1936 as an Orthodox syna-
gogue, it now offers exhibits related to
230 years of Jewish life in Florida.
Open Tuesday to Sunday 10 A.M. to 5
P.M. Adults $4, students and senior cit-
izens $3, families $9, free admission
on Saturday.

The Wolfsonian
1001 Washington Avenue
Miami Beach, FL 33139
305-531-1001
Museum of antiques and objects from
the massive historical and cultural col-
lection of Mitchell Wolfson Jr.
   Closed Mondays. Open Tuesday to
Thursday 10 A.M. to 6 P.M., Friday 10
A.M. to 9 P.M., Saturday 10 A.M. to 6 P.M.,
Sunday noon to 5 P.M. Adults $7, stu-
dents and senior citizens $5.

CORAL GABLES — Dade County

Suggested Dining and Lodging

Il Ristorante
1200 Anastasia Avenue
Coral Gables, FL
305-445-1926

La Palma Ristorante & Bar
116 Alhambra Circle
Coral Gables, FL
305-445-8777
Mediterranean-inspired trattoria located in the historic La Palma Hotel.

Restaurant St. Michel
162 Alcazar Avenue
Coral Gables, FL
305-444-1666
Parisian cafe atmosphere. Located in a
restored 1926 European style hotel.

Biltmore Hotel
1200 Anastasia Avenue
Coral Gables, FL 33134
305-445-1926 or 800-727-1926

Hotel Place St. Michel
162 Alcazar Avenue
Coral Gables, FL 33134
305-444-1666

European-style inn built as the Sevilla Hotel in 1926.

For Information

Historic Preservation Department, City of Coral Gables 405 Biltmore Way Coral Gables, FL 33134 305-460-5216

Other Historic Attractions

Coral Gables City Hall
405 Biltmore Way
Coral Gables, FL 33134
305-442-6400
Spanish Renaissance oolitic limestone building completed in 1927. Contains a mural depicting Coral Gables' early days.

Coral Gables House
907 Coral Way
Coral Gables, FL 33134
305-442-6593
George Merrick's boyhood home. Open Sunday and Wednesday 1 P.M. to 4 P.M. Adults $2, children 50 cents.

Venetian Pool
2701 DeSoto Boulevard
Coral Gables, FL 33134
305-442-6483
A former rock pit that George Merrick transformed into a beautifully-landscaped public pool with caves and fountains. Open Tuesday through Friday 11 A.M. to 5:30 P.M., weekends 10 A.M. to 4:30 P.M.

Vizcaya
3251 South Miami Avenue
Miami, FL 33129
305-579-2813
Palatial Italian Renaissance winter home of industrialist James Deering. Open daily 9:30 A.M. to 5 P.M. Adults $8, children $4.

KEY WEST — *Monroe county*

Suggested Dining and Lodging

Cafe Marquesa
600 Flemington Street
305-292-1294
Located in the Marquesa Hotel, which was an old boarding house.

Flagler's Restaurant and Bar
1500 Reynolds Street
305-296-3535
Located in the Marriott Casa Marina Hotel, which was built in 1921 by Henry Flagler.

Kelly's Caribbean Bar & Grill
303 Whitehead Street
305-293-8484
Actress Kelly McGillis's restaurant is located in the old Pan American Airways building and features an aeronautical museum.

Louie's Backyard
700 Waddell Street
305-294-1061
Wrecker Capt. James Adams's former home, built circa 1910.

Pepe's Cafe and Steakhouse
806 Caroline Street
305-294-7192
Established in 1909 and touted as Key West's oldest restaurant.

The Artist House
534 Eaton Street
Key West, FL 33040
A restored Queen Anne Victorian mansion built in 1890.

Courtney's Place Historic Guest Cottages and Inn
720 Whitemarsh Lane
Key West, FL 33040
305-294-3480 or 800 UNWIND-9

House and cottages that are more than one hundred years old.

Curry Mansion Inn
511 Caroline Street
Key West, FL 33040
305-294-5349 or 800-253-3466
A beautifully restored bed-and-breakfast inn, circa 1899.

Eaton Manor Guest House
1024 Eaton Street
Key West, FL 33040
305-294-9870
A renovated 1890s Conch house in a garden setting.

Gardens Hotel
526 Angela Street
Key West, FL 33040
305-294-2661 or 800-526-2664;
FAX 305-292-1007
Turn-of-the-century homes converted into a luxury European style bed-and-breakfast inn set amidst the historic Peggy Mills Gardens, a tropical botanical garden.

Incentra Carriage House Inn
729 Whitehead Street
Key West, FL 33040
305-296-5565
A nineteenth-century former home of a horse-and-buggy operator.

Island City House Hotel
411 William Street
Key West, FL 33040
305-294-5702 or 800-634 8230
Three historic Victorian guest houses joined by brick pathways and tropical gardens.

Key West Bed and Breakfast
415 William Street
Key West, FL 33040
305-296-7274 or 800-438-6155

A Victorian-style former home of William Russell. Built circa 1898.

Marriott Casa Marina Hotel
1500 Reynolds Street Key West, FL 33040
305-296-3535 or 800-228-9290
An elegant Spanish Renaissance-style hotel built in 1921 by railroad tycoon Henry Flagler.

The Nassau House
1016 Fleming Street
Key West, FL 33040
305-296-8513 or 800-296 8513
A three-story, picket-fenced, hundred-year-old guest house.

The Pilot House Guest House
414 Simonton Street
Key West, FL 33040
305-294-8719 or 800-648-3780
Built in the 1800s.

Southernmost Point Guest House
1327 Duval Street
Key West, FL 33040
305-294-0715
Circa 1885 Victorian mansion.

Whispers Bed and Breakfast
409 William Street
Key West, FL 33040
305-294-5969 or 800-856-7444
The former Gideon Lowe House, built between 1845 and 1866 in a combination of Greek revival and Victorian styles.

For Information

Key West Chamber of Commerce
402 Wall Street
Key West, FL 33040
305-294-2587 or 800-275-4597

Old Island Restoration Foundation
P.O. Box 689
Key West, FL 33041
Produces a brochure titled Pelican Path, A Guide to Historic Key West, a detailed walking tour. Call 1-800-FLA-KEYS for information about the Upper and Lower Keys, or 1-800-LAST-KEY for information about Key West.

Other Historic Attractions

Audubon House
205 Whitehead Street
Key West, FL 33040
305-294-2116
Open daily 9:30 A.M. to 5 P.M.
Adults $7, children $4.

East Martello Museum
3501 South Roosevelt Boulevard
Key West, FL 33040
305-296-3913
A former Civil War fortress, this 1862 brick building depicts Key West history. Open daily 9:30 A.M. to 5 P.M. Adults $5, children $1.

Ernest Hemingway House
907 Whitehead Street
Key West, FL 33040
305-294-1575
Built in 1851, this house was purchased by Hemingway in 1931. Open daily 9 a.m. to 5 p.m. Call for admission fee.

Fort Zachary Taylor
West end of Southard Street
Key West, FL 33040
305-292-6713
Holds Civil War artifacts, plus the country's largest collection of Civil War cannons.
Open daily 8 A.M. to 5 P.M. Guided tours.

Heritage House and Robert Frost Cottage
410 Caroline Street
Key West, Fl 33040
Open daily 10 A.M. to 5 P.M.

Key West Cemetery
Passover Lane and Angela Street
Key West, FL 33040
305-292-8177
Humorous headstones dating from the 1800s, and a monument to soldiers who died aboard the U.S.S. Maine, which sank in Havana Harbor in 1898, igniting the Spanish American War.

Lighthouse Tower & Military Museum
938 Whitehead Street
305-294-0012
Key West, FL 33040
A lighthouse built in 1847, and 1887 clapboard lighthouse keepers' quarters.
Open daily 9:30 A.M. to 5 P.M. Adults $3, children $1.

Maritime Heritage Museum
200 Greene Street
Key West, FL 33040
305-294-2633
Gold, silver coins, jewelry, and other artifacts from the wreckage of Spanish treasure ships Atocha and Santa Margarita.
Open daily 9 A.M. to 6 P.M. Adults $6.

The Wreckers' Museum
322 Duval Street
Key West, FL 33040
305-294-9502
Open daily 10 A.M. to 4 P.M. Adults $3, children 50 cents.

FORT MYERS — *Lee County*

Suggested Dining and Lodging

The Veranda
2122 Second Street
Fort Myers
941-332-2065
A turn-of-the-century boarding house converted into a restaurant. Inside walls are decorated with photographs and memorabilia of early Fort Myers.

Cabbage Key Restaurant and Inn
P. O. Box 200
Pineland, FL 33945
941-283-2278
Built atop an Indian shell mound in 1938 by playwright and novelist Mary Roberts Rinehart. Accessible only by boat at Channel Marker 60. Six guest rooms, several guest cottages, and a marina. The wallpaper inside the restaurant is made of autographed $1 bills worth an estimated $20,000.

Wedding Inn Bed and Breakfast
2135 McGregor Boulevard
Fort Myers, FL 33901
941-332-5668
Built at the turn-of-the-century by William Dowling, who operated the Dowling Lumber Company in North Fort Myers. The inn is furnished with antiques and period furniture.

Historic Attractions

Edison and Ford Winter Estates
2350 McGregor Boulevard
Fort Myers, FL 33901
941-338-2261
Open daily except Thanksgiving and Christmas. Monday to Saturday 9 A.M. to 5:30 P.M., Sunday noon to 5:30 P.M. Adults $10, children $5.

Sanibel Historical Village and Museum
800 Dunlop Road
Sanibel Island, FL 33957
941-472-4648
Displays and exhibits relate the history of Sanibel Island. Free admission. Call for museum hours.

Fort Myers Historical Museum
2300 Peck Street
Fort Myers, FL 33901
941-332-5955
Housed in the restored Peck Street Depot, which discontinued train service in 1971 after sixty-one years. The museum features displays and exhibits of several Indian tribes, a collection of art, carnival, and depression glass. Open Monday through Saturday, 9 A.M. to 4:30 P.M., Sunday 1 P.M. to 5 P.M. Closed on Saturdays from May 31 through October 31. Adults $2.50, $1 for children under 12.

Murphy-Burroughs Home
2505 First Street
Fort Myers, FL 33901
941-332-1229
A Georgian revival-style house built in 1901 by wealthy cattleman John Murphy. The house was purchased in 1919 by entrepreneur Nelson Thomas Burroughs.
Tours are conducted Monday through Friday from 10 A.M. to 3 P.M., every hour on the hour.

Koreshan State Historic Site and Koreshan Unity Foundation and Library
South U.S. 41
Estero, FL 33928
941-992-0311 or 941-992-2184 for more information.

The remains of the Koreshan Unity religious sect, established here in the 1890s by Dr. Cyrus Teed, a Union Army Medical Corpsman who envisioned a 300-mile city of ten million followers. Sixteen buildings remain, including Teed's home. There is also a hollow globe illustrating Koreshan belief that man resides on the inside surface of the earth, gazing at the solar system within. The site is open daily from 8 A.M. to 5 P.M.

For Information

Greater Fort Myers Chamber of Commerce
P.O. Box 9289
Fort Myers, FL 33902
941-332-3624

Lee County Visitor and Convention Bureau
P.O. Box 2445
2180 West First Street
Fort Myers, FL 33902-2445
800-237-6444 or 941-338-3500

GLOSSARY OF
ARCHITECTURAL TERMS

Eclectic architectural styles cover Florida's structural landscape. Here is a brief description of the most popular styles you will see as you walk through historic districts.

Art Deco/Streamline Moderne

The style was inspired by the Exposition Internationale des Arts Decoratifs et Industriels Moderne in Paris in 1925. The art deco movement influenced jewelry, clothing, furniture, and architecture. It featured angular and geometric shapes such as porthole circles, chevrons, and zigzags. Art deco buildings were commonly built with oolitic limestone and included decorative ornamentation and motifs. The art moderne or streamline moderne style grew out of art deco and included curved walls and glass bricks. The style reached its peak of popularity in the 1930s.

Beaux Arts

This classical form of architecture evolved from the eighteenth century Ecole des Beaux Arts. Features include concrete freestanding statuary, heavy stone columns, grand staircases, and decorative swags and garlands.

Bungalow

Gustav Stickley influenced the popularity of this style via his popular 1909 book, *Craftsman Homes*. The style was popular between 1900 and 1930 and featured tapered piers, exposed rafters, a porch, and a low-pitched gable. Bungalows were usually constructed of wood, but also of brick or stone.

Carpenter gothic

Carpenter gothic homes were made of wood by local carpenters and cabinet-makers using newly-developed scroll saws and lathes. The homes featured machine filligree and decorative carved shapes.

Classical revival/Greek revival

A two-story structure with low-pitched gables and fluted, heavy columns topped with decorative capitals. The front of the structure often resembled a Greek temple.

Colonial revival

Assymetrical, two-story structures with classic-columned verandas.

Conch (pronounced "conk")

Conch homes, built by islanders and native Key Westers, were woodframed and tin-roofed and often had louvred shutters. The conch style combined Bahamian and Victorian influences.

Cracker

Some say the term "cracker" referred to Georgia backwoods people who cracked their own corn. Others claim it referred to cattle drivers who prodded mules and cattle by using the low, sharp crack of a whip. A cracker house was similar to a dogtrot style house and was of wood construction. It usually had ample porches.

Craftsman/arts and crafts

An offshoot of the bungalow style popular in the late 1890s, this style was popularized by Gustav Stickley, a furniture maker and publisher whose *Craftsman* magazine, published between

1901 and 1916, promoted simple construction, devoid of ornamentation. Features include banks of windows, an open floor plan, and low, broad proportions.

Frame Vernacular

Refers to buildings constructed of simple wood framing and influenced by the builder's experience, the climactic conditions, and the architectural style that was locally popular at the time. Masonry vernacular refers to commercial buildings.

Gothic revival

This was a popular architectural style for churches and schools. Distinguishing features included pointed arches and vertical lines.

Jacobethan revival/Tudor revival

Derived from the architecture of the reigns of Elizabeth (mid- to late sixteenth century) and James 1 (early seventeenth century), the Jacobethan style features tall chimneys, parapets, rounded arches, and windows grouped together and divided by slender vertical bars. The Jacobethan revival style was commonly used in brick churches, schools, and mansions. The Tudor revival style was similar to the Jacobethan, but principally domestic. Constructed of brick or stone and decorated with wood timbers, the Tudor revival style included wood half-timbering, leaded glass windowing, and projected second stories.

Mediterranean revival

A combination of Spanish and Italian architecture, this style gained immense popularity in Florida during the 1920s and 1930s. Distinguishing features include balconies, loggias, terra-cotta barrel tile roofs, bell towers, arches, and wrought iron balconies and gates.

Mediterranean revival buildings were of masonry or concrete with stucco finish.

Mission

A Spanish style simpler than the Mediterranean revival style. It evolved from the mission churches of California during the late 1700s. It features flat roofs, terra-cotta tile roof overhangs, heavy wood front doors, and wrought iron hardware.

Neo-classical

Similar to the neoclassical style, Georgian and colonial revival buildings included classical detailing, symmetrical facades, and a columned portico or veranda.

Prairie

Frank Lloyd Wright led the way for this style which gained immense popularity in the early 1900s. Usually built out of brick or stucco, the prairie-style house had horizontal bands of windows, and a broad, overhanging roof.

Queen Anne/Victorian

This style became popular in the United States beginning around the 1870s, paralleling the Victorian and Queen Anne eras. Common features of the style include assymetry, turrets, scroll work, fishscale design, gingerbread trim, verandas, balconies, towers, and widow's walks.

Shotgun

A simple, one-story wood cottage consisting of three rooms, one behind the other. It got its name because a shotgun could be fired from the front door, down the side hall, and straight out through the rear door.

SUGGESTED READING

(LISTED BY COUNTY)

ALACHUA COUNTY (GAINESVILLE, HIGH SPRINGS)

Buchholz, F. W. *History of Alachua County*. St. Augustine, FL: The Record Company, 1929.

Hildreth, Charles H., and Merlin G. Cox. *History of Gainesville, Florida, 1854-1979*. Gainesville, FL: Alachua County Historical Society, 1981.

Pickard, John B. *Florida's Eden: An Illustrated History of Alachua County*. Gainesville, FL: Maupin House Press, 1994.

Pickard, John B. *Historic Gainesville: A Tour Guide to the Past*. Gainesville, FL: Historic Gainesville, Inc., 1990.

Proctor, Samuel, and Wright Langley. *Gator History*. Gainesville, FL: South Star Publishing Company, 1986.

BREVARD COUNTY (MELBOURNE, EAU GALLIE, COCOA, TITUSVILLE)

Caidin, Martin. *The Cape*. New York: Doubleday, 1971.

Cleveland, Weona. *Crossroad Towns Remembered*. Melbourne, FL: Florida Today, 1994.

Melbourne Area Chamber of Commerce Centennial Committee. *Melbourne, A Century of Memories*, 1980.

Shofner, Jerrell. *History of Brevard County*. Melbourne: Brevard County Board of Commissioners, 1995.

Stone, Elaine. *Brevard County: From Cape of the Canes to the Space Coast*. Northridge, CA: Windsor Publications, 1988.

BROWARD COUNTY (HOLLYWOOD)

McIver, Stuart. *Fort Lauderdale and Broward County: An Illustrated History*. Woodland Hills, CA.: Windsor Publications, 1982.

McIver, Stuart. *Glimpses of South Florida History*. Miami: Florida Flair Books, 1982.

Ten Eich, Virginia Elliott. *History of Hollywood 1920-1950*. Salerno, FL: Florida Classics Library, 1966; reprinted 1989.

DADE COUNTY (CORAL GABLES, MIAMI BEACH)

Ashley, Kathryne. *George E. Merrick and Coral Gables, Florida*. Coral Gables, FL: Crystal Bay Publishers, 1985.

Antrim, Lorraine, Charles Chase, Mark Ormond, Michael Spring, and Woodrow W. Wilkins. *The Biltmore Revisited*. Coral Gables Metropolitan Museum and Art Center, 1981.

Capitman, Barbara Baer. *Deco Delights: Preserving the Beauty and Joy of Miami Beach Architecture*. Dutton: 1988.

George, Dr. Paul. *A Walking Tour of East Little Havana*. Miami: Historical Association of Southern Florida, 1991.

George, Dr. Paul. *A Journey Through Time, A Pictorial History of South Dade*. Donning Publications, 1995.

Kleinberg, Howard. *Miami Beach, A History*. Miami: Centennial Press, 1994.

LaRoue, Samuel, Jr. and Ellen J. Uguccioni. *Coral Gables in Postcards: Scenes from Florida's Yesterday*. Miami Dade Heritage Trust, 1988.

Redford, Polly. *Billion Dollar Sandbox, The History of Miami Beach*. Dutton, 1970.

Rodriguez, Ivan and Margot Ammidown. *From Wilderness to Metropolis, 1825 to 1940*. Metro Dade County, 1992.

Scheinbaum, David. *Miami Beach: Photographs of an American Dream*. Miami: Florida International University Press, 1990.

DUVAL COUNTY (JACKSONVILLE, RIVERSIDE AND AVONDALE)

Wood, Dr. Wayne. *The Living Heritage of Riverside and Avondale*, Jacksonville, FL: Riverside/Avondale Preservation, Inc., 1994.

ESCAMBIA COUNTY (PENSACOLA)

Bowden, Jesse Earle, Gordon Norman Simons, and Sandra L. Johnson. *Pensacola, Florida's First Place City*. The Donning Company, 1989.

Muir, Thomas Jr. and David P. Ogden. *Ft. Pickens Story*. Pensacola: Pensacola Historical Society, 1989.

Parks, Virginia. *Pensacola: Spaniards to Space Age*. Pensacola: Pensacola Historical Society, 1986.

Parks, Virginia and Judith Bense. *Underground Pensacola*. Pensacola: Pensacola Archaeological Society, 1989.

Parks, Virginia and Sarah Johnson. *Pensacola: The Old and the New*. Pensacola: Pensacola Historical Society, 1988.

GADSDEN COUNTY (QUINCY)

Avant Jr., David. *History of Gadsden County*. Tallahassee: L'Avant Studios, 1985.

Womack, Miles. *Gadsden, A Florida City in Word and Picture*. Quincy: Gadsden County Historical Commission, 1976.

HILLSBOROUGH COUNTY (TAMPA, YBOR CITY)

Mormino, Gary and Anthony P. Pizzo. *The Treasure City of Tampa*. Continental Heritage Press, 1983.

Pacheco, Ferdie. *Ybor City Chronicles, a Memoir*. Gainesville: University of Florida Press, 1994.

INDIAN RIVER COUNTY (VERO BEACH)

Newman, Anna Pearl Leonard. *Stories of Early Life Along Beautiful Indian River*. Stuart, FL: Stuart Daily News, 1953.

LEON COUNTY (TALLAHASSEE)

Avant, Fenton Garnett Davis. *My Tallahassee*. Tallahassee: L'Avant Studios, 1983.

Ellis, Mary Louise and William Warren Rogers. *Favored Land Tallahassee*. Donning Company, 1988.

Ellis, Mary Louise and William Warren Rogers. *Tallahassee and Leon County, a History and Bibliography*. Tallahassee: Florida Department of State, 1986.

Historic Tallahassee Preservation Board. *Capitol, A Guide For Visitors*. Tallahassee,

Florida Department of State, 1982

Jahoda, Gloria. *River of the Golden Ibis*. Hold, Rinehart and Winston, 1973.

MANATEE COUNTY (BRADENTON, FOGARTYVILLE, MANATEE, PALMETTO)

Abel, Ruth E. *One Hundred Years In Palmetto*. Palmetto, FL: Centennial Association, 1967.

Matthews, Janet Snyder. *Edge of Wilderness: A Settlement History of Manatee River and Sarasota Bay*. Tulsa, OK: Caprine Press, 1983.

Schofield, Arthur C. *Yesterday's Bradenton*. Miami: Seemann Publishing Company, 1975.

Warner, Joe. *Singing River*. Bradenton, FL: Manatee County Historical Commission.

MARION COUNTY (OCALA)

Martin, Richard A. *Eternal Spring, Man's 10,000 Years of History at Florida's Silver Springs*. St. Petersburg, FL: Great Outdoors Publishing, 1966.

Ott, Eloise R., and Louius H. Chazal *Ocali Country*. Ocklawha, FL: Marion Publishers, 1966.

Quinn, Jane. *Catholics of Marion County*. Ocala, FL: Mission Press, 1978.

MONROE COUNTY (KEY WEST)

Cox, Christopher. *A Key West Companion*. St. Martin's Press, 1982.

Kaufelt, Lynn Mitsuko. *Key West Writers and Their Houses*. Sarasota, FL: Pineapple Press, 1986.

McIver, Stuart B. *Hemingway's Key West*. Sarasota, FL: Pineapple Press, 1993.

White, Louise and Nora Smiley. *History of Key West*. St. Petersburg, FL: Great Outdoors Publishing, 1959.

Williams, Joy. *The Florida Keys: A History and Guide*. Random House.

OSCEOLA COUNTY (ST. CLOUD)

Florida Cattlemen's Association. *Florida Cowman, A History of Florida Cattle Raising*. Kissimmee, FL: Florida Cattlemen's Association, 1976.

PALM BEACH COUNTY (DELRAY BEACH, BOYNTON BEACH, WEST PALM BEACH)

Britt, Lora Sinks. *My Gold Coast: South Florida in the Early Years*. Palatka, FL: Brittany House Publishers, 1984.

Farrar, Cecil W. and Margo Ann Farrar. *Incomparable Delray Beach, Its Early Life and Lore*. Boynton Beach, FL: Star Publishing Co., Inc., 1974; 1991.

Greater Delray Beach Chamber of Commerce 1895-1995, *Delray Beach Centennial: The Early Years*. Delray Beach: Greater Delray Beach Chamber of Commerce, 1995.

SARASOTA COUNTY (SARASOTA)

Brogan, Bernice Brooks. *Sarasota Times Past*. Miami: Valiant Press, 1993.

Marth, Del. *Yesterday's Sarasota*. Miami: Seemann Publishing Company.

Matthews, Janet Snyder. *Sarasota, Journey to Centennial*. Continental Heritage Press, 1985.

Pursell, Kate and Patti Pearson. *Insiders Guide to Sarasota and Bradenton*. Bradenton, FL: Bradenton Herald, 1996.

ST. JOHNS COUNTY (ST. AUGUSTINE)

Griffin, Patricia C. *Mullet on the Beach, The Minorcans of Florida 1786-1788*. St. Augustine, FL: St. Augustine Historical Society, 1991.

Manucy, Albert. *The Houses of St. Augustine*. St. Augustine, FL: St. Augustine Historical Society, 1962.

Manucy, Albert. *Menendez: Pedro Menendez de Aviles, Captain General of the Ocean Sea*. Sarasota, FL: Pineapple Press, 1992.

Nolan, David. *The Houses of St. Augustine*. Sarasota, FL: Pineapple Press, 1995.

Smith, James M. *Before the White Man: A Prehistory of St. Johns County*, Florida. St. Augustine, FL: Historic St. Augustine Preservation Board, 1985.

Waterbury, Jean Parker, ed. *The Oldest City: St. Augustine, Saga of Survival*. St. Augustine, FL: St. Augustine Historical Society, 1983.

Wright, J. Leitch Jr. *British St. Augustine*. St. Augustine, FL: Historic St. Augustine Preservation Board, 1975.

WALTON COUNTY (SEASIDE, DeFUNIAK SPRINGS)

Brooke, Steven. *Seaside*. Gretna, LA: Pelican Publishing Co., 1995.

DeBolt, Dean, "The Florida Chautauqua." Florida Endowment for the Humanities *Forum*. Fall 1990, 6-10.

Mohney, David and Keller Easterling. *Seaside: Making aTown in America*. Princeton, NJ: Princeton Architectural Press, 1991.

GENERAL NONFICTION ABOUT FLORIDA HISTORY

Bartram, William. *The Travels of William Bartram*. ed. Francis Harper. New Haven: Yale University Press, 1958.

Brown, Robin C. *Florida's First People*. Sarasota, FL: Pineapple Press, 1994.

Burnett, Gene M. *Florida's Past: People and Events That Shaped The State*. 3 vols. Sarasota, FL: Pineapple Press, 1991.

Chandler, David Leon. *Henry Flagler: The Astonishing Life and Times of the Visionary Robber Baron who Founded Florida*. MacMillan, 1986.

Davis, Karen. *Public Faces, Private Lives: Women in South Florida 1870s-1910s*. Miami: Pickering Press, 1990.

Gannon, Michael. *Florida: A Short History*. Gainesville, FL: University of Florida Press.

Haase, Ronald W. *Classic Cracker: Florida's Woodframe Vernacular Architecture*. Sarasota, FL: Pineapple Press, 1992.

Hiller, Herbert L. *Guide to the Small and Historic Lodgings of Florida*. Sarasota, FL: Pineapple Press, 1991.

Jones, Maxine D. and Kevin M. McCarthy. *African Americans in Florida*. Sarasota, FL: Pineapple Press, 1993.

McCarthy, Kevin M., Editor. *The Book Lover's Guide to Florida: Authors, Books and Literary Sites*. Sarasota, FL: Pineapple Press, 1992.

McIver, Stuart B. *Dreamers, Schemers and Scalawags: The Florida Chronicles Volume 1*. Sarasota, FL: Pineapple Press, 1994.

McIver, Stuart B. *Murder in the Tropics: The Florida Chronicles, Volume 2*. Sarasota, FL: Pineapple Press, 1995.

Morris, Allen. *Florida Place Names: Alachua to Zolfo Springs*. Sarasota, FL: Pineapple Press, 1995.

Ruff, Ann. *Backroads of Florida*. Houston, TX: Gulf Publishing Company.

Shofner, Jerrell. *Florida Portrait: A Pictorial History of Florida*. Sarasota, FL: Pineapple Press, 1990.

Singer, Steven D. *Shipwrecks of Florida*. Sarasota, FL: Pineapple Press, 1992.

Stewart, Laura and Susanne Hupp. *Historic Homes of Florida*. Sarasota, FL: Pineapple Press, 1995.

Tuckwood, Jan and Kleinberg, Eliot. *Pioneers In Paradise*. West Palm Beach, FL: Palm Beach Post Publishing, 1994.

If you enjoyed reading this book, here are some other books from Pineapple Press on related topics. For a complete catalog, write to: Pineapple Press, P.O. Box 3899, Sarasota, FL 34230 or call 1-800-PINEAPL (746-3275).

Book Lover's Guide to Florida edited by Kevin M. McCarthy. Exhaustive survey of writers, books, and literary sites. A reference, guide for reading, and literary tour guide.

Classic Cracker by Ronald W. Haase. A study of Florida's wood-frame vernacular architecture that traces the historical development of the regional building style as well as the life and times of the people who employed it.

Cheap Thrills, Florida: The Bottom Half by Frank Zoretich. Humorous and informative sketches about excursions, attractions, and points of interest in Florida that can be enjoyed for less than $10 per person.

Florida Island Hopping: The West Coast by Chelle Koster Walton. The first tour guide to Florida's Gulf coast barrier islands, including a discussion of their histories, unique characters, and complete information on natural attractions, shopping, touring, and other diversions.

Guide to Florida Lighthouses by Elinor De Wire. Photographs and descriptions of these architecturally diverse structures.

Hemingway's Key West by Stuart McIver. A rousing, true-to-life portrait of Hemingway the man and the writer in 1930s Key West. Includes a two-hour walking tour of Ernest Hemingway's favorite haunts.

Historic Homes of Florida by Laura Stewart and Susanne Hupp. Seventy-four notable dwellings throughout the state tell the human side of history. All are open to the public and each is illustrated by H. Patrick Reed or Nan E. Wilson.

Historical Traveler's Guide to Florida by Eliot Kleinberg. More than sixty travel destinations in Florida of great historical significance, all in the spirit of fun and exploration.

Houses of Key West by Alex Caemmerer. Eyebrow houses, shotgun houses, Conch Victorians, and many more styles illustrated with lavish color photographs and complemented by anecdotes about old Key West.

Houses of St. Augustine by David Nolan. A history of the city told through its buildings, from the earliest coquina structures, through the colonial and Victorian times, to the modern era. Color photographs and original watercolors.

Visiting Florida's Most Interesting Small Towns by Bruce Hunt. From Carabelle to Bokeelia, these out-of-the-way but fascinating destinations are well worth a side trip or weekend excursion.